Congratulations!

By purchasing this book, you also receive TWO valuable tickets to my "Highest and Best Real Estate Investing" Boot Camp!

The "Highest and Best Real Estate Investing" Boot Camp is a powerful event that will help you immediately use the techniques contained in this book. It is a two day camp, and is held all over the country. You can find a full calendar of upcoming Boot Camp locations at www.MikeWatsonInvesting.com.

In the place of tickets to my boot camp, your FREE TICKET VOUCHER can also be redeemed for two tickets to any of my "Super Camps". *The "Super Camp" ticket offer is only valid for investors who are new to the MWI system.*

Happy Investing!

~ *Mike Watson*

FREE TICKET VOUCHER

MIKE WATSON
INVESTING

This voucher is good for TWO tickets to Mike Watson's

"Highest and Best Real Estate Investing"
Boot Camp

~ OR ~

TWO tickets to any MWI Super Camp

Visit www.MikeWatsonInvesting.com to see a full calendar of upcoming "Highest and Best Real Estate Investing" Boot Camps and Super Camps

To use this FREE TICKET VOUCHER, you will need to pre-register before attending your Camp

ONLINE	PHONE
To register online, visit www.MikeWatsonInvesting.com	please call us toll-free at (866) WATSON-5

Use your book reciept # _______ when you register

This offer is open to purchasers of The "Highest and Best" Real Estate Investment, by Mike Watson with Jennifer Hawkins. Free "Super Camp" ticket offer is only valid for investors who are new to the MWI system, and have not yet attended a paid MWI event. Original proof of purchase may be required. Pre-registration required, by going to www.MikeWatsonInvesting.com, or by calling (866) WATSON-5. This voucher can be redeemed for two tickets to the MWI Boot Camp OR for two tickets to an MWI Super Camp (One voucher can be redeemed for two tickets to the Boot Camp OR two tickets to a Super Camp, not both events). Seating is limited, and available on first come first serve basis.

THE "HIGHEST AND BEST" REAL ESTATE INVESTMENT!

How to make
Million Dollar Profits
in the 21st Century

MICHAEL P. WATSON
with
JENNIFER HAWKINS

Published by: Mike Watson Publishing L.L.C.

For more information regarding this book and the authors, please contact the
Mike Watson Companies at (866) WATSON-5, or visit www.MikeWatsonCompanies.com.

FIRST EDITION

Designed by Nathan Stitt

Library of Congress Cataloging-in-Publication Data
Watson, Michael P.
The "Highest and Best" Real Estate Investment!:
How to Make Million Dollar Profits in the 21st Century.
Michael P. Watson with Jennifer Hawkins

Library of Congress: 2008902692
ISBN-13: 978-0-9800827-2-2
ISBN-10: 0-9800827-2-2

Acknowledgements

This book is dedicated to my beautiful wife Heather Kristine Watson and my wonderful children Madison, Jaylin, Chloe, Hunter and Isabel. I also dedicate this book to my parents Brent and Pam Watson who taught me to dream big and fight hard. Thanks to my wonderful staff at Mike Watson Investing LLC who have helped immensely with this project. I also dedicate this book to the fantastic student investors who have given me more than I'll ever be able to give them. Lastly to Jennifer Hawkins, my co-author, who has tirelessly worked to bring our dream to fruition.

- Michael P. Watson

Thank you for your unwavering support, Connie Randmaa (Mom), Mark, Connor, and Brannon Hawkins. Thanks to my extraordinary assistant Grayson Griffin (You are groovy). Lisa Ducote, Nate Stitt, Joseph Diosana, Ryan Rude, Mike Stambaugh, my "Power Team" and all of the inspiring student investors at MWI you make this work possible and a pleasure. And finally, thank you Mike Watson, for your never-ending belief and faith in others.

- Jennifer Hawkins

CONTENTS

Letter from a Student Investor

At one point or another in everyone's life a person looks back and reflects on significant events and significant people that have had a major impact on their life. Although it's barely been two years since I first learned about Mike Watson I can honestly say my life as well as my family's life has already been forever altered for the better.

My wife often mentions how she had never seen me more excited than I was when I was first introduced to Mike's system "The Foundation to Success". She also mentions how my excitement in this new endeavor has continued to grow and how much more confident and knowledgeable I've become after two full years of studying and applying Mike's principles.

Basically, Mike has changed my life by showing me a real estate investment system that truly works. He has opened my eyes to opportunities I could never have seen before. His system has forced my mind to overcome obstacles and think outside the box in a completely different way than more traditional thinking. Most importantly his system has taught me the means to provide for my family, friends and loved ones in a way I never dreamt possible.

I hesitate to put a total dollar amount on the significant profits I've made utilizing "The Foundation to Success" as I feel it would take away from what I believe to be are much more important attributes I've taken from his system. These include:

1. I have formed and am now living by a personal "Red Button Statement".
2. I now have the knowledge that my own personal and financial well being will follow naturally by helping and sharing this system with others.
3. Through experience on deals provided exclusively by "The Foundation to Success" I have gained the confidence to step out of my comfort zone and take on projects I never could have

even imagined.

4. I now have a large network of new close personal friends and professional counterparts all of whom are fellow students that strive to see each other succeed.

In conclusion, over the past two years I have completed a large number of varying transactions because of the simple, repeatable aspects of "The Foundation to Success". These transactions include a "square footage fixer upper", a "density fixer upper", several remodels including two "Flixers", two bank owned purchases and several new home builds which are currently in process utilizing new modular techniques. All of these transactions were possible only because of Mike Watson and his real estate investment system, "The Foundation to Success".

I've profited more in the past two years than I had in the previous 5 years combined and have also been able to start a long-term cash flow stream that will continue for many years to come.

Thank you Mike, for not only changing but for greatly enhancing my life, as well as the lives of those around me.

Roy Meyer
Investor
Blaine, Washington

Are you ready to be a Real Estate Tycoon?

When I was a kid our family would play a board game called "Life". I loved that game. The goal was to experience all of life's trials and tribulations and finish the game with the most amount of money.

But there was one other way to finish the game. It was to hit the spot called "Real Estate Tycoon". The most exciting thing about that spot was that when a player hit it, everyone else kept playing. If everyone hit that spot everyone won. My absolute favorite way to win was not by getting the most amount of money. It was by racing to the end as fast as I could to land on that magic space called, "*Real Estate Tycoon!*"

I have had the immense fortune to have become a successful real estate tycoon in real life. It is going to be my pleasure to show you how to become one, too.

Have you ever wondered if there was a way *you* could become a *huge success* investing in real estate? What would it be like to be able to see tons of amazing opportunities all around you *today*? Imagine being able to look at property in a way you had never considered before, in a way that would create *enormous* profits now *plus* long-term *passive* income forever (without property management). Imagine being able to do all of this in spite of how the market moves.

Does this sound too good to be true? If so, hold on for a wild ride. The system I will teach you will change how you invest forever. It will change your life and and the lives of those around you. It already has for thousands of my students.

You may already be a great investor. You may have made millions with real estate, or you may just be starting down your path of investing. If you are either one of these or anywhere in between, this book is for you.

Being an incredibly profitable investor means you know the answer to the two most important questions, "What *is* a fantastic deal?" and, "How do you find *lots* of them?" Most investors' answers to these questions are, "I look for properties for sale at below market prices which I can fix up and flip for a quick profit" or "I look for properties that will offer some cash flow so I can have some income".

In both cases they make the mistake of looking at a property for exactly *what it is*. In addition, when they evaluate their deal they typically make a bad assumption that during their ownership the market will stay the same or go up. And finally they only look to buy what is for sale right now.

I am going to teach you how to avoid these mistakes. I will teach you exactly what a fantastic deal is. I will also teach you simple ways to find so many of them you will be *overwhelmed* with the possibility for profits no matter where you are or what the market does.

How the "Highest and Best" use was literally revealed to me.

In 1995 I was a real estate agent and had been helping people buy and sell homes for several years. One day I was at work in my office and a fellow agent called me and said, "I have a property for sale that I think might be a good investment. Do you want to come take a look at it?"

My first thought was, "Then why isn't anybody buying it?" But, I was a little intrigued so I continued to listen. He said, "It is a small house on a very large lot. I think it can be split into two lots. If so, you could sell the front house and sell the back lot separately and make a pretty good profit."

At this point I had another thought, "Then why isn't he buying it himself?" But I brushed it off and decided to check it out anyway. I drove over to look at the property. What I saw looked interesting. It did seem as if it was larger than most of the lots in the area and was on a corner so I figured this idea might work. It is worth mentioning that if the agent had not brought it to my attention I would not have noticed anything different about this property.

I didn't want to jump into something without knowing what I was doing so I drove to the city development assistance center to talk with someone about this idea of splitting the lot. The woman I met with said "There is definitely enough land to legally subdivide it into two lots." I was starting to think this might be a good investment.

On a whim I said, "What would *you* do with the property if it was yours?" Her answer surprised me and I wondered why she wouldn't have told me this in the first place. She said, "I'd subdivide it but would make the front lot with the home on it smaller and the back lot larger. That way you could build a twin home or duplex style home on the back lot."

At this point I started to get very excited. If I could subdivide the property in this way I knew it would increase the value of the back lot significantly and therefore my returns as well. Going from one home to a home and a duplex lot was a much "Higher and Better" use. I decided this was not just a good deal but a *fantastic* deal and went ahead and bought the property.

I followed through with the subdivision process at the city development center. Soon after, I sold the front home. Within weeks I sold the back lot to a builder who built a twin home on it. My net profit on the deal was over $40,000 less than 30 days after the plat was recorded at the city!

This deal really excited me because I had found a way to make a property worth *a lot more* without doing any physical fix-up to it. Also I loved the fact that it didn't matter what the market did while I owned it. I would have made money regardless. I had *forced the property to have a higher value* (by changing its "use") even though I did nothing physical to it and the market did not change.

I was so thrilled about this deal that all I wanted to do was go out and do a bunch more of them. The only problem was, I didn't know where to find more of them. I called the agent who sold me the property and said, "I want to do some more of those deals. Why don't you go get those types of listings and I'll buy *all* of them." His answer was not what I wanted to hear. He said, "I don't know of any more of those. That was the only one I had."

After I got over being upset, I moved my search elsewhere. I started to do some more research at the city to see where I might be able to find properties like these. What I found not only made me wild with anticipation but infuriated me as well.

I found out that there were many other properties in the area that were large enough to be subdivided. Because of this I was thrilled. The infuriating part was that after I did some more research in that area on the development standards I realized I had made a *horrible mistake*. I had left quite a bit of money on the table.

While I was studying the development standards I realized that the original lot was large enough to have built *8 units on it!* Had I sold that idea to a builder I would have made approximately $50,000 more on the same property without doing any more work. That was the true "Highest and Best" use of the property.

Luckily you are reading this book after I've had 12 years to make these types of mistakes. During that time I have refined the process of finding, purchasing, changing, selling and even holding properties with a "Higher and Better" use into a science.

I am going to share with you my method ("The Foundation to Success") in as much detail as possible so you can also become a *huge success*. You will no longer worry about where to find your next deal. You will not have to rely on appreciation. Nor will you need to have any fear of market conditions. Instead you will see deals *everywhere*, make massive profits, and create huge passive income investing in real estate. All by finding properties that are not currently realizing their *"Highest and Best"* use.

But let's go back to the beginning for a minute...

In order for you to understand a little about me and also to know you *can* do this I want to give you a little background. When I was in college I mowed lawns for a management company to earn a living. I had no idea what I wanted to do with my life. I was a psychology major and wasn't sure where I was going with the degree. One day as I was riding the mower I had an inspiration. My parents were part time real estate investors and told me how much money they made on properties where I was mowing the lawn. I decided that I would become a real estate investor, too. I thought, "How hard could it be? Don't all investors make a bunch of money?"

So I went to my parents and told them my plan. They thought I was too young and said I shouldn't go into the business. I have never been one to enjoy being told what to do so I became an investor anyway. Thinking back now I wonder if my parents knew me better than I thought. Maybe they knew their response would help propel me toward success.

So, at a very young age, without any help from anyone, including the bank (more on that later), I bought my first investment property. It was a condominium that I rented out for a very small positive cash flow. It was what I would call today a "traditional" type of investment. And even though it turned out OK it was not a big money maker. At the time I thought I would buy a bunch of those types of properties and in 30 years when the loans were paid off *I'd be rich.*

After I finished college I got my real estate license. My thought was that I'd be an insider for real estate investing and could make a *fortune* that way. *Unfortunately* I made the mistake of becoming a "traditional" real estate agent as well. What that meant was that I didn't do many of my own investments. Basically I only had time to work with buyers and sellers.

After a couple of years in the business I started to get frustrated. It's funny because actually I was making quite a bit of money. The problem was that I was completely stressed out and overworked, not to mention unhappy.

I realized I had gone WAY off the path of my purpose of being an incredible real estate investor. I'd done a little investing but had not committed to that part of the business. Unfortunately it was the investing side of real estate that was my true passion.

I thought back on all of my deals and was struck with the truth. The truth was that both working with clients and investing was working for me. However one was much more *lucrative* and *leveraged* and it was the one I had intended to pursue exclusively when I began my career.

Right then I decided to dedicate myself to the investing side of the business much more actively and let go of the customer side. That's when I got the call from my fellow agent about the house on the big lot and the investing really started to explode. As I look back now I realize it was the conscious decision to *commit to the investing* that changed everything.

After only two short years of focusing exclusively on investing I looked up from what I was doing and was a *multi-millionaire!* How did I get to that stage so fast? What was the secret to my incredible success in such a short time? First let me tell you what else happened.

Why would I write this book and give away my system?

One day I went to a closing where I was going to make over $100,000 on one deal that I had started only 6 months before. We were all sitting around the table and I was feeling quite proud of myself. The person leading the closing was a friend. When we got to the paperwork where it showed my profit I put it in front of her and said, "What do you think?"

She looked up at me and said, "I hate you."

Shocked at her answer I said, "Are you kidding?"

She said, "No, if you are so smart why don't you help me do these kinds of deals too?"

At that moment the room seemed to shift. My perception slowed. The truth slammed me in the gut and everything became clear. My path was being shown to me. I didn't want people to hate me for being a success. I wanted to have people around me who are also successful and I *knew* how to get them there. Who was I not to help them? Who was I to hoard my knowledge?

There were *so many* of these types of deals in my city alone that it was *ridiculous* to keep this information to myself. I could never do all of the incredible deals myself in a lifetime. I knew at that moment I was meant to share my investing knowledge with other people.

Because of this experience I decided to share *all* of my secrets to success. I decided to tell everyone I knew exactly how I had made my profits. Because of this the official real estate investing program "The Foundation to Success" was born.

> The more you ***share*** your knowledge the more success you will have!
>
> **~Mike Watson**

"The Foundation to Success" has produced hundreds of very profitable deals over the last 14 years. It has made me a multi-millionaire many times over. It has created a portfolio that will support my family for my, and quite possibly their, entire lifetime. But why should you trust me based on my experience alone? Isn't the real proof in what my investor students have accomplished? Here are just a few stories from students around the country.

"What can I say? My path has been forever altered. Since learning and implementing Mike's "Foundation to Success" system within the last 2 years, my brother and I "Flixed" a property for a $70,000 profit, having owned it for only 113 days. We have since joined forces with 2 gifted and talented MWI students. We have a conservative $300,000 equity position currently, and will more than triple that with FREE and CLEAR property within the next 6 to 9 months. We are creating incredible cash flow in Southern California in 2008, amazing!"

Mike Stambaugh
Blue Ocean Company LLC
Whittier, California

......

"Because of Mike Watson I am now working as a full time developer. My sons and I have several projects in the works. We're developing 2.69 acres near Hemet, CA into 47 townhomes, 3.32 acres in San Bernardino into 45 townhomes and 1.86 acres in San Jacinto into 24 townhomes. We also have three subdivisions under way in Riverside for a total of 16 lots! *I expect to earn between two and seven million dollars over the next 18 months.*"

Tim Huyck
Riverside, California

……

"Just over one year after I attended Mike's 2-day seminar I am working on several fantastic projects and I am so excited! I have introduced Mike's system to two of my son-in-laws and their friends. I also have a "Power Team" of eight people and we are all excited! I never knew I would want to do something like this at the age of 64.

One of my deals is to change one home into a six unit apartment complex. It is on a half acre near a hospital. Another deal we bought is an old building on 1.29 acres. On this property we currently have a plat for 54 condos units and 2 floors of commercial!

I am so thrilled to be a part of Mike Watson's system of investing. The level of support he and his company provide is astounding. If you are interested in real estate investing in any way, get involved now."

Darlene Morgan
Salt Lake City, Utah

……

"Our first purchase was 3.82 acres of vacant land in Bloomington CA. We are currently subdividing the property into 15 single family home lots. Our current short-term equity position is $350,000 and long-term profits at build out will be $1.3 million.

Our second purchase was 4.6 acres of vacant land in Colton CA. We are working on a plat for 68 units of 3 bedroom 2.5 bath townhomes. This property was purchased at $13,500 per door. It has short-term equity or profits of $464,000 and long-term profits of $3.8 million at build out.

Our favorite thing about Mike's program is that we no longer spend all of our time "earning a living". Instead we are able to help other people. This is something we have dreamed about since we married 25 years ago."

Vernon and Vickie Alderson
Big Bear, California

……

"Since Oct 2006 we have 14 closed transactions with a volume of $6,896,000. We have only spent $8,000 of our own money. The total future value of the properties is $59,230,000. Part of the above purchases was 145 cash flowing units. We have a $17,747 per month net positive cash flow after all expenses and debt service just on those 145 units. Finally we now have 9 employees and 27 members on our 'Power Team'.

All of this is because of Mike Watson."

Jim Stephens and Kevin Liu
Houston, Texas

……

"Since attending Mike's seminars I think outside the box, see properties for their "Highest and Best" use, and leverage other people's time and money. My husband and sons are involved with my team. We have bought properties whose equity doubled overnight with Mike's techniques. We bought a two bedroom home that is now land for 28 senior apartments. We also bought a two bedroom home that is zoned to be 25 townhomes. We bought a church on five acres. We separated the acreage and subdivided 16 home lots and sold the church. This deal alone has a profit of $300,000! Because of Mike Watson I am now a developer with an incredibly bright future."

Diane Hull
Redlands, California

......

"Following "The Foundation to Success" has enabled us to experience amazing personal and business growth. It didn't happen overnight, but our "Red Button Statements" gave us the strength to persevere. Our "Power Team" has grown from one to five very active members. We have two active deals that should net roughly $2 million in profits and seven other deals entering the pipeline. We've never felt more excited and productive in our lives!"

Supin and Laura Ko
Seattle, Washington

......

"Since learning Mike's "Foundation to Success" less than two years ago, I now own 36 properties, have a net worth of $780,000 and an estimated short-term (12-15 months) net worth of $4,470,000. I am working on 19 active developments. If they go to completion they will have a value of $16,900,000.

Because of Mike Watson I have knowledge and confidence like I've never experienced before. I have a bullet-proof deal evaluation process and a repeatable system to find and profit from real estate investments.

Mike Watson is a passionate man with a heart of gold and a genius mind for real estate investing. He pushes you like a coach, cares for you like a father and supports you like a grandfather. From the bottom of my heart, thank you Mike."

Ryan Rude
Riverside, California

......

"The Foundation to Success" has changed my life by providing me with tools, support and the opportunity for Partnerships with MWI. Actually that is what hooked me. When I found out that Mike would partner with me on a project I knew his system was for real. He is a teacher who talks the talk AND walks the walk with his students.

The real gem of his program is the benefit to my friends, family and close clients. One of my team members found a 14 unit apartment complex that we have under contract and will be able to do a condo conversion. The evaluated profit on that is about $980,000!

Our first project was a 2.48 acre parcel that had 2 beat up duplexes on it. We bought it for $625K which was about $200K under market value. The acreage will hold 42 units with a future value of $8.1 million. We then 'door knocked' and found an adjacent 5 acre parcel which we are currently under contract. Potential profit in the short-term is about 570K and the long-term is over $3 million. Can you say, Hoo-Rah!"

Marleigh Manzo
Queen Creek, Arizona

......

"The Foundation to Success" is the best real estate investing system you will find anywhere. I guarantee it. If you follow the "Foundation to Success" exactly as it is written you will be a success. If you are not, I will refund *every penny you paid for this book.*

"The Foundation to Success" will not only make you rich it will teach you how to *rejuvenate your cities*. It will show you how to *help many families* own their own homes that could not otherwise have done so. It will *empower* you to create the life of your dreams.

For the last 4 years I have been teaching this system to thousands of people across the country. I am now writing this book because I felt I *had* to reach an even wider audience. You were meant to pick up this book.

Can you hear the doubts screaming in your head?!

Are you thinking, "It may have worked for you and your students but it won't for me because..." Fill in the blank. Some of those things may be, "the market is bad", "the market is too good", "you can't do those things here", "I don't understand the details of how it all works", etc.

Whatever your doubts may be at this time I challenge you to set them aside until you finish reading this book. "The Foundation to Success" is *not* based on location, market timing, or appreciation. It works in spite of all of those things. I have used it successfully over and over in markets across the country to create enormous wealth for myself and *many* others. I have used it in up, down and flat markets with unbelievable results across the board.

My intention is for you to finish this book and go out and make your life and those around you better. You will have all of the tools you need. I will make sure of it. I will provide all of the details you need to become a wildly successful real estate investor.

You will not finish this book and wonder where to begin. You will not finish this book and say "What now? What do I do next?" *You will know*. I will give you very specific tools that you will be able to use immediately. All it requires is for you to *take action* with the information you will have and follow "The Foundation to Success". If you do, you will be a success.

It is my intention to teach you how to succeed. Then I will teach you how to help others join you and reach their dreams, too. "The Foundation to Success" will show you how to find more deals than you could ever do on your own. Therefore there is no reason not to bring others in and teach them. With more people "The Foundation to Success" has the ability to change more of the world into its "Highest and Best" use.

OVERVIEW

"THE FOUNDATION TO SUCCESS"

"THE FOUNDATION TO SUCCESS"

What is this remarkable system called, "The Foundation to Success"?

By now I would imagine you are thinking this system must be pretty complex. You are probably saying to yourself "I'm going to have to study for months or even years to understand the ins and outs of how it could all possibly work". But, here it is. These are the steps, yes, it really is this simple.

1. *Know* "The Foundation to Success"
2. Create your "Red Button Statement"
3. Find Incredible Properties (Competing and non-competing methods *no one* else is using)
4. Evaluate Properties For Their "Highest and Best" Use (Plus 6 other key characteristics)
5. Buy the Property Using the *Two* OPM's (Never use your *own* cash again.)
6. *Expose* the vision! (Immediately put it back up for sale)
7. Create and Enhance Equity (Change the use, and *explode* your profits.)
8. Sell the Property for a Profit (Short-term *fast cash*)
9. Refinance for an Equity Position (Long-term strategy for *Passive Income*)
10. Prosper and Share with Others (Give back and create *leverage* with "*Power Teams*")

The Three Secrets to Why it Works

How can these ten simple steps guarantee your success in real estate investing?

Let me tell you the three main secrets to why this system works so well and works everywhere. There is not a city in the country and probably in the world that does not have a need for improving real estate. Drive around your city, all around it and look closely at what is there. I have a student in Monterrey California who is finding distressed properties left and right. If she can find them there, you can find them in your town.

Imagine being given very specific ways to find the niche in your market that will make you rich. Once you understand the workings of "The Foundation to Success" you will be able to find a hidden *treasure trove* of potential profits in your city. You will learn how to look at a property for what it could be, rather than what it is. I will teach you how to find properties with incredible hidden value that other people look right past.

The second secret is this system works in any type of market. You will no longer worry about what the market is doing. I will teach you how to *create equity* in your property, thus you will explode your profits! As a matter of fact a bad market is better than a good market. I will go into six specific reasons why this is true.

The third secret to why "The Foundation to Success" works so well is that there is an exit strategy for the short-term and the long-term. You will never have to wonder, "What happens if this deal doesn't sell?" As a matter of fact, if the property does not sell quickly or at all it will be an even *better* deal than if it does. "The Foundation to Success" and the deal evaluation system I teach will virtually guarantee this.

Buying Property with the "2 OPM's"

Another exciting aspect of "The Foundation to Success" is that embedded within it is a powerful method of buying property *without* your own cash, income or good credit. I didn't want to mention this on the first page because this type of teaching is hard to believe. It is true though, there are student investors all over the country who have no cash and little or poor credit and are buying multi-million dollar properties.

You may be saying to yourself, "I don't need *any* of my own cash, credit or a good income to do this? There is NO WAY!" Well, remember when I was mowing lawns for a living? I was making $4.75 an hour working 20 hours a week. I had no tax returns. I didn't have any money to use for down payments. I didn't have bad credit. I had no credit at all.

Imagine being 22 years old and being in my situation. Imagine going into the local bank to see about getting a loan to buy investment real estate. Well I did just that. In the process I pretty much got laughed out of the building.

I walked into the bank and sat down in the office of the loan officer. After explaining my situation she sat back in her chair and said, "You are in no position to get any type of financing." She also suggested in not so many words that I was wasting her time by being there. As you can imagine I was quite shaken up when I left the bank.

However I was not going to let her stop my future so easily. I knew I had simply asked the wrong person or the wrong question. (Later you will understand why it was both) I wasn't going to let a simple thing like, a loan officer thinking I was off my rocker, derail my success. I knew I would just have to find another way to make it happen and boy did I ever!

I did not need to have money or good credit and neither do you. "The Foundation to Success" will teach you how to use *two* OPM's (Other People's Money). The first OPM is other people's *money*, or "raising capital" and the second is other people's *mortgages* also known as "seller financing".

You will learn how to seller finance just about *anything*. After all, seller financing is better for the seller than it is for the buyer. You will learn how to raise capital of your own you didn't even know you had and how to help others invest with you. When you use these two techniques together you will easily be able to do deals with no money out of your pocket from day one to payday. When I combined the two OPM's I was able to buy three properties during my first year of investing at the age of 22.

By now I'm sure you are beginning to understand "The Foundation to Success" is a system that anyone can use anywhere. There are only two things you need to make it work. The first is to *have an incredible appetite for success* and the second is to *be willing to do what it takes to make things happen*. Hearing the word "No" should never again stop you but rather compel you on to success.

> "When someone says "No" you are just asking the wrong person or the wrong question!
>
> **~Mike Watson**"

When? When? When?

Many people ask me, "How long will it take me to make a lot of money with your system?" or "When should I quit my day job?" I am always tempted to say, "Go for it! Jump out on a limb and make it work now!" But the truth is, it is much smarter to ease out of your day job as you ease into investing. Real estate can take time to purchase and sell again. The rule of thumb I suggest is, "Don't abandon your current vehicle for income until you have investment income to replace it."

There is one instance when I do *not* give this advice. Instead I say, "If you are in any type of field that has to do with real estate don't get out of your day job ever." (See Step 4 on Deal Evaluation and Step 10 for "Power Teams" as to why this is true)

The final thing I would like to say here is it is possible to make a lot of money fast with my system. How quickly you succeed will depend on how much effort you exert, how quickly you learn the system, your creativity, resilience and perseverance. It may take you a while to get going but remember, once you have a deal or two under your belt it will be far easier to keep the momentum going.

> "Don't abandon your current income until you have investment income to replace it.
>
> **~Mike Watson**"

A Revolution in Real Estate Investing

I've given you a few of the ideas I'll explore but why is "The Foundation to Success" different than other real estate investing systems? So far it might sound similar to other programs you may have heard about. You might see some attributes and think, "This is just another get rich quick scheme that won't work for me." Keep reading. I am confident you will soon feel differently. Let me give you just four of the many points right now that show why "The Foundation to Success" is different from anything else you have ever read.

The first point is the "Non-compete" method of finding properties. You will learn ways to find properties which are incredible investments and you will be the *only* person making an offer to the owner. There will be *no* other buyers, and therefore *no* competition. Imagine what this will do for your negotiating.

The second is that you will learn how to make *every* transaction a win/win proposition. I know this sounds like a cliché but listen to the difference within "The Foundation to Success". When I say win/win I mean you as the investor win and the seller wins. (See the section on "*4-Offer Spreadsheets*" in Step 5) But there is more, I will teach you how to make sure the person who is buying the property *from you* wins too. (See the "Flixer" explanation) And finally you will have a system where everyone who works on the deal meaning contractors, lenders, appraisers, etc. will win. (See the "Power Teams" section)

The third point is that investing is a bigger game than just profits. Profits are "in the moment money". Profits are essential to investing but "The Foundation to Success" goes much further. It shows you how to *create* equity positions, cash flow and passive income *without having to own property!* These three things will give you lifelong security! P.S. You might want to read that paragraph again just to make sure you got it.

The fourth point is you will learn the details. I will personally make sure you have the specific tools you need to go out and do this program successfully. Just one of the tools you have at your disposal is called the "MWI Community Forum". It is a place you can go online to ask any question you may have about any material in the book, or, any of your deals.

MIKE WATSON INVESTING

Online Resources

On the MWI Community Forum you will get responses from other investors around the country, from the Mike Watson Investors coaches and even from me directly. I have posted over 800 answers to questions you can read right now. Anyone can go there and it is FREE. **Just visit www.mikewatsoninvesting.com** and click on the "Forum" today.

Don't sell your house just yet.

I have had many students come up to me and say, "Your program is wonderful, I can see how I could make a bunch of money with it but I don't think there is any way it will work in my town. Maybe I should move to a city with more opportunities."

I always smile and say, "I can guarantee you there are aging properties, need for affordable housing, development opportunities, and areas your city wants to improve *right in your town.* The question is, are you willing to go find them?"

Most systems teach you how to either take advantage of people who are losing their homes, do traditional fixer uppers or find property that is cash flowing as it stands. That means the average investor is already doing these types deals. Therefore there is a large demand for these types of properties. When there is a big demand the prices are usually high.

On the other hand "The Foundation to Success" teaches you how to view property differently. It teaches you how to see property for "what it can be" rather than for what it is. Most investors do not have this skill. There is less demand for this type of transaction. Therefore most cities are *ripe* for success with this program.

You don't have to move to do this program. As a matter of fact the best place to succeed is right in your back yard. That is because you know more about your own area than anywhere else. People that teach investors to go chasing markets all over the country without being highly intelligent about the area are putting those people at more risk than is necessary. I am going to show you exactly how to find lots of deals where you know the area very well. Where better than your own town?

The sky is falling! The sky is falling!

Have you ever noticed how some traditional investors use a hunt and peck system for the next hot market? Their big plan is to buy properties in markets that are moving up and then sell those properties before the market slows or drops.

Unfortunately many investors go through a feast while they are in a hot market, but few get out in time and many are left with properties they can't sell. These properties eat away those initial profits *fast.* In the worst case scenario the investor can lose everything.

One of my favorite attributes of "The Foundation to Success" is its ability to create and protect profits in *any market.* You are going to learn how to change the *value* of a property when you change the properties use. When you do this you will rely much less on the market going up. As a matter of fact it may be completely irrelevant.

With "The Foundation to Success" you will make money in up, flat or down markets by changing the use of property. In fact, I like to say, "Good markets are good, bad markets are much better."

The Seven *Huge Benefits* of a Down Market

Am I crazy? Did I just say huge *benefits* of a *down* market? Can you believe that a down market is really much better for investors than an up market? Does it make any sense at all? Here is why I believe "bad" markets are better than "good" ones for investors. At this point if you are willing to think a little differently you might see some incredible opportunities crop up in your market.

Benefit 1: Terms

Here is how powerful terms can be in a deal. What if you could buy a property with no money down? That is pretty good but what if on that same property you could have *no interest or payments* for 5 years? That is even better. What if you didn't even have to qualify for anything to buy it? Those are some phenomenal terms!

I have students who have done deals with exactly those terms. How is that possible? It is possible because sellers expect to have to do *extraordinary* things to sell their properties in down markets. Those extraordinary things can be outstanding terms for a buyer. Use that knowledge to your advantage. But keep in mind that the seller will still win as well because they *have* to sell and will be able to because of you.

Benefit 2: Rents

Imagine buying an apartment complex you intend to do a condo-conversion on and the rents go up by 30, 40 or even 50 percent in one year. You might consider holding that property for the long-term no matter what.

In a bad market more people have to rent. They may have less cash, plus they may have foreclosures or bankruptcies on their record. When there is a higher demand for rentals in an area where prices were very high for entry level homes the rents *will* go up until it is possible to buy again.

In other words rents will rise until they get much closer to the cost to own. Once they get nearer to that number they will begin to taper off again. If you own rental property during a down market there is a good chance your rental income will go up during that time.

Benefit 3: Prices

When people have to sell their property and there are no buyers what happens? It is a simple economic principal. Prices drop. Not only do they drop, but sellers will accept low offers all day long. They will offer incentives and bonuses. Ask for *the world* in a bad market. Get rock bottom prices or move on to the next deal. You are in the driver's seat. There are deals everywhere.

Benefit 4: Building Costs

What is one of the first things that will occur in a bad market? Who is the first to slow production? Who is the first to cut costs? The answer is: volume builders. They are in touch with the market. They know exactly how many people are buying and when the market slows they tighten their purse strings very quickly.

They offer incentives to buyers and agents to get their inventory moved. In addition they stop building new homes. When this happens they let go of contractors and sub-contractors. The framers, the painters, the dry wall people, the carpet crew, everyone is in need of work.

When there is a glut of contractors needing work, the cost of construction goes down and goes down fast. If these people don't have a job they may not eat. Make sure to get bids redone *frequently* in a down market to make sure you are not paying more than necessary for construction.

Benefit 5: Foreclosures

Foreclosures are properties that the bank or government has taken back from the owner due to non-payment of the loan. When the market is good, foreclosure properties are extremely competitive. People think just because it is a foreclosure you are getting a good deal. This is not typically the case. You could pay market or higher for a foreclosure and not even get to do inspections.

On the other hand, when you have a bad market there are *many more* foreclosures and therefore they can become quite lucrative. Keep your eye on the number of foreclosures in your area and when you see a huge jump it's time to do some checking into the foreclosure and notice of default market. If there are more foreclosures than buyers it is time to get a deal! Keep in mind that the *best* foreclosures to buy are the ones with a "Higher and Better" use!

Benefit 6: Something is always selling

Have you ever noticed that *something* always sells? Even in the worst market something is selling. There is not a city that has had *not one sale* over any length of time. The key is to find out *exactly* what it is that is selling.

If you are a real estate agent or have one on your "Power Team" keep track of every sale in your "Area of Expertise". Once you determine what is selling, find a way to *create* more of that product.

Benefit 7: Less competition

I love it when the market gets soft or bad! Most investors run and hide. Lots of buyers in general wait it out until there is a big upswing. The best time to buy is when there is little or no competition.

> "Good markets are good, bad markets are a ***gold mine!***
>
> **~Mike Watson**"

Online Resources

For more information on the benefits of investing in a "bad" market go to **www.mikewatsoninvesting.com/bookextras** and then click on the audio link for the "Anytime! Anywhere! Presentation" This is a FREE talk given by Mike Watson.

Your "Spark of Inspiration" List

While you are reading this book you might notice an interesting phenomenon. *Your mind will expand and will fire off amazing thoughts.* You will have sparks of ideas and insights. When these sparks occur write them down. You will not remember them later unless you do. If you don't remember them you will not be able to put those magnificent insights into use. I have provided a checklist in the back of the book in the Appendix 2 section that will help you keep track of some of these items.

You will get the most out of this book and those "Sparks" if you take just a moment and write them down *while* you are reading the book. It might even be smart to use a pen as your bookmark. That way those gold nugget thoughts will not be lost forever. As I say, "Knowledge is not truly yours until you use it." By writing down your sparks of inspiration you will cement them into your knowledge base and can draw on them later.

The name of the list is the "Spark of Inspiration List" and it has such items as, types of deals that interest you, areas of town that might work the best, and critical to do list. As soon as you have a "Spark of Inspiration", go to the Appendix 2 and write it down.

Right now you can flip back to the section and fold down a corner or put a tab on the page so it is easy to reference.

> "Knowledge is not truly yours until you ***use*** it.
>
> **~Mike Watson**"

By this time I expect you are wondering about an actual deal and would like some more details. Let me go through an actual deal I did a few years ago. Out of the hundreds of deals I've done on my own and with others this is one of my favorites. I don't like it because I made a bunch of money. I have others where I made much higher profits. I like it because I used quite a few of the principals from "The Foundation to Success".

There will be many times I'll refer back to this example throughout the book. I'm going to call it the "Awesome 15-unit Condo Deal"

"Awesome 15-unit Condo Deal"

I was so excited one day when a member of my team (See *"Power Teams"*) found a neglected 75 year old home for sale on a big lot. The inside was a disaster. The whole yard was either totally overgrown or dead. Almost everything needed to be fixed or changed to make it a nice home. You might be thinking I was crazy to be excited about a dilapidated property but here is one of my secrets: *"Distress equals Dollars."* When you find distress there is a very good chance you have found opportunity.

THE ORIGINAL "AWESOME 15-UNIT CONDO DEAL" PROPERTY

We went to talk with the owner. She said, "I would like to get market price for my home because it is in a good area and if I don't I won't be able to buy another house."

I said, "It is a great price, but the condition makes it a very average deal."

She was getting a little upset and told me, "I will lose the home if I don't sell it and I need the money to buy a mobile home to live in or I might end up homeless" At this point most investors might have seen an opportunity to get a huge deal on the property by just telling her they would save her from a foreclosure.

Most investors would buy the property, put in carpet and paint, clean up the landscaping and try and sell it for a small profit. But luckily because of "The Foundation to Success" I knew the property could be *much* more than an old beat up house with new carpet and paint.

I wanted to set her mind at ease so I told her, "We are prepared to pay full price for your home." You could see the worry and tension leave her body *immediately*. I was so happy to be able to help her.

Let me give you my next secret which is why we could pay her market price for a sub-par home. Before I found this home, I had gone to the city and found an area where we could take property from one use, such as a single-family home, and convert it into a much "Higher and Better" use, such as a condominium complex. This particular area was zoned for 25 residential units per acre.

I got a city zoning map and outlined the streets and properties that allowed for this incredible use. I was pretty sure I could find properties in the zone which were utilizing less than the allowed 25 units per acre. (I will be giving you a very detailed method of how to create your own "Area of Expertise")

Next my team and I searched for all of the properties that were listed for sale in that area of the city. We also researched the expired real estate listings, homes "for sale by owner", properties for rent, vacant properties, and distressed properties. We even checked the Notice of Defaults and list of Pre-Foreclosure properties that were in that specific area.

THE ORIGINAL PROPERTY AND LOT

THE VISION EXPOSED

During our search we always asked ourselves which of these properties were utilizing less than the already approved 25 units per acre. Of the properties we found, one of them was this distressed old house on a .63 acre lot. Because of "The Foundation to Success" we realized this home shouldn't be a carpet and paint rehab, it should be a *15-unit condominium project*. (25 units/acre x .63 acres = 15.75 units, See: Evaluate for "Highest and Best" use section)

Getting back to the story, the owner told me, "I've gotten a lot of very low offers and I was getting scared I would not be able to move into something else. Thank you so much." I gladly paid her the full asking price of $129,900 for the distressed home.

Had I been an average investor I could have put $40,000 into remodeling the home and yard and maybe sold it for a $15,000-$20,000 profit. However that seemed like a lot of work for not much gain. Besides, I saw the property for *what it could be* and knew there was much more profit just waiting to be captured! (It was a Win/Win deal. The owner got their full asking price and we got a property with a huge potential for a very large profit. Plus when we sold, the builder got a fantastic deal on a lot they developed.)

Once we closed on the property, we immediately put the property back up for sale as a 15-unit condominium project *in progress*. We listed it for approximately $70,000 more than we had purchased it for. We then announced to the world, "Come in and do the condominium project for a profit or *I will*." (See: "Flixer", "Create and Enhance Equity" sections)

"The Foundation to Success" makes this whole process fun. I didn't really care if the property sold or not. If it sold I'd make money but if it didn't, I'd make *more*. (Sell for short-term profit or Refinance for an Equity position and long-term cash flow sections)

We listed the property on a Friday. By the following Monday we had 3 offers that were *full-priced or higher*. The one we accepted was for cash and was more than the asking price. We closed 28 days later and made just over $65,000 in net profits after commissions, closing costs, city fees and carrying costs on the deal. We didn't do any physical fix-up, and did *very little* work at all.

The property sold to a builder who wanted to do a condominium project. He was grateful to buy our project because he couldn't find any places to do a project similar to this one. We sold the property for what it *could be* (a 15-unit condo project), not for what it *was* (a beat up old home in foreclosure). From purchase to sale took less than 70 days. We made almost $1,000 per day for each day of ownership. That is what I call an incredible profit!

I will go into much more detail about this transaction throughout the book. For now just notice how simple the process can be and that we did not look at the property for what it was but for what it *could be*. This is basis of the "Highest and Best" use theory, which is the crux of "The Foundation to Success".

> "Always look at a property for what it ***can be***, not for what it is.
>
> **~Mike Watson**"

STEP 1

KNOW
"THE FOUNDATION TO SUCCESS"

STEP 1

KNOW "THE FOUNDATION TO SUCCESS"

Stop! Herein lies the key to success.

Why are some investors successful and some not? Why are some *people* successful and some not? I won't claim to know the full answer to those questions though I do have a few simple tools based on what has worked for me.

The key to my success in real estate investing has been to always remember step number one of "The Foundation to Success". Step #1 is simply to *know* "The Foundation to Success". This may seem a little mundane therefore you might feel like skipping this step. I strongly advise you don't do that. Instead, commit to memorizing all ten steps of "The Foundation to Success". It is not that long or complex. There is no excuse for an incredible investor to not know it.

I teach a *two-day* seminar on the ten steps of "The Foundation to Success". It is called the "Highest and Best Real Estate Investing Boot Camp". At this camp I offer a full money back guarantee that the system works in any market and with any type of real estate. You might say "How can you possibly guarantee the system works for everyone?" I can guarantee it because I know it works. I've seen investor after investor take my techniques and follow "The Foundation to Success" to become a *huge success*.

But how can I guarantee that anyone who really wants to can become a successful investor? I guarantee it by making sure they *know* the system. I am so confident in my system that I include a *lifetime membership* to my two-day Boot Camp when anyone signs up, pays for and attends their first two-day event. Student investors can attend as often as they like for *free* for as long as Mike Watson Investing (MWI) offers the Camp. I have students who have been to over 20 of these camps. They are the most successful student investors in my program. Quite likely, this is because they *know* "The Foundation to Success" better than anyone else.

By knowing the steps you will be able to use them. In addition if you ever get stuck on something in a deal all you have to do is review the steps and make sure you are following them. Step #1 is, take the time to *memorize* all ten steps. After doing this, read this entire book so you understand how to implement the steps in your market. When you follow this simple formula you will be a success!

Let's review the steps so you can memorize them.

1. *Know* "The Foundation to Success"
2. Create your "Red Button Statement"
3. Find Incredible Properties (Competing and non-competing methods *no one* else is using)
4. Evaluate Properties For Their "Highest and Best" Use (Plus 6 other key characteristics)
5. Buy the Property Using the *Two* OPM's (Never use your *own* cash again.)
6. *Expose* the vision! (Immediately put it back up for sale)
7. Create and Enhance Equity (Change the use, and *explode* your profits.)
8. Sell the Property for a Profit (Short-term *fast cash*)
9. Refinance for an Equity Position (Long-term strategy for *Passive Income*)
10. Prosper and Share with Others (Give back and create *leverage* with "*Power Teams*")

At this point you may be thinking, "I wonder if I can just do the steps I want to and ignore the rest?" My answer to that is no. Here is my observation. Sometimes when I'm teaching my camp someone comes up to me and says, 'The Foundation to Success doesn't work!"

My response to them is always, "*Which* step of 'The Foundation to Success' doesn't work?"

At this point their eyes seem to glaze over and they don't have an answer. I always say to them, "When you know the steps to "The Foundation to Success" you will know which step isn't working for *you*. Then you can learn that step better and modify it to fit your market. Do not expect a system you don't know inside and out to work perfectly for you. You must learn it to live it and have incredible success with it."

Many people think all they have to do is read a book or attend a seminar to change their lives. A book or seminar may be the catalyst for change but the only way to experience success is to *apply* what you have learned. I suggest you apply all of the steps, not just the one's you think you need.

Your success depends solely on what you do with the material I provide to you. It is my responsibility to give you as much insights as possible. *Memorizing* "The Foundation to Success" is the first essential step for your success.

Are you committed to your success?

Thinking back over my career, it is surprising how I overcame so many obstacles on my way to success. Beginning with no money, no credit, no tax returns, no real estate education or mentoring, how in the world did I make it work?

The most crucial element to my extraordinary success in investing and life in general is simply my *level of commitment*. Being 100% committed to success and unwilling take "no" for an answer from anyone meant I didn't let obstacles stop me. There was always a way to overcome them. My commitment level was much higher than any hurdle that ever arose.

One of my favorite sayings was and still is, "No means go!" Another one is, "Don't tell me no, show me how." And lastly, "No really means no *competition*." All three of these sayings are a testament to my commitment level. When you commit completely to your own success "No" will never, ever stop you again. You will be much larger than any stumbling block that comes your way. Even if you are lacking in other ways, but still have commitment, you will achieve incredible success. Commitment is *everything*!

> "Once you are committed ***everything*** will happen. By comparison, before commitment very little will occur.
>
> **~Mike Watson**"

The Secret to Pinpointing Your Drive to Succeed

How do you become committed to something? I believe it is by having a deep reason for the commitment. Do you have a compelling reason to be successful? Do you have a reason for finding the true drive within you? I challenge you to make a critical decision right now. Decide if you are ready to live an extraordinary life.

Success isn't for quitters or the faint of heart. Success is for people who make a commitment that is bigger than their own personal limitations. It is for those who are willing to go outside of their comfort zone.

How you create and make your commitment is absolutely fundamental to your success. When I teach my boot camps I start by asking some simple questions such as, "Why are you here?" People raise their hands and give me answers such as "to make money" or "to be rich".

Is that the truth? Are you looking for white paper with green ink on it? Or are you reading this book for something more? If you take the time to look much deeper you may surprise yourself. There are other reasons why you want to be successful. You know it and I know it.

I take quite a bit of time in my camps to help people dig down and get in touch with those reasons. I hear incredibly passionate responses from people as to why they are committed to being a success. Those responses have carried many people through the trials and tribulations of real estate investing. Why? Because their *reason* for being successful is bigger than the *obstacles* they have to overcome. Are your reasons big enough? Have you taken the time to figure out what those reasons are?

Here are some things people have said in my camps. One woman said, "My purpose for being committed to becoming a huge success investing is to provide a better life for my special needs child." Another student said, "I will be an incredible investor in order to help a loved one through cancer". I've heard many say "I want to give my kids the best education possible and this includes teaching them how to provide for themselves." Another one I hear frequently is, "I want to provide an incredible retirement for myself or my parents".

These reasons and ideas are the foundation for making a real commitment to being an incredible investor. If your reasons are powerful enough to *you* they will get you through obstacles, negativity and self-doubt.

> "Make sure your ***reasons*** for investing are bigger than the ***obstacles*** you will come up against.
>
> **~Mike Watson**"

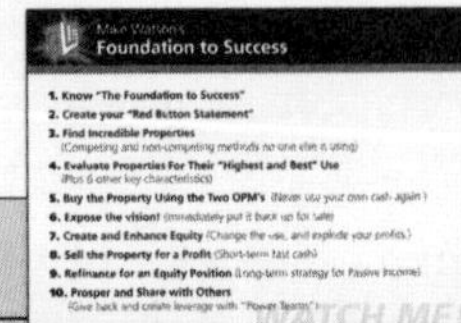

Mike Watson's
Foundation to Success

1. **Know "The Foundation to Success"**
2. **Create your "Red Button Statement"**
3. **Find Incredible Properties** (Competing and non-competing methods no one else is using)
4. **Evaluate Properties For Their "Highest and Best" Use** (Plus 6 other key characteristics)
5. **Buy the Property Using the Two OPM's** (Never use your own cash again!)
6. **Expose the vision!** (Immediately put it back up for sale)
7. **Create and Enhance Equity** (Change the use, and explode your profits.)
8. **Sell the Property for a Profit** (Short-term fast cash)
9. **Refinance for an Equity Position** (Long-term strategy for Passive Income)
10. **Prosper and Share with Others** (Give back and create leverage with "Power Teams")

WATCH ME!

www.MikeWatsonInvesting.com

FREE Online Resources

I have already created a FREE professional looking printout for you. It lists the 10 steps to "The Foundation to Success", ready for you to print and frame.

Go to **www.mikewatsoninvesting.com/bookextras**, and then click on "FTS Printout". Print it and post it in your home or office where you can see it every day. That way it will be easy to memorize and will become a part of your life.

STEP 2

CREATE YOUR "RED BUTTON STATEMENT"

STEP 2

CREATE YOUR "RED BUTTON STATEMENT"

My life's path leads me to the magic formula for strength.

This idea of commitment leads us into Step #2 of "The Foundation to Success" which is to *create* your "Red Button Statement". This statement is your own personal statement that reinforces your commitment to your success. It will provide you with the strength you need when hurdles arise in your path.

To show you how I came up with Step #2 here is some life history. When I was growing up I had two very different parents who added greatly to the man I have become. My mother always told me, "You can do anything you put your mind to". My father said, "You have to figure out how to do things for yourself otherwise you will be a failure".

As a child and young adult I believed these two ideas were very different. I felt my mother's positive outlook meant she was the only one who was supporting me. I unfortunately looked at my father's method as "wrong" and that he didn't believe in my abilities. I caused myself a lot of pain and turmoil due to this belief.

You may be wondering what this has to do with strength. Early in my career I felt I had to prove my father's "doubter attitude" wrong. I honestly couldn't bear the thought of him thinking I couldn't make it in the tough business of investing.

This drive to prove my Dad wrong was my *momentum*. It gave me the necessary "strength" to strive for success. After I had achieved a substantial amount of success in my career, my Dad came to me and said, "I am so proud of everything you have accomplished". I was shocked! I never remembered hearing those words before. I started to get choked up. With his words I realized I had been using this belief of my dad being "wrong" and "unbelieving" as my motivation to be successful.

However, once I realized he was on my side all along, this drive to prove him wrong was gone. The wind went out of my sail and I began to flounder and sputter. I wasn't motivated to fight when things got tough. I was shocked at my own indifference. After about 6 weeks of floating, I decided I had to come up with something very powerful to strive for again to get myself moving towards a higher level of success. I looked closely at my hopes and dreams and as a result set new goals for my life.

I now know I must have a *very* strong reason *"Why"* and a very strong *"Who"* to be a successful investor. I realize a "vendetta" is not going to push me to the level of success I crave, and know is possible. From the flailing came a path I use to this day to reconnect with my drive.

I began to seek out the *real* reason why I wanted to be a success. After much soul searching I realized the reason was two-fold. I not only wanted to achieve success for myself, but I wanted to help others. It was at this point in my life that things all fell into place. This was the path to creating my "Red Button Statement".

When something did go wrong or got tough all I had to do was re-visit my "Red Button Statement" and I became motivated all over again. Nothing could stop me ever again. Because of my "Red Button Statement" I have become more successful than I ever thought possible. It is constantly pushing me to new levels of success. It is truly the "magic" formula for success.

The Only Way to Guarantee Your Success

Think of the last time you saw a movie that was a suspense film. At a certain point everything hinges on whether or not the charismatic main character is going to be able to hit that *red button* in time! When they finally make it through thick and thin and get to that illusive "Red Button" they punch it with all their might. What happens then? In some cases the bomb goes off. In other cases the rocket launches. What I like to imagine is the door that had steel bars across it unlocks and opens.

Why do I like that image? I like it because it is exactly what happens when I go back to my "Red Button Statement". When the going gets tough I read it and the locked door opens. My mind finds a solution to a problem I thought was insurmountable. Issues are solved because I know *why* I am investing and *who* will receive the benefits of my success.

My "Red Button Statement" creates a powerful enough emotion within me to remind me exactly what my life is about. It is the springboard I return to whenever I am stuck. It can be that powerful for you too.

If you don't have a strong personal reason to be successful, you won't be. Real estate investing can be a difficult and competitive business. When you are passionate about the reason you want to be a success you will not let *any* stumbling block stop you from being an absolute success. By creating your own personal "Red Button Statement" you guarantee your success!

> "If you don't have a ***strong*** personal reason to be successful you won't be.
>
> **~Mike Watson**"

Think you already know your "Why"? Just want the guts?

You may be anxious to get to the meat of the program. You may be starting to wonder if there *is* any meat. Don't laugh, I know it's true. I hear it all the time in my camps. Most people do not understand this simple fact; the meat is what *anyone* can learn. But here is the secret; if you are one of the *few* who actually do *this* step your success is inevitable. If you take some time to get in touch with what makes you feel passionate about succeeding and put it into your own powerful "Red Button Statement" for action you *will* succeed, regardless of the meat.

> "Without drive and passion the details will get you nowhere. It's like having all of the parts to the car but no gasoline or spark.
>
> **~Mike Watson**"

Step #2 is to create your "Red Button Statement". You may wonder why I put this before teaching you how to find properties. You might think that evaluating deals is more important than creating your "Red Button Statement". You may even go as far as to say, "I don't need to do this step."

Let me just say *if you skip this step you are playing with fire.* You are risking your entire success with this program if you don't spend some time looking at "why" you are doing this and for "whom" you are doing it. As a tip, if you do make that horrible decision to skip this step and find yourself stumbling with the program, come back and start at the beginning. Do this step and it will pick you up from your stumbling. I guarantee it!

Enough said. I believe if you are going to do this step you will, and if not, you won't. Some people are not willing to take this risk and some are.

If you have trouble with your "Why" I suggest you imagine you already have millions of dollars. Now, figure out what you would do with that money to change your life and those around you. Who would you help and how would you help them? Write this down, "If I had 100 million dollars after taxes I would....", and list everything that comes to mind.

Use the answers to that question to create your "Red Button Statement". Your "Red Button Statement" is not about "money", it is about what money can *do* to change your life *and* other people's lives. Expand your success to include others and you will be instantly fulfilled and much more motivated. When you are able to create wealth and freedom or maybe just security or comfort in another person's life you will never be lonely and you will never be unfulfilled.

You will have a higher energy and your actions will take on a more substantial meaning. Really take some time to figure out your "who". This is a key ingredient to your success. It will keep you motivated when times get tough.

Do you realize the power you hold? Do you realize that investors affect hundreds of people's lives? Do you know that when you decide to invest and follow "The Foundation to Success" you will *greatly* increase your positive influence on others?

Keep this in mind when you are thinking about whose lives will be improved by your investing. When you invest you create more money for yourself, create income for investors, and increase what others earn. You may even provide better living conditions for entire communities.

Your "who" can be as big as you want it to be. It can include family, friends, communities, neighborhoods, a certain sector of society and even cities or nations. Be sure to include in it people for whom you have a deep and genuine feeling and your "Red Button Statement" *will* drive you through thick and thin.

Tips to Create an Exceptionally *Powerful* "Red Button Statement"

Ask yourself these questions and write down the answers.

- "Why do I need to be successful?"
- "Who do I need to serve and help?"
- "Who can I help with this life change and how exactly will they be impacted?"

Take the time to look deep within your heart and find answers to these questions that speak to you. You will be unstoppable!

Once you are clear on the above questions here are the next steps in the process.

1. Decide when you would like to accomplish your success and write it down.
2. Take your answers to the questions above and form those ideas into your "Red Button Statement" by starting with something like this, "I will not stop investing until I ________ and until ________ lives are impacted and blessed.
3. Write your Statement and post it in a conspicuous place for constant reminder.

Even though I feel my own "Red Button Statement" is very personal I am going to share it with you. I know that two things will result from sharing. You will understand better how powerful your "Red Button Statement" can be and I will guarantee my success and achieve my purpose *faster*. That is the *power* of sharing your "Red Button Statement". The more you share your "Red Button Statement" with others the stronger it becomes and the faster it will be your reality.

Note: This would be a good time to go make some notes in your "Spark of Inspiration" list in Appendix 2.

My Red Button Statement

"I will not stop working and investing until my wife lives the life she deserves, my children have the confidence and tools to fulfill their ambitions and dreams, my extended family and future generations live in abundance and prosperity, and until I share the knowledge I've been blessed with from implementing "The Foundation to Success", with all of those who are willing to hear and learn it. In addition, I will liberate people by providing world-class education on the subjects of how to obtain *financial prosperity, a balanced lifestyle, career satisfaction and freedom."*

As you can see, this statement means a lot to me. It includes both my "why" and my "who".

In summary, to help you create your "Red Button Statement", determine which people are the most important to you and single out your driving need to be an investor. Putting these things down on paper will help you keep moving forward *no matter what.* You will know why you are working every single day. You will be literally *moved into action* by your own true motivations and dearly held beliefs. This strength will carry you through anything.

I cannot stress enough how important this step is in your success. As a final note, I suggest you re-work your "Red Button Statement" every 6 months or so. Your life is getting ready to explode and in six months your driving life force will be even stronger than it is now. Not to mention, your comfort zone will have expanded and you always want to keep it growing.

Keep your "Red Button Statement" current with where you are in your success. That way it can continue to be a motivating factor like no other. Once you have created your "Red Button Statement" you are now ready to move on to the nuts and bolts of investing.

FREE Online Resources

I have a FREE tool on my web site where you can insert a photo and your "Red Button Statement". (Some people are visual so a photo of something or someone who motivates you can be very inspiring) Then you can print it and post it where you will see it frequently. Just go to **www.mikewatsoninvesting.com/bookextras** and click on "My Red Button Statement"

STEP 3

FIND INCREDIBLE PROPERTIES

STEP 3

FIND INCREDIBLE PROPERTIES

Finally the Nuts and Bolts

So, you have made it through to the nuts and bolts of this outstanding system. Get ready for a wild ride. I've been told that the flow of information to student investors in one of my boot camps is like trying to drink through a fire hose. You will most likely start to feel this way at different times throughout this book. Hang in there. It will all make sense at the end. You will have a complete understanding and *all* of the tools you need to make a *fortune* in Real Estate Investing.

It's time to find out if you are in or out. It is time to see if you are ready to push up your shirt sleeves and get down to business. Are you going to put on the brakes now or step on the gas? The choice is yours. I *know* you can do it!

Step #3 of "The Foundation to Success" is, "Find incredible properties (with competing and non-competing methods *no one* else is using)". Can this really be true? Are there really no other people using these techniques?

The answer is of course there are. My students are! Just take a peek at the "Forum" and you will know it is true. But in reality the number of people who learn these methods and put them into practice is miniscule compared to the number of investors there are in the market place.

And the further truth is, I'm going to show you how to find so many deals that it won't matter if every investor in the whole world knows these techniques. You will still find plenty of amazing deals totally missed by other investors.

The two most important questions are...

Do you remember at the beginning of the book when I said the most important questions are, "What *is* a fantastic deal?" and "How do you find *lots* of them?" It is time to give you the tricks of the trade.

Listen carefully. *"Distress equals Dollars"* I may be repeating myself from a couple of chapters ago. But maybe I haven't made myself clear, *"Distress equals Dollars."* Oh, and did I mention, *"Distress equals Dollars!"* I think you may be getting the point.

Here is the revelation I am ready to share with you. Most people think a distressed property is a property which needs some kind of *physical repair*. This is only partly the truth. In "The Foundation to Success" any property that is not utilizing its *"Highest and Best" use* is a *distressed property*.

Note how simple this is. Your quest is simply to find properties that have a higher and better use. Once you find these opportunities you can start the change from what the properties *are* to what they can and *should* be.

When you change the *use* of a property you change its *value*. The larger the discrepancy between what a property's use is *now* and what its highest use *could be* the more value is created. Thus the better the deal it is. You might be starting to get a hint of how I'm going to help you create your huge profits.

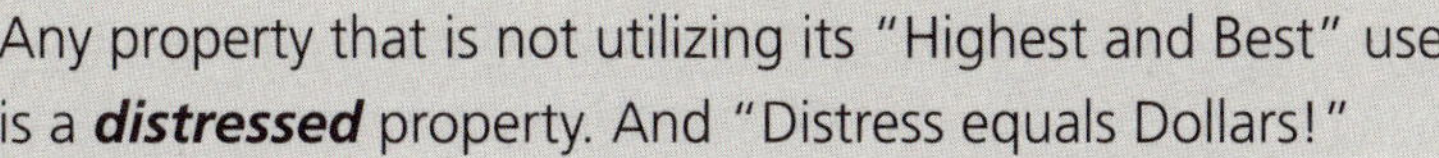

> Any property that is not utilizing its "Highest and Best" use is a ***distressed*** property. And "Distress equals Dollars!"
>
> **~Mike Watson**

Four Ways to Create DOLLAR$

I've already said that "Distress equals Dollars". Now I'm going to show you why. I explained that distress can mean more than just poor physical condition. I've shown you that distress also means a property is not being used for its "Highest and Best" use. But what exactly does that mean?

The simplest way I can explain it is to say, "*Density equals Dollars.*" Did you catch that? I made a slight change to our "*Distress equals Dollars*" equation. It's now "*Density equals Dollars.*"

At this point you are probably thinking I'm a little silly for repeating these catch phrases so often. The whole point I'm trying to make is this: *Distress* means a property is not being used for its "Highest and Best" use. When you learn how to *find* a distressed property and change the use to *where it should be* you can make *huge profits!*

Obviously the key is, "Where do you find these types of properties?" The incredible thing is this, "They are all around you. You just don't know how to see them yet". I am going to show you how easy it is to see them. But I'm getting ahead of myself. First I want to tell you four ways you can create dollars. All of them are ways to increase the density of a property.

My definition of density includes number of units, number of owners, amount of square footage and amount of net rental income. That means you will increase *at least* one of these four things on a property to increase its value. Here is a little more detail.

1. Increase the number of units. 10 Condominiums on a lot are worth significantly more than a home on that same property. As a matter of fact the lot is worth more if it is simply *allowed* to have more units. This is pretty much the case across the board.
2. Increase the amount of square footage to the existing building. Obviously if you add square footage to the property it will be worth more. The key with this technique is to pay less for the square footage you added than the increase in the sales price. (Pay $100 per square foot to build and sell it for $250 per square foot)
3. Increase the net income the property produces. When a property produces income it is valued by that income. When you increase the income or decrease expenses you increase the value of the property. Your income is more "dense".
4. Increase the number of owners, or Tax ID numbers. This is similar to number one but with a twist. If you buy an apartment complex and turn it into condominiums why does the value increase? It increases because there are more owners. When an owner occupant buys a property they can get better financing terms than an investor. Therefore they can pay more per door than an investor. For that reason and a few others we will discuss later, a property is worth more when you increase the number of owners or Tax ID numbers.

> "Find a property where you can ***change the use*** with one of these four methods and you will change its ***value***.
>
> **~Mike Watson**"

How to Put What You Have Learned into *Action*

Let's say that one day you are driving down the road and you see a *little house* on a really *big lot* on a street that has *other* types of buildings. For example there may be a gas station a few doors down, a lawyer's office next door and a small apartment complex at the end of the block.

What would be going through your mind at this point? If you had *not* read this book it might be, "What am I going to have for dinner tonight?" or "Who did I need to call?" or "I wonder what is on TV tonight?"

On the other hand if you had read this book and you came across this situation it might catch your attention. You might think, "I wonder if you could put something else on that lot?" Or even this, "Since there are other things right around here I bet you could put more on that lot than what is sitting there."

You might go so far as to think, "I bet with that big lot you could build something like that apartment complex on it." And with that thought should go, "I *know* that an apartment building is worth more than an old house."

And finally, if you had only read to this chapter you would say to yourself, "What do I do now? I have to know if I can help out that *distressed* property!" If this is what you would be thinking you are on the right track. Just remember to keep your eye on the road.

That All Important Word "Zoning"

Now that you have an inkling of what we are trying to do it is time to learn about the crux of "The Foundation to Success". This concept is what is typically called "Zoning." Most people think of zoning as just being "Where you can build certain things." What you may not realize is that it is a *very precise tool* which cities use to sculpt areas as they wish them to be built, re-developed or re-vitalized.

What do I mean by this? How can zoning be a tool? In reality, cities have very little say about who builds what and where. But, they do have the knowledge of what the city needs. They know where parks are needed, they know where homes are needed, and they know where re-development is needed.

Because the city has this knowledge but very little power to make developers build, they use "Zoning" to have some say in what goes where. By manipulating the zoning in an area they can somewhat control how a city is built and how it is re-built.

When a property is zoned to have a home on it then the value of the land represents that home. When a property is zoned to have a huge retail center on it the value of the land represents that possibility. One has a *much* higher value than the other.

When the city uses the tool at their disposal and changes zoning they are *manipulating* the value of property. When they allow more density in an area, developers will build there because they can make more money when they build 10 or 20 units than they can when they build one home.

This sounds a bit like, "Density equals Dollars."

Isn't everything with "Higher and Better" zoning already built?

At first thought you might think this is true. But here is the exciting news. There are properties all over your city that have either nothing on them or something that should not be there. Or even better the zoning has recently or will soon *change to a higher density* than what is allowed right now!

How do I know this? How can I be sure that in EVERY city these properties exist? Here is why. First, there is not enough housing built to guarantee *affordable* entry level housing to everyone who wants it. If there was there would be nice affordable housing sitting vacant. That is quite rare.

Second, I have driven around hundreds of cities. Not one is completely built to its "Highest and Best" use. You would probably be shocked if you got in your car right now and drove around your city. You would find more vacant or distressed property than you ever imagined.

Third, personnel in almost every city development office I've ever visited have told me there are areas in their city that need re-development. These are areas that are "physically distressed".

Here is the best news yet. <u>In the areas where your city has physical distress the city is most likely offering incentives or higher density just to get people to go build anything new. Find those areas and give them what they want.</u> That is a multi-million dollar tip!

This will blow your mind!

Now that you understand a little bit about zoning I want to give you twenty things you can look for. Remember to look at property for what it can be, not for what it is now.

Look for the following:

1. A home on a lot zoned for more than one home.
2. A home on a lot zoned for a duplex
3. A home on a lot zoned for multi-family (4-plex, 8-plex, apartments, condo's)
4. An apartment complex that can be converted to condominiums (There are more "owners" therefore it is considered more dense, and therefore more valuable)
5. A property, with or without something on it that is large enough to subdivide into multiple lots.
6. A home on a lot that is large enough to subdivide and build a second home.
7. A duplex, triplex, 4-plex, etc. which can be converted into condominiums.
8. A small home in an area where prices are high thereby justifying adding square footage.
9. A home with an unfinished basement which can be turned into living space.
10. A home with an unfinished attic that can be turned into living space.
11. An apartment with "all bills paid" by owners. Possible to separate meters or bill tenants and get higher net income.
12. A commercial property next to a residential property.
13. Physical distress clumping together. Possibly area where more density is allowed.
14. Any type of physical distress.
15. Small homes mixed in with nice big homes.

16. Vacant Lots next to multi-family properties.
17. Single family homes next to multi-family projects.
18. Large corner lots. With or without property on them.
19. Properties with more than one home on them. (For conversion or subdivision)
20. "For Rent" signs. (This is a distressed owner; their property is definitely not being used for its "Highest and Best" use.)

What do all of these things have in common?

They all are examples of property or areas in distress! They all have a "Higher and Better" use. Always keep your eye out for distress. (By the way, this was just a quick list I threw out to you. I have many more where this came from. My goal is to teach you how to spot distress on your own.)

Note: This may be a good time to write down some thoughts on your "Spark of Inspiration" List in Appendix 2.

I *love* all types of distress!

I have touched a few times on the fact that in "The Foundation to Success" we look at distressed property as those properties that are not currently being used as their "Highest and Best" use. But, do we have any use for actual physical distress? Should we just discount it completely? There are three reasons why my answer to those questions is a resounding, "No!"

The first I'll explain with a familiar example. I found a lot that had a home on it where the zoning allowed an "Awesome 15-unit condo complex" to be built there. This home was not in good condition. Even though I was just going to tear out that home I cared about the physical distress because I was able to buy the property for a lower price.

Did the builder who bought the property from *me* care if the home was in bad condition either? No, because they were going to remove the home anyway as well. So, *because* it was in bad condition I actually made *more* profit than I would have if it was in good shape and I had to pay more for it.

The second reason I like physical distress is it throws up a red flag. When I am driving around and I find an area with several properties in disrepair grouped together or near each other I get excited. Why? Because I know I'm going to get to do several fantastic deals in a very small area. Why would that be exciting? Because it is a form of leverage to do lots of deals in one area. First, your contractor is happy. Second, you will be an expert on that area. Third, you don't have to drive all over town!

The last reason I LOVE physical distress is that as these physically distressed properties begin to cluster together, the city will begin to sit up and take note. What happens then? When a city begins to notice an area that needs to be re-developed it will offer special incentives for investors and developers to come in and clean it up, or "redevelop it".

These incentives can sometimes be extremely lucrative. One time I was meeting with a person working at a development office in a city near Las Vegas. They told me that in a certain area, where they wanted re-development, the city would "Guarantee a zoning change to a higher density". I said, "What do you mean *guarantee*?" They said, "If you submit an application for a zone change, pay a $750 application fee and go through 2 hearings in 45 days, you can nearly *double* the number of units as is currently zoned for on that lot. Furthermore, we will allow you to record a new site plan for your project during the same 45 days."

I couldn't believe it. To have *"guaranteed"* zoning is quite rare. I took advantage of the incentive and immediately went out and bought four properties in that area. I did the zoning change and sold them to developers for a *huge* profit. I love distress!

Clues to Help Find "Distressed Properties"

As you are looking for properties, here is a quick list of things that should click in your mind as being signs of distress. If you see several of them in an area make a mental note to do some further investigating of that area.

- Boarded up homes
- Broken windows
- Weeds, dead grass
- Cars on blocks
- Appliances in yard
- Full mailbox
- Piles of newspapers
- Notices/stickers on windows/properties
- Variance notice
- Utilities turned off
- Lights always on or off
- Blinds always open or shut
- Dilapidated roof
- Holes in walls
- Homes that are "For Sale by Owner"
- For rent/lease signs
- Out of area phone numbers on signs
- Vacant properties
- Notice of Defaults
- Condemned properties
- Health Department Notices

If you <u>believe</u>, get ready to explode your profits!

We are getting ready to get into a lot of details. Understand that the details are necessary, but the truth is "The Foundation to Success" is simple. All you have to do is find and buy a property that is not being used for its "Highest and Best" use. Then put the property back up for sale and make the change into it's "Highest and Best" use.

The way you do that is by doing one of four things, increasing the number of *units* on the property, increasing the amount of *square footage*, increasing the number of *owners* or Tax ID numbers or increasing net rental *income*.

As soon as you do one of those things your property is worth more. As a matter of fact it is worth more the MOMENT you spot the discrepancy of its use. Some people find that statement hard to believe. Here is a true story about one of my students.

Lynne had been learning about "The Foundation to Success" for about 4 months. During that time she found a property that had a duplex on it. It was in an area where there was a shortage of affordably priced homes. She thought that by doing a condo conversion on the property it would be worth more money. (In other words, she increased the number of owners from 1 as a duplex to 2 as two condo's)

She put the property under contract to buy but was petrified that she was making a mistake. The bank required that she get an appraisal on the property. She asked the bank if she could do it "subject to" the condo conversion. They said they would prefer that because then they would know what it was worth when she completed the conversion.

The day Lynne got the appraisal back (even before she bought the property!) she was in shock, relieved and amazed! The purchase price of the property as a duplex was $275,000. However, the appraised values of the two condos were $210,000 and $215,000 for a total value of $425,000 WITHOUT DOING ANY PHYSICAL WORK TO THE PROPERTY!

She got up in front of the classroom to share her story and was almost in tears. I asked her if she had actually believed it was that simple. She admitted that "No, I didn't truly believe it was so simple until after I got the appraisal. Even then I had to look at it 3 or 4 times before I believed it. Now I do."

It is that simple. Change the use, change the value.

> Believe it! When you change the use you change the ***value***, sometimes dramatically.
>
> **~Mike Watson**

How to Be an Expert

You might be wondering what else you need to know. You also might want to know how the system has evolved over the last 12 years. And finally you might want to know how you can do *lots* of these deals.

Here is the ultimate answer to those questions: You build an "Area of Expertise". That is it. There is nothing more. Let's begin with my definition of an "Area of Expertise". ("AoE")

An "Area of Expertise" is a small area you specifically choose that will be the site of your first 5-20 deals. This area should be small enough for you to truly be an expert about it. This means you will know each property, every owner, and all of the details about zoning and development in your "AoE".

I suggest you keep your area to a 1x1 mile or 2x2 mile square at the most. More than this will be very difficult to handle. Plus, there will be deals galore even in this small area. I strongly believe your chance for success is improved if you focus on a smaller area.

Are you asking, "How do I choose my area?" If so, that is the key question for it is *vital* to your success. Pay close attention to the next few tips. They will make or break your deals.

Typically the best area to start with has older properties. There are three main reasons why this is true. First, in new areas you will not find much *redevelopment* opportunity. Second, in older areas there are usually *smaller homes on larger lots*. These larger lots may offer the possibility for higher density zoning. The third reason is that in many cities these areas may be *somewhat close in* to the city center. When you build new properties in those areas the values are usually higher based on location alone.

> "The smaller and older your "Area of Expertise" the easier it will be to have outstanding success.
>
> **~Mike Watson**"

Let me explain the reason why we are looking for an older area with smaller homes on larger lots. Many of your deals are going to exist because of what is called "infill". Infill occurs when a city grows out so far that the traffic becomes unbearable. As this happens cities offer developers incentives to come back in toward the center of the city and add more housing where it was missed as the city was developing outward. The city does this in an attempt to relieve some of the commuter traffic.

In addition areas that are older may have physical distress and need redevelopment. The city may offer fantastic incentives to get builders, investors and developers to come in and give the area a face lift. The most compelling incentive is usually higher density allowances or zoning.

Three Things to Remember When You Choose Your "Area of Expertise"

First, consider the zoning! Ideally your area will have at least *6 different types of zones*. Why is this important? You want multiple zones because in these transition areas cities will often let you be more flexible in your design and outcome. Allowances may be made for more density or square footage than in other areas. This can be a very good thing.

Does it have to be six? "No, but absolutely make sure you *do not* choose an area with *only* residential or *only* commercial zoning!" (I will go into fantastic detail in later sections on how to get this information. For now just absorb the basic concept.)

Second, pick an area *where you already have some knowledge.* It could be near your home, office, child's school or any place you drive through frequently. It might be somewhere you lived in the past. Try to keep the area as near to your home as possible but do make sure the criteria fits. My first "AoE" was the trip between my home and my office. I had so much fun driving to work. I would take a new way every day and find deals that made me more money than my "job."

Finally, make sure your area does *not* have Homeowner's associations or CC&R's (Codes Covenants and Restrictions). As a matter of fact avoid these like the plague. These areas usually have already been developed to the highest density allowed. This means "No profit potential!" Homeowner's associations usually maintain the properties in the area to a high enough standard that the city has no real reason to offer incentives for urban renewal. When you see an HOA just think, "Keep Out! No investors allowed!"

P.S. Don't go too far outside of the area you live or work. It's harder to get contractors. It's harder to keep your pulse on the market. It's harder to be at your deals when necessary. Investing close to your home is always best.

> "When you choose your "AoE", pick an area with 6 or more zones, an area with which you are familiar, and one ***without*** an HOA.
>
> **~Mike Watson**"

It's time to push up your sleeves and get down to business.

The fact is that investing takes a lot of hard work. I would imagine you are starting to realize this. Obstacles come up in every transaction and they take a certain amount of tenacity to overcome. When I talk about the *simplicity* of the system and the fact that everyone can use it do not confuse those things with it being *easy*.

You will have to work to make the system work. Once you have completed a few deals it will become easier and easier. Your knowledge will expand and your techniques will improve by using the system in your own marketplace. The only way to be a *huge success* is to take *huge action*.

All of this said, I am going to do my best to make it simple and exciting. Are you ready for some details? Are you ready to make this system your own? Are you ready to become an *expert*? Let's do it!

The first thing is not so huge but it is necessary. Go to the store and buy a 4 inch thick 3 ring binder and get at least 15 tabs for sections. This binder is for you to gather your "Area of Expertise" *vital* information. This binder will enable you to have this vital information at your fingertips when you are out looking for properties and evaluating deals. Go to the store now. Do not read any further until you do that step. You won't be overwhelmed if you have a place to put the huge amount of information I'm about to give you.

Did you go? OK. Now that you have your binder, here is what you will put in it.

15 *Vital* Pieces of Information You Need Right Now

What follows is an exhaustive list of the *vital information* you want to have in your binder. I will explain each item, why it is important and where you can find it. In some cases I will give you an example or a photo. If you start to feel a little overwhelmed remember this, "You are becoming an expert just by *making* your binder!"

FREE Online Resources

If you want to have the 15 tabs to print out just go to my web site at **www.mikewatsoninvesting.com/bookextras** and go to "AoE Tabs".

Tab #1 "Current Zoning Map"

What is a current zoning map? It is a map of your city which shows the different zoning areas. It is usually done in color. You can find the current zoning map at your city or county development office.

You will begin to pick your "AoE" from this map. Choose an area based on the tips previously discussed. Get the largest copy available of your area. (Once you choose it) You want to be able to see each property individually within your "AoE" and how each one is currently zoned.

EXAMPLE OF A CURRENT ZONING MAP

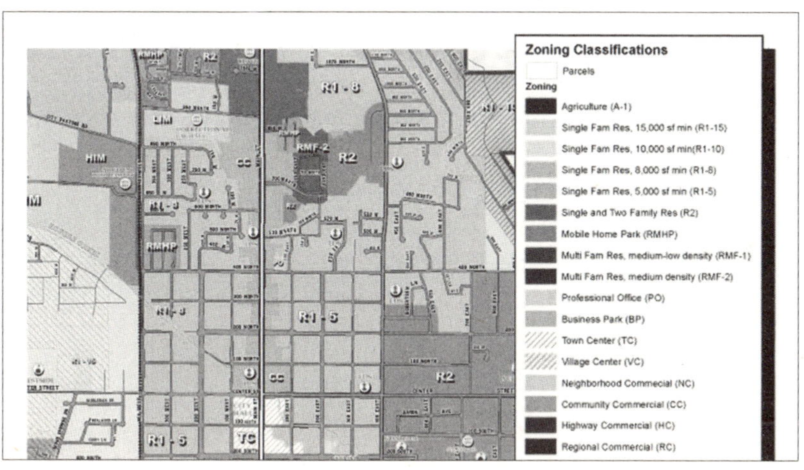

Tab #2 "Future Zoning Map" or "Future Land Use Map"

I know it sounds a little sci-fi but, "The Future Map" of your city is your key to riches. I'll explain it in a minute but remember, the beauty of your "Future Map" is that most investors have *no idea* what it is or how to use it properly to find amazing deals. You soon will.

The "Future Land Use Map" is a map showing what the city or county wants to see created in the *future*. Almost all cities are working toward change and redevelopment in certain areas. Typically the city will offer *higher density zoning* to incentivize the developers to build in those areas. This zoning is shown on the "Future Map."

Here is an amazing secret. "If the city wants it in the future, they really want it *now*." What does this mean for you? You can find areas where more density is desired and give it to them now.

You will find this map at the development office or city planning office. They may have a different name for it but it *is* there. You may run into a lot of people that don't know what you are talking about. Don't give up! I have seen it called the Future Plan, the 20 year plan, Neighborhood Plan, the 2020 plan, Future Land Use Map, General plan, comprehensive plan, etc. The best thing to do is to find someone who is in charge of zoning and they will know what you're looking for. Get the map for your particular "AoE". Be diligent. Find that map. It is your main treasure map to riches.

> "The "Future Zoning Map" is your main ***treasure map*** to riches.
>
> **~Mike Watson**"

Tab #3 "Zoning Breakdowns"

Wait! Don't leave the city development center yet. While you are there make sure you pick up a copy of the "Zoning Breakdowns" These are the written explanations of the intention for each zone and a simple explanation of what can be built in each zone.

For instance, in one area there is a zone called MF-3. In this certain area the intent is to put multi-family (MF) properties on the lots with up to 24 units per acre. In other words, you could build a 24 unit apartment complex on the lot if it was one acre and all other standards were met.

If you have trouble finding the "Zoning Breakdowns" they can sometimes be found online if your city has a development web site. But the best way to get any information is from an individual who works there. You can ask them questions and find out more about your city.

Tab #4 "Use Chart"

These sound so boring. Don't nod off now because use charts are *awesome*. These charts show all of the different types of property that can be put on a lot with certain zoning. For instance, if you look at the top and it says R-2 then look down the column it will show you what *can be* (permitted) put on a lot which is zoned R-2.

It will also show you what *might* (conditional) be put on that lot. And finally what *cannot* (unpermitted) be put on a lot with its particular zoning. In order to follow the path of least resistance, always look for permitted uses.

This is a fantastic tool coupled with your zoning maps. These two together are what you need to determine the "Highest and Best" use of a property. Use Charts are also available at your development office or online.

EXAMPLE OF A USE CHART

LAND USE MATRIX

LAND USE KEY P=Permitted Use C=Conditional Use Blank Box=Not Allowed

PERMITTED USE	ZONING DISTRICTS																		
	A1	R1-15	R1-10	R1-8	R1-5	R2	R-MHP	R-MF1	R-MF2	PO	BP	VC	TC	NC	CC	RC	HC	L-IM	H-IM
Accessory Apartment					C														
Dwelling - Mobile Home							P												
Dwelling – Multiple-Family						P		P	P			C	C						
Dwelling – Single- or Multiple-Family above First Floor (Mixed Use)						C		P	P	P		P	P						
Dwelling – Single-Family Attached						P		P	P										
Dwelling – Single-Family Detached	P	P	P	P	P	P	C	P	P										
Dwelling – Single-Family Detached, Manufactured	P	P	P	P	P	P	P	P	P										
Dwelling - Two-Unit (Duplex)						P		P	P										
Mobile Home Park							P												

Tab #5 "Development Standards"

As any good architect knows these are the *key* to the treasure map. Luckily you don't have to be an architect to take advantage of this treasure. At some point you will probably want an architect on your "Power Team".

As for "Development Standards"; These are the standards your city requires you to follow when you build, add onto or remodel an existing property. For instance, your development standards will tell how much parking you are required to put on your lot based on what you are going to build. It also includes such vital information as how far back you have to be from the road in order to build (these are your "setbacks"). You will need this basic information for each type of property you may buy in each zone.

These standards can usually be found on your development web site. Talk with the city and find out what the standards are in your "AoE". They may be different in different areas.

Stay with me here. We are going through a lot of material very quickly. These first 5 items are the basis for what we do from here on out. They are the basic development information you need about your city. They are what you will use to help you start to pick out your "AoE". What follows gets a bit more detailed and specific to certain areas within your city. It's about to get *really* fun!

Tab #6 "Special Zoning or Economic Incentives"

These are *crucial* programs your city offers that you need to learn. Make sure you find the right person to talk with at the city planning department. Many have no idea what we mean by an incentive. I've had a person at a city look me in the eye and say, "We don't have any development incentives at all," only to find out that they had an area of town where they did not require *any* parking. Do you know what that does for a project? It can increase the number of units you can build *dramatically*.

There are many types of incentives such as, increased density, automatic variances, and low interest loans for both the buyer and the developer. Some cities offer down payment assistance or may offer to pay for utilities or roads if you build affordable housing. Some cities allow you to build taller buildings, have lower parking requirements and on and on.

Find out what kinds of incentives are being offered in different areas of your city. These incentives can make a deal very lucrative. Some investors even find the areas where incentives are being offered and just make *those* areas their "AoE". I highly recommend considering this as a technique for finding your "Area of Expertise".

P.S. Update this information every 3-6 months

> "Development incentives are so powerful they can actually ***determine*** your "Area of Expertise"
>
> **~Mike Watson**"

Tab #7 "<u>Overlays</u>"

Overlays are exciting! Overlays can be worth millions of dollars, but be careful. Overlays can also kill a deal very quickly. Overlays are simply additional zoning or regulations that have been "laid over" an area, which either aid in development or hinder it.

Make sure you know about any overlays in your city and especially in your "AoE" once you have determined its boundaries. That way you won't miss an incredible opportunity or make a decision to purchase a property based on only partial information.

You can sometimes find overlay information online if your city has an extensive development web site. However, it is always better to go into the development office and talk with someone who is familiar with your area.

Sometimes overlays are a part of the future plan. When they are part of the future plan, overlays can have incredible incentives for developing properties to their "Highest and Best" use.

For instance, I have a student who found an area that had an overlay that allowed what is called "Mixed Use" zoning. This type of zoning allowed the person who owned the property to build both commercial and residential on the same lot and with a *much higher density* than was allowed without the overlay. Needless to say this became their "AoE".

The time has come to make a decision.

By the time you put the first seven sections of your binder together you should be formulating your plan of attack. The first thing to do in your plan is to decide *where* to attack.

So what does this mean for awesome investors? It means you should be starting to notice some areas with potential for massive "Higher and Better" uses that can be your "AoE". As a matter of fact, if you don't have an area by this time you should go back and review the information in the first seven tabs again. In addition you should review the section on how to choose your "AoE".

As a final tip for picking your area, "Concentrate on those areas of your city where there are incentives and overlays" This is where you will get the most bang for your buck in the *distress and density equal dollars* equation.

It will be quite difficult to get the rest of the information for your binder until you have narrowed down a small area in which to work. Pick an area now. If you have to change it later that's OK. Just pick one so you can move forward with your binder.

Note: This might be a good time to make some notes on your "Spark of Inspiration" List in Appendix 2.

A sticky question

One day when I was teaching a Degree Camp a student asked me, "What if all of the areas with incentives are in 'really bad' areas? Should I still buy property there?" My answer was this, "First of all, you should never spend time in an area where you consider your health and safety to be at risk. However, most areas with incentives will be areas where you want to work. Cities don't offer incentives in areas that don't have problem properties."

Then I was asked, "How bad is too bad? How do I know?" What I said was, "I have always tried to judge an area by people's willingness to live in the area. In other words, how much of the area is occupied?"

A really good way to answer this question is with *vacancy rates*. If the normal vacancy rate in your city is 8% and a distressed area has a rate of 20% or more, you should typically not invest there. Those numbers indicate a problem. For some reason or another, people don't want to live in that area. New housing probably won't fix the problem by itself.

On the other hand, if the vacancy rate in a city is 8% and your "rough" area has a 12% vacancy rate or less, you should explore that area further. Assure yourself that you don't feel at risk there and proceed with analyzing your deals.

Everyone needs a place to live. Sometimes the neighborhoods I was most concerned about resulted in the best investments and the happiest neighbors. Don't judge a neighborhood until you look at it a little more closely.

How to be a Super-Sleuth

Now that you are an expert on your city in general, know some things about your zoning and development standards and have picked your "AoE" it's time to be a Super-Sleuth. The fastest way to be a success is to do what successful people are already doing. How can we apply that idea to real estate investing? That brings us to Tab #8, the "Super-Sleuth" tab. It doesn't sound that intriguing yet, but just wait.

Tab #8 "Subdivisions, PUD's, Zone Changes, Variances and Special Use Permits"

At this point you may be saying, "What *are* all of these things?

Have I gotten in way over my head?" The answer is, they are ways to *mimic* others who are making incredibly profitable deals happen. Stick it out just a bit longer and everything will become clear.

All of the things listed above are what *others* are doing to *change the use* of property. (Remember, when you change the use you change the value.) Now that you know your "AoE", go to the city and ask for copies of all of the things listed here that are happening in your area. Then you will see what others are doing so you can do them too.

A subdivision means someone is just taking a large parcel of land and dividing it into smaller parcels.

A PUD is a "Planned Unit Development". I like to call a PUD "Make Sense Zoning". When you have a piece of land with the correct zoning but that doesn't fit exactly into the development standards for the area, and it makes sense to develop it, you can usually ask to do a PUD.

I did a PUD on one of my projects. There was a piece of land that was large enough for 12 units based on the zoning and lot size. The only problem was that it did not have enough land on the street (required frontage). Technically I couldn't do *anything* with the lot.

I went to the city and said, "I know this lot does not have enough frontage to build according to your standards, but it is a very large lot. Can I do a PUD?" They said, "Yes. If you put in a playground, a picnic area, and fence the entire property you can build 12 units." Everyone else thought the property was worthless. I built two fourplexes and two duplexes. *I Love PUD's.*

A zone change is just that. It is when a person asks the city to change the zoning of a property so they can build something different. I don't usually suggest doing a zone change as they are not typically guaranteed. I like to suggest you always follow the path of least resistance in your investing. The path of least resistance is not normally through a zone change. Though as you may remember when the change is *guaranteed* it can be worth *a lot* of money.

A variance is when there is just one or two things that don't work with the development standards on a project. For instance, maybe there is only room for 16 parking places but the standards require 17.

At this point if you were building this project you would have to ask special permission from the city to continue. What you are asking for is a variance. The problem most times is that with a variance you have to make sure the neighbors agree with your project. If they do great, if not you may have spent a lot of time and money for nothing.

This is why it is important to find out what variances are getting approved. With this information you can get a good idea of what the city and neighborhood will allow and why.

A special use permit is used when you want to build something on a property that is not allowed in the zoning. For instance, if you want to put an apartment on a piece of property that is zoned for industrial use only. You would ask the city or county for a special use permit to allow you to build the apartment.

Now that I have explained all of the items on this tab let's again go over *why* you want these things in your binder. When you go into the city offices you want to ask about all of these that apply to your "AoE". You want to find out how others are making huge profits and mimic them. (See the Laws of Mimicry below) Most of the items in this tab are ways to *increase density*. If others are getting projects with higher density approved you can too.

All of this information is public information. You can ask for copies of all material the city has that was submitted by developers, architects and engineers. Find out what is being done currently and what has been done in the last 6 to 12 months in your "AoE".

P.S. Update every 3-6 months for new info and projects to mimic.

You Will Become a Local Hero

Tab #9 "Minutes from City Council Meetings"

Why in the world would I have you collect minutes from your city council meetings? What possible good use could come from them?

Have you ever been to a city council meeting? If you have you might notice they are time consuming and not all that exciting. (I will change that thought shortly.)

Quite often the city council is the entity that *determines* development issues. They approve zoning, they decide on variances, they rule about issues that will *make or break* a project. At the very least, make copies and read the minutes from the city council meetings that have anything to do with your "AoE" for the last 6 to 12 months.

These minutes often can be found online. If not, ask the people at your development offices where you can get a copy. In addition to getting copies of past minutes I recommend that you *go* to the meetings and get to know the people on the city council. Sometimes the meetings are shown on local television stations. The benefit to watching it on television is you can skip over the parts that have nothing to do with development. On the other hand you won't get to know the people.

Now that you have spied on other investors and projects it's time to be a super incredible sleuth and find out what your *city* wants you to do. Talk about following the "path of least resistance." If you find out what they want and go do it you will be a hero. City councils are used to developers coming in and shoving ideas down their throats. It is the rare developer or investor, who will ask their opinion. If <u>you</u> do this you will be heavily rewarded.

I have a student in Southern California who went to her city meetings regularly. The council took notice because she was the *only* person from the general public in attendance. After one of the meetings they asked her, "Why are you here? You could just watch this on television". She said, "I come to the meetings to find out in person what the city wants to see developed."

They were so shocked and excited by her answer they said, "We will stay for an hour after the meeting and answer any questions you have." From this meeting alone she has several deals going. One of which is on land that the city is *donating* to her!

It may be time consuming to go to the city meeting but it is full of golden nuggets. When you find out what the city council is or is not allowing other people to build and you give them what they want, you will be a local hero.

> Go to your local city meetings. You will end up being a "Local Hero".
>
> **~Mike Watson**

Tab #10 "Subdivision Deed Restrictions"

What is a "Subdivision Deed Restriction?" A deed restriction is created when the original person who built in an area subdivided the land. When they subdivided they created rules of the subdivision. These rules apply *first*. Even zoning is secondary to deed restrictions. If there is a rule in your deed restrictions you must follow it. If you don't your neighboring owners could sue you.

Let me show you how important these rules are. One investor attending my classes found a property and put it under contract. Her intention was to build another unit on the property. The zoning allowed her to do this. As a matter of fact the city said, "We will give you *building permits* to build the unit." The only problem was that the Deed Restrictions (that were *55 years old*) stated no more than one unit could be build on any property in that subdivision. As you can imagine this presented some challenges on her deal.

Luckily she had a person on her "Power Team" who was familiar with this type of situation and she found a way to amend the restrictions and save the deal. The point is to know your restrictions *prior* to going under contract. If you have a relationship with a title company you can ask them to pull up the deed restrictions in your "AoE". Or, at the very least pull them up on any property on which you are seriously considering making an offer.

It's Time to Get Down to the Nitty-Gritty

We have gone from very general information down to some specific information for your "AoE" By now your binder should be getting pretty full. At the same time you are slowly becoming an expert. It is now time to move to individual properties and start looking through a magnifying glass at the possible deals in your area.

Tab #11 "Names of all Property Owners by Address"

Yes, you really are going to get every name of every owner in your entire "AoE" This is one of the reasons why I want your area to be relatively small. If you have chosen an area that has over 2000 properties it will be hard to do this step. Do not make this mistake. Pare down your "AoE" at this point if necessary.

This list will be very handy when you get to the "Non-Compete" methods of finding incredible deals. Make sure you get all of the properties in your area and the owner name and address which may or may not be the address of the property. You can find this information at your county property tax appraisal district records. In most cases this is online.

If you are a real estate agent or know a real estate agent (or have one on your "*Power Team*") you may have access to a title company that can, for a small fee, pull up all of this information for you and organize it.

Tab #12 "Tax Information on each property"

What are the benefits of having the tax records of the properties in your "AoE?" They are many. You may be able to see if there is an existing loan on the property and how much it is. You may be able to see exactly what the size of the property is. You can find out when the owner bought the property.

It will give you some general information about what buildings are on the property and their condition. All of these things will help you find property, owners and deals! This information will also help when you are negotiating your purchases.

These records are available online in most areas. If not, you can contact your tax district and find out where you can get this public information. And again, your real estate agent will have access to these records as will a title company.

Two More *Incredible* Treasure Maps

Tab #13 "Property Plat Maps"

Property plat maps are an *awesome* way to find opportunities! I consider them to be one of the two additional treasure maps for real estate investing (The future map is number one). A plat map is basically a map of a subdivision showing the *boundaries* of each lot and sometimes the measurements of the lots. The plat map may also have tax ID numbers and the subdivision name on it.

EXAMPLE OF A PLAT MAP

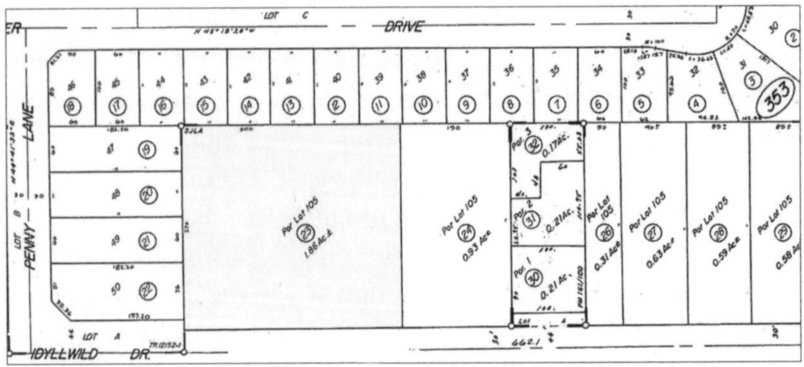

Some fun things to look for on plat maps are flag lots, oversized lots, skinny lots, landlocked lots, condominiums and corner lots.

A "flag" lot is a lot that has been subdivided into two lots. One is in the front by the street, the other is in the back with a long driveway to the street. The back lot actually looks like a flag with a flagpole. Thus the name "flag" lot. Why should you look for flag lots? When someone created that flag lot they were essentially creating *density* where it did not exist before. There had been one house on a lot before and they subdivided into a "flag" lot and built a second home.

EXAMPLE OF A "FLAG" LOT

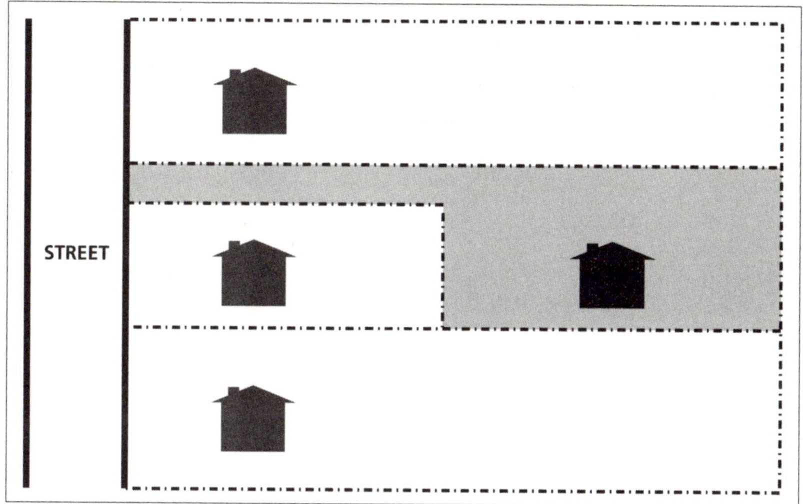

If you see any "flag" lots in your "AoE" you know that it is possible to use this technique on other lots in the area. Keep an eye out for "flag" lots on your plat maps.

An *oversized* lot could be split into two or more lots or could possibly have something with more units built on it. *Skinny* lots that may seem unusable to others may be quite valuable if combined with other adjacent lots. *Landlocked* lots can be remedied. When you make a lot useable that is essentially useless, you will create value! Landlocked lots can be given easements or combined with other lots.

Corner lots are fun, especially when they are large because they can often times be split into two legal lots. When you find a big corner lot you may have found a deal. You may be able to see if others have split corner lots on the plat map. Keep looking for treasure.

How do you know if there is a condominium on a parcel by looking on the plat map? In most areas condominium units have individual tax id numbers. These will all be shown on the lot with the condominiums. Why is it important to know where Condominiums are? Because their presence indicates that it is likely you could turn apartments into condominiums. When you increase the number of owners from 1 (50 unit apartment complex) to 50 (50 condos) you will increase the value tremendously.

The property plats can sometimes be found online at your tax appraisal district site. If you can't get them there you may have to go to the county courthouse or appraisal district office. Get your hands on that treasure map!

Tab #14 "Aerial Photographs"

As you may know an "Aerial Photograph" is simply a picture of property taken from overhead. But don't worry you don't have to get in a helicopter and take them yourself. Someone else has already done that for you for free. Aerial photos are so much fun. I can spend hours just looking at them. I consider these pictures the third of the three treasure maps for finding outstanding deals (Future Map, Plat Map, and Aerial Map).

Aerial photos are fun and exciting because they literally tell the story of *infill*. When you look down on a property from above you can see exactly where you can add density. Imagine looking at a neighborhood from above and being able to see where there are empty lots, small homes on large lots, multiple properties on one lot, etc.

You can see where a building is situated on a lot. You can see how much space there is to build other structures. You can see adjoining lots that are vacant. You can see properties that have more than one structure on them already (to mimic). In a nutshell you can see *opportunity*. Do not skip Tab #14. It is the tab that will illuminate your world with the techniques taught in "The Foundation to Success"

EXAMPLE OF AN AERIAL MAP

These photos can usually be found online at your city development web sites. Most have some sort of mapping system, possibly called a GIS map, with aerial photos of properties that you can print. You can also find free aerial photos on many other web sites. Take the time to get aerial photographs of your whole "AoE". Then sit down and take a really good look at what is there.

You will see areas with room for more properties to be built that you could not otherwise see, even by driving by. Aerial photos combined with plat maps are super powerful tools you can use to find amazing deals.

> Your other two treasure maps, Aerial Photo Maps and Plat Maps, can be a goldmine for deals. Have fun with them finding opportunities for infill.
>
> **~Mike Watson**

At Last the Final Tab!

If you have done this work correctly you may have had to go buy another binder. I realize there is a lot of information you have to gather. I also know that this information has the power to make you *wildly successful*. Let's keep going and finish it up.

Tab #15 "MLS Info"

You now know about your city, about your area and you are starting to learn about the individual properties in your "AoE" There is only one section of vital information you are missing. You must know the *market* in your "AoE."

There is only one way to get this information. You must either be a real estate agent or work with one. You need information on all of the properties that are for sale or for lease right now. You also need to know what was for sale or for lease within the last six months to a year.

Why do you need this information? First, you need to know exactly what previous properties have sold for in the area. This will indicate the market value of what you are going to buy. This also helps you know the market value of what you will end up selling. You cannot evaluate a deal properly without this information. Get it all.

Don't just get it all and leave it at that. This information will need to be updated on a regular basis. If the market is very hot or very cold, you must update very often.

At this point you are probably saying, "I can see why I need to know what is for sale and what has sold but why do I need to know about rentals? The rental market is important should any of your deals go long-term and you hold them for rental cash flow.

Finally, I am going to have you gather all of the Expired, Withdrawn and "For Lease" properties. They will be used when we talk about our "Competing Methods" of finding incredible deals.

All of this information is best gathered by a real estate agent. They can pull up your "AoE" and get you all of these statistics and listings in a reasonable amount of time. If you are not one, you need to find a good one who understands investing. I will help you with this later. I highly suggest either paying them or offering to partner with them on transactions. Your other option is to sign a buyer's agency agreement so they are paid commissions every time you buy and sell.

Motivate your real estate agent. They will be invaluable when gathering information and evaluating property. As a matter of fact they will end up *bringing you deals* when you teach them how. (See "Power Teams")

Right Now *you* are the Smartest Person on the Block

Before I continue I want to say something. You are doing awesome. This is a big task and for those of you who have completed it "Congratulations!" You are well on your way to being a *huge* success as a real estate investor. I can say without a doubt that you are officially an expert in your "Area of Expertise".

Now it's time to have some real fun! You have gathered all of the information and you are ready to rev up your engines and take off. With this information you will be able to know very quickly whether or not you have a fantastic deal. You will *not* have to go back to the drawing board every time you find a new deal. You will have at your fingertips all of the information about properties you need to implement "The Foundation to Success".

You will be able to make timely offers, have shorter times for closings, make better offers and know a deal when you see it. This is true *power* when it comes to real estate investing. The creation of your "Area of Expertise" binder is the guts of this program. The better and more complete your binder the more success you will guarantee yourself.

> "Congratulations! When you have completed your "Area of Expertise" binder ***you*** are now an expert and you have done the ***guts*** of the program.
>
> **~Mike Watson**"

Some Final Tips for Creating Your Binder

Tip #1 "Always talk to people rather than a computer"

I've had some students say, "I can find all of this information on the development web site or online somewhere. Why do you suggest I physically go into the city? Isn't that just a waste of my valuable time?" My answer is, "It is always smarter to go talk to someone in the flesh. That way you can ask questions and interact with those who can help you the most."

But the main reason is this, "By talking to a real person you may be able to find out about changes that are coming or ones *not yet* on the web site." This information alone can make you hundreds of thousands of dollars. Isn't that worth a little of your valuable time?

Tip #2 "Meet with a city planner"

Go into your city and talk with a planner. It does not have to be the senior planner. Just get face-to-face with someone who is in the trenches giving advice to others on development. Make an appointment. Your city may have walk-in hours but I've found that most people in those offices usually are there to say "no".

The other problem with the walk-in area is that it is difficult to build a long-term relationship with the personnel. You will most likely talk with different people every time you go in. The final reason is they are going to be less excited to help you because they want you to have a certain property on which you are already working. They don't like to talk in general terms. They'd rather answer specific questions.

So make an appointment and go in and talk with a city planner. Always remember to ask the people you talk with what they would do. Get names, numbers and email addresses of everyone you speak with and take detailed notes.

Have a little fun. Investing can be fun and *exciting*. Get ready to find some amazing deals!

Tip #3 "Take a list with you to the city"

When you go to the city planner's office take the list below with you. Tell them you are going to be doing several deals in a small area. You may be referred to other people or to specific web sites. Make notes and follow up on any information provided. Planners will give you more golden nuggets to add to your treasure chest.

What to do or ask about at the City or County Office:

- Get zoning delineations and breakdowns.
- Get zoning maps.
- Get a "future map" (often called General Plan or Comprehensive Plan).
- Obtain a plat map.
- Ask about tax records and properties.
- Get aerial views.
- Get phone numbers of everyone you talk with.
- Ask about recent developments, PUD's, variances, zone changes special use permits etc. in your "AoE" (See The Laws of Mimicry below)
- Get the minutes of the City Council/Planning Commission that refer to anything in your area in the last year.
- Get development flow charts. (These explain the time line for going through the development process at the city.)
- Meet the city planner.
- Go to city council meetings.
- Ask everyone you meet, "What would YOU do?"
- Ask about areas of urban development or renewal.
- Ask about infill zones.
- Find out about any available Economic Stimulus Packages.

Note: This might be a good time to make some notes on your "Spark of Inspiration" List in Appendix 2.

Tip #4 Remember the "Laws of Mimicry" at all times

I've mentioned "The Laws of Mimicry" several times. By now you are probably wondering what they are. "The Laws of Mimicry" can be the *fastest* way to success. "The Laws of Mimicry" will show you how to do bigger and better projects. The first and foremost step is to *find out what other developers are doing in and around your "AoE"*, then you will be able to profit by mimicking them.

- Law One – Find out how others do the things they are doing.
  This is done easily by getting information from your city about projects in your "AoE"
- Law Two – Learn where you can do the same things.
  See if you can do what others are doing when it is any type of increase of density.
- Law Three – Figure out how you can do these things better!
  Once you find out what the city is allowing and not allowing you can take that information and use your new knowledge to create outstanding deals!

What does doing a project or investment *better* really mean? In the eyes of the city doing it better may mean using better architectural flair, or better materials, adding more amenities, providing more affordable housing or using green materials.

Doing it better as a successful *investor* means making sure you either get more units, a more affordable sales price, more square footage or income, out of your project. These things will be the bargaining tools you will use with the city when you have a project to show them. It is your job to learn what others are bargaining with and getting. When you do this you can then use those same strategies on your projects. The "Laws of Mimicry" are a fantastic tool that will enable you to work smarter.

> "The "Laws of Mimicry" can be the fastest way to extraordinary success.
>
> **~Mike Watson**"

What do you actually *do* with all of this information?

We have gotten to the point where you have gathered a ton of information about your city, your "AoE" and the actual properties in your area. What do you do now? How do you take this information and profit from it?

Drive around your "AoE" regularly!

I will talk at length about this technique in the "Non-Compete" methods of finding deals. For now the idea is to look at other projects that are currently in progress. Also, keep an eye out for any of the things we have talked about, such as small homes on large lots, and all of the types of distress.

In addition, go look at any of the projects the city told you about. This will be an eye opening experience. Find out what the city is allowing. There is an implied willingness to allow another of the same type of project on another lot in the same vicinity.

Make yourself a regular fixture at city planning and zoning meetings and at city council meeting.

These meetings are where the city gives their ideas for supporting or not supporting projects that are submitted. Knowing the city's mindset, focus and direction is the basis for good mimicry.

Human relationships can make a very big difference. Many city councils see developers and investors as the people who can bring to fruition the redevelopment and urban renewal of their city. This is why mimicry is crucial. If projects get approved, the city will usually approve more similar ones. By being at the meetings you will learn exactly what your city wants and does not want. Remember, it is always best to go on the path of least resistance and give the city what it wants.

Learn about your zoning.

Zoning is the key to this entire process. I suggest you actually read through the zoning regulations for your area. That way you will know what the city wants.

Remember that *zoning is law*. Therefore, conforming to the zoning that is in effect is absolutely essential when you develop a piece of property. What I mean by that is you must find out what is allowed now or will be allowed in the future and follow those regulations. That way you won't have to fight with neighbors, associations or even the city council itself. If you follow zoning as it is written nobody can stop you from developing the property.

Make sure you always check your deed restrictions as they are one thing that supersedes zoning.

There are plenty of properties out there which are under utilized just based on their current use and *currently* allowed zoning. If you become an expert at knowing what each zone is and what can be built in that zone you will instantly know when a property has a *huge potential for profit*. Learn as much as you can about the zoning in your "AoE".

Get a good feel for the "development standards" in your "AoE".

It is crucial that either you understand or you *have access* to someone (usually an architect on your "*Power Team*") who understands the specific development standards that go along with each type of zoning.

Development standards are the guidelines and restrictions for projects, homes and new developments. The city uses these standards to implement its vision. When a city turns zoning into law, it is in essence, planning how the city will be developed or redeveloped over time.

Why would you want to be intimately familiar with these standards? Let's say, for example you found an area where you could build eight units where currently there was only one home. How important would the standards be?

If the standards said you had to have 3 parking places for each unit or they said you had to have 100 feet of frontage and the house you bought did not have these things you'd be sunk!

The more familiar you are with the development standards the more likely it will be that your projects will get accepted by the city. If you don't know your standards you may not get approved through the city. If this happens you may lose a lot of money on deals.

Development standards include things such as the amount of units you can put on an acre, handicap requirements, building height limits, parking requirements, landscape standards, fencing, exterior building materials, setbacks and floor to area ratios.

These are the things that bring your projects to life. If you start to feel overwhelmed with all of the information you need to know just remember to *involve others* who are professionals.

Talk to an architect, an engineer or a permit expediter. Those types of people do this every day and will be happy to sit down and talk with you about the ins and outs of your project.

Get intimate with your "Future Map".

The future zoning map is a glimpse into the future. Remember it is your main *Treasure Map* to riches. When you compare the current zoning map and the future zoning map and you see *any differences* there will typically be an opportunity for profit.

If you know your zoning you will instantly know which properties will have a *higher* zoning in the future and thus a significant chance for a profit. In these areas the city is saying that it *wants* higher density in the future. Why would they not allow you to do that *now* if they want it there in the future? There is good argument that they *will* allow it now.

Study the difference between the current zoning map and future zoning map. Find discrepancies and you will find opportunities for *outstanding profits!* It really is that simple.

Read up on the incentives and opportunities your city is offering for redevelopment.

Cities take great pains to plan for future development especially in areas with distress. Often they want to see areas changed and improved that developers have neglected, avoided or simply don't know about. To help address the needed changes, cities often give incentives or bonuses to create a better opportunity, (read *profit*) for developers and investors to work those areas.

There are all kinds of development incentives. Some allow for a higher density. There may be development standard waivers, lower or no city fees for permits. Sometimes they allow for a shorter city process time, waived hearings, tax credits, utility credits and or city-paid improvements to support your development.

These incentives can cause development and investments to go much faster and therefore be far cheaper. As you can imagine, faster developments means less holding costs. Cheaper developments means more *profits*.

I have a current project in a city in Arizona that wants an area of their town redeveloped so badly they are offering a $5,000 bonus to any investor who *tears out* an old existing building. In addition they offer a $5,000 bonus per unit for the number of units the builder *replaces* on the lot.

On our project, we are tearing out an old building and adding in almost 30 new ones. As a result we will receive approximately $150,000 of extra profit just because of the incentive being offered by the city. That is a huge incentive to develop in the area and the city loves it because they are helping make a distressed area much nicer.

I am aware of another city in Arizona where the city offers a 10% density bonus over the base density and charges no city fees for development. Also 5 of the 8 required meetings and reviews for the projects to get through city approval process are being waived.

We have another project in a city in Northern California whose incentives include only one parking stall required per unit in their downtown core. They also allow developments to go through the city process in *45-60 days* instead of the normally required *2 years*. The lowered time for having to do the project will shave off approximately $200,000 of holding costs. Talk about an incredible deal!

Development incentives can go a long way towards the viability and profitability of a project. Most cities offer them. Make it your business to find out where those opportunities exist and capitalize on them. These incentives can often be worth a lot of money and/or time. *Do not* start your investing without being familiar with the incentives in your area. Doing that is like throwing money out the window.

> "Development Incentives are so ***powerful*** they can create deals where they otherwise didn't exist.
>
> **~Mike Watson**"

The First Under-Utilized Way to Find Deals

We are finally to the point of finding your specific deals. Everything up to now has been about learning *what* to find. Now we are going to go *find* it.

As a quick review, you are looking for properties that are in "distress". In other words you are looking for properties that have a "*Higher and Better*" use than what is currently sitting there. Remember that "Higher and Better" is defined as one of four things; more units, more square footage, more owners, or more net income.

When I teach investors how to find properties I focus on two main sets of techniques. The first is called "Competing Methods", and the second is called "Non-Competing Methods". I will discuss both of them in detail. Let's start with "Competing Methods".

By definition "Competing Methods" are methods of finding properties that others are also using. Therefore you are *competing* for the same *properties*. However, even though you are using the same method, you now know how to look at the properties differently. Just because of this you will get different results. In addition I am going to teach you how to use the competing methods *themselves* differently so you will find properties that others will not.

I'd like you to think back to our example at the beginning of the book where I bought a home and sold it as an "Awesome 15-unit Condo Complex". When I found that property I used a "Competing Method". What I did was look for properties at the county courthouse and in newspapers that were in foreclosure or which had a Notice of Default status.

A Notice of Default is filed against a property's title when the property owner fails to make several payments. The lender considers the loan to be in default and files a notice at the courthouse. The property owner must then "cure" the notice by paying the required reinstatement amount to the lender to avoid the property going into foreclosure.

Many investors look at properties which are in a state of financial distress. We often compete against people that have located a property the very same way, but our bidding techniques and pricing format are usually very different.

This is where thinking differently comes in handy. Most people would come in and bid the house down from the seller to get as good a deal as possible, but that is a weak way of doing business. You should not take advantage of someone who is in foreclosure or notice of default. They should be helped as much as possible. Remember if you're not able to create a win/win transaction you're not following "The Foundation to Success."

Here's how a typical investor would see the possibilities on this deal.

Purchase Price after Negotiation (Asking Price $129,900)	$115,000
Cost to fix up for a flip	$28,000
Holding and End Closing Costs	$12,000
Total Costs on Home plus work	$155,000
Value of home after work done	$180,000
Total cost of home plus work	< $155,000 >
Total Profit	**$25,000**

Most investors would *not* do this deal. There is too little profit for the amount of time and risk. However, as previously mentioned, we decided to look at the property in a different way than most other investors. We looked at the property for what it *could be* instead of what it *was*.

Let's look at our numbers.

Through research on our "AoE" that we had in our binder, we realized the property had a much higher and better use. Therefore, we were able to come in and pay *full asking price* for the property. The seller was able to get all of their remaining equity and leave with some dignity intact and some money for a fresh start. We still got the property at a fantastic price and made a huge profit and here's how.

Purchase Price	$129,900
Work on Property (Platting, site planning, city fees etc.)	$4,100
Holding and closing costs	$10,000
Total Costs on Project	$144,000
Offer from Subsequent Buyer	$210,000
Less total cost of the project	<$144,000>
Total Profit	**$66,000**

As you can see, we saw the property *differently* and therefore had different results than other investors. We were even able to help the seller.

So the first thing to remember about finding property using competing methods is that you will be looking at the property differently. That means you will see things others will not. When you see things others do not you will see deals others do not. Therefore it is extremely valid to look at all of the properties that are for sale.

My *Twist* on "Competing Methods"

Remember the story I told about a local real estate broker calling me about a listing he had which potentially could be subdivided into two lots? Remember how I bought it, subdivided it and sold the home and the lot separately? Remember how I made a *huge profit* fast?

Well, that was not the end of the story. When I finished that first deal I was so excited I decided I wouldn't work with clients anymore. I thought from then on I would just be an investor. However I didn't have any more deals to do. Remember how I called the agent and he said he didn't have any more deals like that?

Do you also remember that I was devastated? I knew I had to figure out where to find more of those types of deals. Here is what I did. After I calmed down I remembered two things. The first was the property was listed on the *Multiple Listing Service* (MLS). I figured there were probably others like it on the MLS. I just needed to figure out a way to determine which ones could be subdivided.

The second thing I remembered was the city planner gave me a list of uses for the property's zone. I realized that if I found other properties in the same zone they would have to have the same available uses. That is when I excitedly began scouring my MLS based on *lot size and zone*. In this way I found many more properties to buy.

Using the MLS was a competing method. Basing my search on property zone and lot size was the twist. Thousands and thousands of people use the MLS but very few (other than my students) use it *this* way. Once I started thinking differently, my career results changed dramatically. Within a one mile radius of that first property I completed over *30 deals in the next two years.*

*Note: Whenever you find an outstanding deal use it as a "Portal" to an area for more fantastic deals. In other words use it as a sign post that says, "Look in the immediate area and you will find more similar awesome deals".

> "Use the "Competing Methods" ***differently*** in order to find deals others won't.
>
> **~Mike Watson**"

Eye-Popping Automated MLS Searches

Here are some outstanding searches you can use to find properties in the MLS that are "distressed". Have your real estate agent put the searches in and automate them to email to you automatically when something becomes available.

These searches will result in lots of properties you can analyze based on what you know about the area and zoning. Then you can decide if they have a "Higher and Better" use.

Have your real estate agent set up a search for the following words in the "Remarks" or "Property Description" section of the MLS. When you find these words in the listing there may be a possibility that the property is distressed. It will take a minute or so to determine if it is a possible deal. Time spent looking for possible deals is time *very well spent*. The following words or phrases are often signposts of distress or opportunity.

MLS Word Search List

- Apartment – This may have a garage apartment which could be condo-converted.
- As is - This may be a distressed property.
- Auction, bank, or short sale – This may be a property in foreclosure or owned by a bank.

- Carry - Meaning the seller may finance some of the purchase price.
- Change or possibility– We are looking for change of use, so check for these words.
- Condo or conversion – You may find a property that is either zoned for condo's or that can be converted.
- Density – The granddaddy of all search words!
- Duplex, Triplex, Fourplex – You might find a home that is a duplex but you have to get it legally permitted in order to sell it as a duplex.
- Extra room - You may find something that has room for another living or bedroom.
- Huge/large or big yard – There may be room to add on to the property or build another unit.
- Lot or Lots - The property may come with more than one lot.
- Multi-family – This may have conversion possibilities or income possibilities.
- Opportunity
- Plat or Plat Map – When you see these words the property may have a plat for something with more density, it is worth investigating further.
- Potential, fixer, or handyman special
- R1, R2, R3, R4 - This may be different in your area, it just means to look for higher density zoning within the wording, in some areas it's MF, or SF, you need to be familiar with the zones to utilize this technique.
- Seller Finance -Terms can make or break a deal. (See more info in the "Seller Finance" section)
- Subdivision – This might be a sign that you could subdivide something
- Tax ID Number, TIN, PIN, Separate, Multiple – These might give you a property with more than one lot that you could sell separately.
- Tenants - When you see the word tenant it tells you the prop-

erty is not owner occupied. Owners tire of property management and vacancies and may be willing to sell for a low price.

- TLC. Tender loving care, as in, it needs a lot of work.
- Variance – You may find a property that has a variance or is getting a variance for more density.
- Zone or zoning – Owner may be changing it or agent may be talking about better zoning.

The majority of these words are best used on *residential* properties.

Investing Tools

We have CD's that give you very detailed searches for both residential and multi-family properties. Just go to our web site at **mikewatsoninvesting.com** then "Products", and go to the "Top MLS Searches" CD.

As an additional tip you should check for these MLS words in some other locations on a normal basis. You can check web sites, bank properties for sale, courthouse listings, yard signs, FSBO (For sale by owner), "For Rents" and classified section of the paper, NOD Lists (Notice of Default) and regular advertising. These words can and *will* lead you to deals.

The other thing you will want to do is have your real estate agent set up a search that pulls *all properties* that come up for sale in your "AoE". That way you will know immediately when something is available. Once you learn how to analyze your deals you will be able to make offers on these properties immediately!

Finally, go back through your "AoE" book and review the properties that were taken off the market. Either they were *withdrawn* or *expired.* These are fantastic people to contact. If those properties have a "Higher and Better" use and the seller wanted to sell at one point and didn't, there is a good chance they may sell to you now.

P.S. The MLS can be a fantastic "Portal" to an area with lots of profitable deals. Find a property on MLS that would be an outstanding deal if the price was right, and then go find other properties in that same area using the "Non-Competing" methods to follow.

How to Find Deals that *No One Else* Can

Before I started using "Non-Competing" methods to find deals I was spending hours on the MLS looking for deals. When something popped up I'd run out the door and make an offer immediately. Unfortunately many times I did not get to buy that property because someone else beat me to the punch. I began to get tired of this and decided to take matters into my own hands.

It is time to introduce you to my "Non-Competing" methods of finding amazing deals. By definition you will not have to compete with *anyone* else when you buy a property. That is a huge advantage.

The key to "Non-Competes" is that most of the properties you research and make offers on will *not openly be on the market.* If they are not on the market and you are the only buyer you will have much more leverage when you negotiate. You will have more time to analyze, more time to negotiate and less stress. I *love* "Non-Compete" deals.

I've taught you how to find properties that have a potential for profit. I've shown you some ways to find "Competing" properties that are *for sale.* You can evaluate these and buy the one's that you can change to a higher and better use.

You may find at some point that you are out of exceptional deals in your "AoE" yet you still want to do more deals! If you are savvy you will start the "Non-Compete" techniques at the same time you do the "Competing" methods. My guess is that once you do "Non-Competes" you will not spend as much time on the properties that are for sale.

"Non-Competes" are *that* good.

The key to being the *only buyer* is to make contact with people who own properties with a "Higher and Better" use. Contact them even if their property is not currently for sale. I recommend you actually do the following things on every property within your "AoE".

7 Tricks-of-the-Trade with "Non-Competes"

1. Go Door Knocking – Yes, I mean go to your "Area of Expertise" and knock on doors. (I will go into this in great detail in a later section.)
2. Drive Around – Drive around your "AoE" and look for distress. Oh, and by the way, if you find something that looks interesting refer to trick #1.
3. Call Every Sign - One of the most powerful things you can do when driving around is to "call every sign every time". Whenever you see anything with a phone number on it in your "AoE" pick up the phone and call it. Use the same questions as you will for door knocking. (See later section)
4. Send Letters – Make contact with owners via letters on a normal basis. By sending them monthly or every other month you will make sure that when someone wants to sell they will have your contact information right there in front of them.
5. Call Owners – Put together a list of the owner's phone numbers in your "AoE". You can get the numbers from the tax records and sometimes online. You are allowed to call someone if you want to "buy" something from them. Just not if you want to "sell" something to them.
6. Sphere of Influence – You can teach the people in your "AoE" and who you are close to, how to find properties for you. That way you will have many eyes out looking for deals instead of just your own.
7. "Power Team" (We will discuss this further in step #10 of "The Foundation to Success")

Isn't that just simple stuff anyone can do?

At this point you may be asking yourself, "Those things don't sound that new or interesting. Aren't there other people doing the same thing?"

I have to admit that making phone calls, driving around and door knocking is not exactly rocket science. However, unlike others we aren't necessarily driving around and door knocking on any old property. You are only going to talk with people who own properties with a *"Higher and Better" use.*

Honestly I don't think there are very many people who actually take the time to go around and talk with owners and neighbors in person. Remember the "Awesome 15-unit Condo Deal"? That was a physically distressed old home on a big lot. Some people might stop and knock at their door looking for an opportunity for a carpet and paint fixer or just to get a below market price. We drove around the area and knocked on the door because of the 25 units per acre.

The house could have been in excellent condition and it still would have been appealing to us due to the existing zoning. We liked the distress for the lower price but we would have knocked on the door anyway.

Very few investors are familiar with zoning and the opportunities it creates in all cities. Even fewer investors are out *knocking on doors* and looking for properties based on zoning information. If you actually do these things you *will* find deals that no other person is researching. You *will* buy properties that never go on the open market. And you may never go back to finding deals exclusively using "competing" methods.

How to get Astounding Results Just from Driving Around

In a nutshell the best use of your time is to go find deals. Driving around is the definition of finding a deal. I suggest you drive around your area *once a week*. When you drive around make sure to take your "AoE" binder with you. That way you will have the maps you need and the owner information right at your fingertips.

Spend a little time before you drive around your "AoE" to look at the current and future map. Make sure to go look at any property that is going to be zoned higher density. While you are out driving keep an eye open for the following things:

- Distressed properties – Not being used for their "Highest and Best" use!! (In addition to actual physical distress)
- Vacant properties – These are obviously distressed, contact owners.
- Scrapes / Tear-outs – May be either a project to investigate or might be going up for sale.
- Fixer uppers – Especially if they have a "Higher and Better" use.
- Vacant lots – Almost all vacant lots have a "Higher and Better" use.
- "For Sale by Owner" signs – Call them when you are there! They could be distressed owners who can't afford a real estate agent.
- For Rent/Lease signs – Call them NOW! These are distressed owners because the property is only being used for its "Highest and Best" use if it is fully rented at the going market price. A high percentage of owners with vacant rental units will consider selling their property.
- Other signs with phone numbers – Take these down and call them. The person on the end of the line will most likely know information about the area. Ask them the key questions that follow in the "door-knocking" section.

You will see things when you drive around that are impossible to see any other way. When you see a property ask yourself, "Is it being used for its 'Highest and Best' use?" If not, the next step is to do a quick evaluation on the other uses for the property.

If you determine there is potential for a good profit then contact the owner to see if they have any interest in selling. You can also just stop and knock on the door while you are driving around. Some of the properties you see will be so compelling you will want to know more about them *immediately*. Driving around and knocking on doors can be a lot of fun, especially when you find your first deal!

> "Use ***any*** time you have in the car as time to look for deals! Watch for key opportunities to relieve ***distress*** and you will be a success.
>
> **~Mike Watson**"

More Suggestions for Successful Driving/Knocking

It may seem silly but when you are driving around call the numbers on every sign. Call "For Rent", "For Sale", "Car For Sale", and even "Business Signs". CALL EVERY SIGN – EVERY TIME. You will be amazed at the information you can collect this way. I have bought several properties by calling these signs. Act like you are a detective looking for information on the area. People love to talk about other people. Give them the chance.

Use a flyer campaign.

In other words, when you go door knocking take a flyer that shows your interest in purchasing property in the area. Leave it on the door when people are not home. Or if you do find them at home, you can give them the flyer and use it to help start a conversation.

FREE Online Resources

There are several samples of flyers that students have posted on my web site mikewatsoninvesting.com on the area called "The Forum". Feel free to go there and "mimic" those samples if you wish. There is no charge for them. Just pull up a search on the word "Door Knocking Flyer" and see what comes up.

Just visit www.mikewatsoninvesting.com, and click on the "Forum" today.

Interview people on the spot.

Drive around your area until you see people out on their property then stop and interview them on the spot. "Driving Around" is a form of door knocking. When people are out in their yards they can't hide behind a locked door. Another handy thing about driving around and talking to people who are outside, is if it is really HOT or really COLD you don't even have to get out of your car… though it might be worth it to actually go to a door once in a while.

Use the Laws of Mimicry.

Learn from what has already been done in your area. How did those other investors do it? Find out how they did the work. Make a point to notice projects while you are driving around. Follow up on those projects at the city planner's office to see exactly what is being done.

Begin writing offers on every deal you see.

Do your evaluation and if it works at all make an offer at a price that makes you a good profit. Be a finisher – if you see an opportunity, take it through to the end.

Really get to know the market in your "Area of Expertise".

Go visit property that is currently for sale and for rent. Establish what the market prices are for sale, and rentals. This way you will know if a higher income is possible on a property just from raising rents. You will also know immediately if you are getting a good price on a property.

Pick a use for a zone (from your use chart)

Then, go find properties that are not currently using the highest use for their zoning. For example a vacant lot equals a condo project. Or, a small home on a big lot equals a fourplex.

Drive your area once a week!

You may be thinking, "Why in the world should I drive around the area so often. Gas prices are outrageous. Isn't there something better I could be doing?"

Honestly, the answer is "No". When you drive your area frequently you will become extremely aware of the properties, people and zoning. The more you drive your area, the more intimate you will become with what exists. This will help you focus on what can be changed to a "Higher and Better" use. It will allow you to get to know the local people and learn information from them about things which might not be public knowledge.

When you drive this often, you will know right away of any changes that are happening in the area. If a property goes up for sale or for rent, you can be the first one to call. If a zoning sign, variance sign, or public hearing sign goes up be the first one to investigate.

And finally if a property burns down or some other physical distress happens to it you will be the first to learn about it and be the first one to begin negotiating. If a new project starts you can analyze it with the Laws of Mimicry and discover what other properties in that neighborhood or zone would allow an even better project to go in.

Drive around once a week or more. It is actually the most captivating part of "The Foundation to Success". Being out in the field is exciting! Take someone with you and see who can find the most deals. Make it a game. You will be rewarded handsomely.

> "Drive around your area with a friend and see who can find the most deals. Enjoy the ***game*** of investing.
>
> **~Mike Watson**"

Tongue-tied?

The first time I knocked on a door and asked the owner if they wanted to sell I was a nervous wreck. The thousandth time it was a breeze. Let me explain how I'll shorten the time frame significantly for you.

Between those two different knocks I had a few tough experiences and learned quite a bit about human nature. I also ran into a few challenging pets. That is why I have Rule #8 of door knocking, "Never go door knocking alone and always take someone who runs slower than you." But I'm getting ahead of myself.

What I learned first is that people will talk to you if you get them talking about someone else. They don't like to answer the door and have you say, "Can I buy your home?" Typically when this happens they will put up a huge stubborn wall of negativity.

I have three simple rules for you to follow that will walk you through how to talk with people and break through their barriers. My three rules of thumb are, "Build a relationship of trust by finding something in common." Secondly you should, "Always be up front about your reason for being there." And finally, "Talk about something or someone else".

Once you have developed a bit of a rapport with the person you can start with these questions, in this order:

1. Do you know of any vacant or distressed properties in the area?
2. Do you know of any distressed property owners in the area? (i.e. divorced, job loss, death etc.)
3. Do you know anyone who is considering selling or buying property in the area?
4. Have you considered selling or buying any real estate.

I like this set of questions because it does two things. It gets you information about property you may have missed in the area. And, it helps you find out if there is anyone you could help. (Many times selling a property is extremely helpful.)

These questions are not threatening to people who might be considering selling at sometime in the near future. In addition if you find someone who wants to buy in the area you might have a buyer for one of the properties you may be selling.

I use these questions when I talk with anyone. It does not matter if I am driving around, knocking on doors, calling a sign or writing a letter. They are excellent tools for gathering information. Use them.

The Rules of Door Knocking

1. Do not ever go door knocking alone. Take at least one other person and let others know where you will be at all times.
2. Only knock on doors when it is light outside.
3. Wear "business casual" clothes while door knocking
4. Smile!
5. Start and keep conversations going.
6. Talk about other people and other people's property. Initially

they will not want to talk about their own property.

7. Have Fun.
8. Always go door knocking with someone who runs slower than you do.

Get Your Phone to Ring with Owners *Ready to Sell*

One of the other things I suggest you do as a "Non-Compete" method of finding deals is to send letters directly to owners.

If you decide to write your own letters make sure you get your message across clearly. The first message is that you are an investor and you want to get them involved in investing.

The second message is they can participate and profit in this business just like you are. The third message is that you are looking for properties, people and investing partners. Try and shape the messages in a way where the people who receive your letters can easily understand and see their participation in your business.

Share the excitement and enthusiasm you have for investing with them. Try and make them feel like they are a part of your "team" because if they live in your "AoE" they *are*.

If you want to get more responses from your letters then use a first class stamp and hand-write some or all of the address or letter. Or even better, I suggest you hire a teenage neighbor to do the writing for you. One of my students has her "Power Team" write, send and take calls from the letters. She then does the evaluation, makes the offer and they are on their way. Her team has done several deals from those letters alone.

Hang in there.

Your head might be swimming at this point. You may think I've given you a full time job just with what I've shared so far. It is important for you to keep reading and to *start* the "Non-Compete" process. I will teach you a way to leverage this work so you can invest in many properties and still have a life. (See Step #10 on "Power Teams") Just remember that "The Foundation to Success" process is simple. Putting it into action requires some work but it will all be worth it in the end.

STEP 4

EVALUATE PROPERTIES FOR THEIR "HIGHEST AND BEST" USE

STEP 4

EVALUATE PROPERTIES FOR THEIR "HIGHEST AND BEST" USE

You have found a property with potential *and* a willing seller. What now?

By this time you are probably thinking, "I am an expert in my area and I know how to find properties that might be profitable deals. I've even found a seller who wants to sell their property. The only problem is I'm not sure it is a fantastic deal. How do I know?"

Well, if this is what you are thinking you are right on track. That is because...

You have learned Step #1 *know* "The Foundation to Success", Step #2 *create* your "Red Button Statement", and Step #3, "Find Incredible Properties". Now you are ready for Step #4 of "The Foundation to Success" which is: Evaluate properties for their "Highest and Best" use (plus 6 other key characteristics).

Before I get started with how Step #4 works I want to tell you why I created it. One of the first short-term investments I did ended up with a profit of only $2,300. Needless to say I was a bit nervous that I was going to *lose* money. I was less than two more mortgage payments away from not having any profit.

If I had misjudged by even a little more on my expenses I would have lost money. By the end of the deal I was grateful to have escaped the project with a small profit. I was grateful but I was extremely upset with myself. I decided to analyze why I had come so close to this financial fiasco. I wanted to guarantee it would *never* happen again.

Ever since that deal I have taken a hard look at *every* project to learn where I could have performed better. I do this even when I make a load of money. There is *always* room for improvement.

The worst thing that could happen on a deal is being unable to sell the property for a profit and being forced to keep a long-term asset *without* positive cash flow. I've created a deal evaluation process that covers those issues. You can *only* be an expert investor if you are an expert at *evaluating* deals. I will soon show you the seven steps of "Incredible Deal Evaluations".

Is bullet-proof investing possible?

Honestly, no. Investing is never 100% without risk. If you make mistakes you can face horrible losses. However, one of the blessings of the extensive deal evaluation process you will learn is it makes you *nearly* bulletproof in your investing. If your deal passes the evaluation with flying colors you can rest assured you have a winner.

The main thing I recommend is that you be very *honest* and *conservative* with your calculations and estimates of value. You may think it sounds funny when I say, "Be honest with yourself", but here is the truth; "If investors with good intentions overvalue their properties, undervalue their expenses and/or under-calculate the time needed for the investment it can be disastrous!"

> "Remember, "Conservative Evaluations" lead to "Liberal Returns".
>
> **~Mike Watson**"

The Deal Binder

When you find a property you are going to start your "Deal Evaluation" process. At this point I suggest you create a "Deal Binder". You are going to be collecting quite a bit of information and paperwork over the next month or so, especially if you make an offer, get under contract, purchase and "Change the Use" of the property you have found.

The best way to put the binder together is to create Tabs for the main items of a deal. The main items of a deal are:

1. Overview – This section will contain the basic information about your project. What it is now and what your vision is for the property.
2. Contracts/MLS/Title Report – Keep your contracts, amendments, addendums and anything you negotiate in this section. In addition if the property is listed in MLS then keep a copy of the full printout of the listing here. Finally attach the Title Report.
3. Financing/Cost to Change – All information about loans with banks and lenders will be in this section. This also includes work bids for the "Change of Use".
4. Zoning/Development – Keep all current information about the zoning and development standards in this section. In addition any work you do on either of these items would go here. Such as, architectural renderings, new plats, engineering work etc.
5. Maps/Photos – Have a picture of the property, an aerial, and any maps of the area. Include your zoning map and future zoning map here.
6. Comparables – This section is full of your comparable sold and available properties. Include both sales and leases if applicable. Keep this section up-to-date.
7. Critical Paths – Maintain time lines for all contract items and changes you will do in this section.

8. Demographics – Have your real estate agent pull demographics of the area of your property.
9. Management and Leasing – If your property has any management or leasing needs keep that information here. Such as, leases, deposit amounts, rent rolls, utility info on the property etc.
10. Miscellaneous – Put any additional pertinent information in this section of your "Deal Binder".

When you have created your "Deal Binder" it will be very simple for you to keep all of the data on your deal organized. In addition you can show your "Deal Binder" and "Area of Expertise" binder to people when you are talking to them about being on your "Power Team" or investing with you. These binders will make a strong statement about how serious and thorough you are with your deals!

I have students who have met with multi-million dollar investors who have told the student, "This is the most comprehensive presentation I've ever seen on a deal". Use these systems to keep your deal organized and to be professional. Let's move on to the seven essential steps you will take when you evaluate your deal.

The 7 Essential Elements of a Solid Deal Evaluation

1. Determine the "Highest and Best" use of the property
2. Compare your *purchase* price with your *appraised* value
3. Evaluate your current and possible future cash flow
4. Explore and exploit terms
5. Determine the "Future Potential" of the property
6. Evaluate your short-term *and* long-term plans
7. Remember to ask, "Is there any Professional Application?"

If you are wondering which of these is the most important, the steps are listed in order of importance. However, all of the steps should be considered extremely important because they all play a significant role in the outcome of your deal. The key is to make sure *all* of the steps work and have a positive result *before* you move past the point of having significant money at risk.

What exactly is the "Highest and Best" use?

The most important step in evaluating a property is the first step of our deal evaluation system. "Determine the property's 'Highest and Best' use." *Most* properties are not used to their full potential. The key to determining if a property is currently using its "Highest and Best" use is to have a strong understanding of your zoning and development standards. In addition, having your "Use Chart" handy will prove helpful.

Usually the "Highest and Best" use is the most dense option for the property. The more units there are on the lot typically the more the property is worth. So, the goal is to maximize the lot for what the zoning allows.

Let's go back to our "Awesome 15-unit Condo Deal". In that case a single family home on a .63 acre lot was *not* the "Highest and Best" use for the property by a long shot! The "Highest and Best" use according to the zoning was a 15-unit condo complex.

You might be thinking that you know there are other uses but wondering, "What is the *'Highest and Best'* use?" The way you figure that out is to look at what the property is currently being used for and compare it to all other possible uses. Get out your "Use Chart" from your "AoE" binder, look at that particular zone and compare the current use to the accepted uses. Then determine which of the uses will allow for the highest number of units on that property. "VOILA" you have your "Highest and Best" use. Remember however, there are *four* types of density and that a *significant improvement in any of our four areas* from what is currently in place will typically yield excellent profits.

Another way to determine the "Highest and Best" use is to take the current zoning map and compare it to the future zoning map. The current zoning map tells you the area zoning as it sits now and the future map tells you what the city planners want the area's zone to become. Often, the zoning intent for the future is a "Higher and Better" use than the current zone. Find those properties and evaluate them! Many will be *incredible* deals.

I want to make sure you get that last paragraph. Please go back and read it again. I don't think you got it. If you did you would be out driving around comparing the current map to the future map and looking at what is standing on the lot right now! This simple process is the fastest way to riches I have *ever* found!

P.S. Both of those maps are already in your "AoE" binder.

> It's good to be dense.... if you are a piece of land.
>
> **~Mike Watson**

Let me make a prediction and save you a ton of time

If you are one of those people who takes action fast I want to give you a little sneak peak. My prediction is if you apply what I have taught you so far *you will find many properties that have a "Higher and Better" use.*

You might think, "This property has a 'Higher and Better' use. It must be a great deal. I'm going to buy it!" I love your enthusiasm and have to say that it will get you far. But here is a warning that goes along with the prediction. Finish reading this entire deal evaluation section before you make an offer.

Why? If you go buy *any* property that has a "Higher and Better" use you may find some that are not great deals. Verify the property you are interested in makes it through all 7 steps of the deal evaluation prior to making an offer and you will be in fantastic shape.

Here is an example. If you find a single family house in a zone which allows for a duplex, the property would absolutely have a "Higher and Better" use. However, if you have to pay $175,000 for the house and a duplex in that area only sells for $225,000 you will *not* have a good investment on your hands.

You will have to tear the house out, build the duplex, put in site improvements and still make a profit all for less than $50,000. This would be a horrible investment. It would not be possible to make any money at all. Take every deal you find all the way through the deal evaluation process prior to making an offer. There are plenty of deals that will make it through this process. If you find one that doesn't make it through all of the steps just move on to the next one.

> "There are deals everywhere but not all of them will make it through this evaluation process. Make sure yours does before you spend a lot of time or money on it.
>
> **~Mike Watson**"

Is it *really* a deal?

In order to determine this you have to move on to the second step of our deal evaluation. Step number two is, "Compare your *purchase* price with your *appraised* value". This step will help you determine if you are purchasing the property for a good price. Most investors will tell you they don't like to pay full price for a property. However, if the property has a much "Higher and Better" undiscovered use, then the sales price when you buy it isn't as important as what you can do with the property.

In the "Awesome 15-unit Condo Deal" example, I paid *full asking price* for the distressed property because I knew how profitable it could be and I didn't want to lose out on the opportunity.

That said, you want to make sure you are not over-paying for the property. You do want to know how much below present value you might be able to purchase a property. Any discount you can get at purchase will enhance the profit or equity position you have at the end of your investment.

There are several ways to get a discount. One is to find *physically distressed* properties. Other ways are to put down *large earnest money*, or make cash offers. You can do *quick closings*, purchase multiple properties in one transaction and remove all or most of your purchase contingencies. All of these things make your offer more attractive to a seller.

This may be helpful information but how do you find out if you are getting a good deal in the first place? Really the only place to get correct market information is from a real estate agent. They have easy access to the most recent statistics on sold properties in the area. This is the most vital information you can attain when you are assessing a property's value.

You never want to go too far back in the past when you are looking at sales prices because markets are always fluctuating. You also want to make sure that you are looking only at properties that are extremely similar to what you are going to buy. In other words, make sure your comparable properties have similar square footage, lot size, age, style, and location.

In addition to recent sales information you want to look at what is pending, and available. This information will help you assess your competition when you go to sell your property in the short-term. It can also help you find other properties that may be available that are similar to the one in which you are interested. This information is *not* as useful as the "sold" information when you determine value. Appraisers never use anything except for "solds" to determine value and neither should a competent investor who wants to be *bulletproof!*

Keep in mind there is no better resource than a real estate agent to help you assess your market and value of your property. They will also be instrumental in helping you make good offers. It is extremely important as an investor to have an experienced real estate agent who can help you when you need it. Make sure they either have some investing experience of their own or they have read this book. Ideally they are students of my program.

The *Ultimate* Back-Up Plan

The third step of the "Deal Evaluation" system is, "evaluate your current and possible future cash flow". You might wonder why you must evaluate the property for cash flow when I have made such a big deal about changing the use of a property. Where does cash flow enter the formula at all?

First, cash flow is extremely helpful when you have carrying costs. If you buy a property with a fourplex on it and plan on tearing it out to build a mixed use 20 unit condo complex plus 10,000 square feet of retail space, you will be working with the city on plans for 6 months to 2 years. It could even be longer. My point is this; "Why pay for the property while you are going through that process? Why not have the current tenants pay for some or all of your carrying costs during this time?" See where I am going with this?

Second, "Cash Flow is the *Ultimate* Back-Up Plan!" All successful investors try their best to have positive cash flow regardless of whether they will change the use of the property or not. You should attempt to have all of your properties at least pay for themselves. Any residual monthly income is a bonus. Positive cash flow is also extremely helpful if you end up keeping the property for the long-term.

The Cash Flow formula

Since cash flow is so important I'd like to give you a way to figure out if the property you are going to buy *has* any. To determine cash flow you take the gross operating income (GOI) and subtract out all of the operating expenses. This leaves you with the net operating income. (NOI) You should then subtract the monthly debt service from the NOI. This will leave you with a positive or negative cash flow. Keep reading, I'll say it in English in a minute.

The Cash Flow Formula:

Gross operating Income - Expenses = Net operating income

Net Operating Income – Debt Service = Cash flow (+ or -)

In other words *add up* all of the money you will *receive* from rents, utility reimbursement, laundry rooms, etc. and then *subtract out* all of your *expenses* such as, utilities, maintenance, management, repairs, yard care, insurance, taxes etc. Finally *subtract out* the full payment you will have on any *debt* on the property. If you are unable to determine all of your expenses at this preliminary evaluation a rule of thumb is to use 25%-30% of your gross rents plus your taxes and insurance. If you go under contract make sure to verify these numbers during your due diligence time frame prior to closing.

If the final number is above zero you have a *positive* cash flow. Keep in mind that if there is a huge profit possible on a deal, it might be wise to buy a property even though it doesn't have a positive cash flow, as long as you know you can *increase* the cash flow if something unforeseen happens.

Two Awesome Lists to Increase Cash Flow

There are two basic ways to increase cash flow. You can *increase* the income or *decrease* the expenses. Here are two simple lists of some of the things you can do.

"Increase Rents" by doing any or all of these:

- Improve flooring
- Add new appliances
- Add parking
- Add covered parking
- Create storage
- Add washer/dryer or connections or laundry room
- Improve the floor plan
- Increase number of bedrooms or baths
- Change an existing office, formal dining or garage into a bedroom
- Improve landscaping
- Add central air conditioning or heat
- Add fencing, or privacy fencing
- Lease to room mates for higher per room rates

Keep in mind a little tip. If you rehab a property do not over-do it. I have found that when you upgrade a unit you don't necessarily get more rent. You will usually get a *better tenant* but it may not increase your cash flows. Most of the items mentioned above are adding *amenities*, not rehab. Keep to these items and you will be able to get more rent.

"Decrease Expenses" by doing any or all of these:

- Allow the tenant to do work on the property
- Add sub-metering to have tenants pay utilities

- Fight your tax evaluations if they are set too high
- Increase efficiency in windows and insulation
- Decrease the debt service through refinancing
- Ask for larger non-refundable deposits to lower your make-ready expenses
- Hire a better priced property manager
- Get multiple bids on all maintenance issues to insure proper pricing
- Use a different utility provider for lower costs. (If available in your area)

The more positive cash flow you have, the more you will want to invest in property. Make sure all of your properties cash flows can be positive in case you decide to keep your investments for the long-term or for some reason they don't sell. Remember this is your "Ultimate Back-Up Plan!"

> "***Decreasing*** property expenses is as valuable as ***increasing*** property income.
>
> **~Mike Watson**"

Cash flow is nice but it's *not* King

I was teaching my deal evaluation system in a Boot Camp one day and an investor raised her hand and said, "I have been taught that cash flow is *all* that matters. How can you say it is only the *third* most important piece of the deal evaluation?"

My response was, "Imagine you find a duplex that costs $250,000 and has rental income every month of $1600. Would you buy it?" She said, "Probably not because it obviously doesn't have positive cash flow and I would be losing money every month."

I said, "You're absolutely right. If you evaluate this property like most investors it does not seem to be a great deal. However what if you were able to do a condo conversion and make it worth $400,000? Or, what if it comes with a vacant lot that you can build a fourplex on? Would you still say you should not buy the property?"

She was starting to see my point so I continued, "In addition, what if you could add covered parking or washer dryer connections and put separate meters on the units. Then you could increase rents, decrease expenses and have a cash flowing property".

She answered, "I guess then it would be a very worthwhile deal"

Remember, it is always smart to have positive cash flow but keep in mind that positive cash flow is not the *only* way you should analyze your deals. What is most important is to make sure your deal will cash flow if you end up holding it in your long-term portfolio.

Terms are your *secret weapons* for superb investing.

The fourth step of your deal evaluation is to explore and exploit possible terms. Know your terms, they can make an ordinary deal incredible, but can also kill a deal just as easily.

Always remember, in real estate *everything* is negotiable. When you are looking at a deal you have the ability to influence and even determine exactly what *all* of the terms will be. Don't believe me? Read on.

What do I mean by terms? Terms are all of the *details* of the contract that most people take for granted. Terms include how much your payment is (yes, really), when your closing will happen, what your interest rate will be (yep, this too), what a seller may contribute to your deal, and whether or not the seller will be the bank. (yes, you read that right!) In a nutshell "Terms = Value." So let's learn some amazing terms and how to use them as your secret weapon!

Most people think of terms as the price and the timing of a transaction. Terms are much more interesting than just those two items. Well thought out terms can make it *easy* for you to buy properties. They can create *huge cash flow* during ownership and can even make your deal *sell faster* in the future.

Terms are so important to your deal that they can literally make or break it on their own. If you learn how to think differently you can create phenomenal deals with terms.

The first thing you must understand is that *you* have complete control over any of your deals. What I mean by that is *you* make the decision to buy or not. Therefore you are in control. With this control comes the power to negotiate. But what specifically should you negotiate?

When you are looking at buying a property it is wise to ask the seller about different options for terms before you even go to the negotiating table. But first you must know what some of those options are and how they can benefit you. Here are some terms you can use to negotiate with sellers in order to make the deal work better for *both of you:*

- Seller financing – This is my absolute favorite term to negotiate. Why? Because when you negotiate some or all of the purchase as seller financing you can negotiate your financing terms. But why is that important?

  Let's say you want to buy a 20 unit apartment complex for $2,000,000. Most lenders will ask for $600,000 as a down payment and will make you do a loan that is only for 15 years. When you do this type of loan your payments, and therefore carrying costs, will be quite high, and your cash flow will be low.

  On the other hand if you negotiate to get financing from the seller you can negotiate your own terms. This means you could ask for $100,000 down and an interest only loan. This way you lower your out-of-pocket cash and your payments. (Thus increasing your cash flow)

- Low interest rates – Interest rates can significantly affect your deal. Look at what happens to your payment on a $500,000 loan when you have interest-only payments and the rate is 10% versus 6%.

  With a 10% interest rate your monthly payment is $4166.67. With a 6% interest rate your payment is $2500. That means you are paying $20,000 less *per year* for the property!

  Negotiate the best interest rate possible on any seller financing you obtain. Keep in mind that if the rate is reasonable, seller financing is almost always better for both buyer and seller.

- Delay in payments – How exciting would it be to buy a property that you are going to develop and not have any payments for 5 years? I have a student in Florida who has done just that. The seller was willing to forego any payments on his seller financing for 5 years in order to lock in the price now. The amazing thing is that this student is going to do some paper changes to the property and make it worth close to double the purchase price and then sell it prior to his payments starting! You can do this too.

- Seller finance and mortgage combos – Dare I suggest there are better terms than the ones already mentioned? Here we go. What if you buy a property that has a loan on it, take over those payments and have the seller finance their equity to you? In that case you would be buying a property for Zero Down! I see this done quite often amongst my investor students. Keep reading to learn exactly how.

- Assumptions in seller finance notes – Don't let the fancy words make your head swim. This is just a simple way of saying that if the seller gives you seller financing they will let the next buyer take over that financing.

  If you can get a seller to allow you to sell the property and then let the new buyer assume the financing from the original seller you will have a very marketable property.

  Anyone can buy this property, regardless of credit issues or income. This is a very attractive deal for many investors. In addition it can be much cheaper than getting new financing. Typically there are no points or loan closing fees.

- Extended closings – This is when you negotiate to go under contract now but will not close on the property for several months.

  Why would it matter if you close in 60 days rather than 180 or more? In some cases it doesn't matter at all, however on some deals you can get a portion of the changes completed prior to having any carrying costs.

  For example if you are going to buy an apartment complex to do a condo conversion you could do some of the work with the city to implement the conversion before you even own it. In other words, your carrying costs would be free during that time! This could make a difference of tens of thousands of dollars or more on one deal.

- Access to property to perform work before ownership – On most deals you will have some access to the property prior to closing. You will have to do inspections, surveys and appraisals among other things. But that is not what I am talking about here. What I am talking about is having access in order to perform physical work to the property. Why in the world would you take a risk and do physical work (costing you money) to a property you don't even own yet?

The answer is the same as in the extended closing. You could virtually wipe out all carrying costs if you do your changes prior to ownership. How much does it cost you to make payments on a property on which you don't even have a loan? Nothing. This technique combines well with the "Extended closing option mentioned above".

At this point I imagine you are starting to see why the terms of your offer are extremely important. These terms and many others will literally be used as your "weapons of war" in real estate investing. Use them with care and responsibility and you will create the most incredible win/win transactions for yourself and others!

They *will* give you your terms.

When you get out in the field and start making offers you will find that many sellers and even real estate agents may not be that familiar with some of the terms with which you are now armed. I have a little advice.

If you genuinely find out the needs of the seller and make sure *they* are met then in most instances the seller will go along with whatever else you offer. That includes seller financing, low interest rates, delayed closings and all of the other formidable terms you can negotiate.

Why will they do this? Because their needs have been met. Most sellers only have two or three real needs. If you meet these needs and then create terms around them that make the deal work for *you*, why wouldn't the seller agree? The truth is they will.

In the next chapter, I am going to give you a tool called a "Four Offer Spreadsheet". This tool will help you uncover the specific needs of any seller. With it you will be unstoppable with your negotiating.

Let me give you a real life example of how this works. One day I got a call from an owner of a 12 unit apartment building. He said, "I heard that you are interested in buying property in the area around my apartment complex. Would you like to take a look at mine?" My answer was of course, "Yes. I'll be right over."

After looking at his property I did like it. But his price was a bit high for what I wanted to do. But then he said the magic words, "I will do *anything* to get rid of this building if I can get *full price*." The reason he wanted full price was he wanted to invest his proceeds elsewhere to get some cash flow to replace the loss of his rental income. In essence he wanted to get rid of the burden of being a property manager without losing his monthly income.

His building was priced well for him, but unfortunately, under the terms of a *new loan* it would not cash flow for me. Based on our discussion of "terms", what do you think I did? I bought the building with *no money down*. I also got him to agree to seller finance the whole purchase price for 6.5% interest with a 30-year mortgage. This solved everyone's problems!

It allowed him to get the full price he wanted and allowed me to have a nice cash flow since I was paying such a low fixed interest rate. But why would he do this? Where was his income from the investment he wanted to do with his equity? He got it from *my payments*.

He wanted those payments so badly that he asked for a $10,000 prepayment *penalty* for ten years to guarantee himself the income for that long. In other words, I would have to pay $10,000 if I sold the property or refinanced it before the 10 years was over. I countered his request by asking him to allow me to offer the loan as a *simple assumption* to any subsequent buyer. That way I could pass his prepayment penalty along to someone else should I decide to sell prior to the ten year pre-payment period.

This is a perfect example of how you can use terms creatively to make a sensational win/win deal for everyone. In a nutshell "How well you understand terms is equal to how successful and profitable you will be with real estate investing".

> "Terms are your "Weapons of War". Understand them and use them responsibly to create unlimited Win/Win deals.
>
> **~Mike Watson**"

The Realistic Crystal Ball

Once you determine a property's "Highest and Best" use, its best market price, and that it has a positive cash flow and win/win terms what is next? Step 5 of the Deal Evaluation process is to determine the "future potential of the property". It's time to get out your crystal ball. A crystal ball will show you what is going to happen in the future.

How is this done? Through research! You research what is going to happen in the area for the next five to twenty years. Find out what the city, county, and state's master or future plans are for the property and the immediate *surrounding area.*

The future potential is different from the current "Highest and Best" use in that it would involve some sort of *change* in regulations or zoning from what is in place now.

Here are some of the questions you should ask of your city, county and state in order to determine the future potential of your project:

1. What developments are proposed in the area?
2. What zoning changes are coming?

3. What annexations may happen to impact the property?
4. What stores, commercial developments or residential developments are coming that may increase or decrease the value of the property?
5. Will there be any change to the road system near this property?
6. Will schools be built near by?
7. How will the adjacent properties change over time?

If you are buying a property solely because of something you expect to happen in the future you must make the change ASAP! Keep in mind that future plans are not always guaranteed. They can and do regularly change.

You should check for these things because they may not all be positive changes. This study will help insure you're buying a good investment if you end up keeping it for the long-term.

If you haven't already,
get out your calculator NOW!

If you find a property and it fits into the criteria up to this point, you are very close to writing an offer. As a matter of fact once you have read this whole book you could probably get a property under contract at this point in your analysis and do the final steps during your feasibility period.

The next step is to get out your pen, paper and calculator. You may have done some of this already but this is where you will need to really crunch some numbers. Step #6 of our deal evaluation is to "Evaluate your Short-term and Long-term plans"

The first thing you must understand is how to calculate your returns. If you don't understand this section read it over and over until you do. Without this basic knowledge you will be unable to determine if a property can make you a profit. *Do not invest* if you are unwilling to do this step.

There are several different ways to calculate returns in the investing world. I do it a little differently than most. The reason is that I invest a little differently than most. I calculate how much equity I will have in the property when all of the changes are completed. My back up plan of holding a property long-term absolutely *requires* that I calculate returns this way.

I refer to this calculation as "Refinance Returns". What this means is the number you come up with will be a *percentage* of the *property value* when all changes are finished. The percentage is the equity you have in the property at that time.

If there is enough equity you will be able to refinance the property, pay off all of your investors and short-term loans (more later on these loans) and not use any out-of-pocket money to close. If this can be done you can keep the property in your long-term portfolio for cash flow without having *any* of your own money in the deal!

Let me explain how important this is. If you do not have enough equity in your deal and you need to refinance because it did not sell, the result could be that you have to bring a very large sum of money to the table just to be able to *keep* the property. I'm sure you can see how important it is to have the right amount of equity left in your deal.

Let's learn how to calculate these returns.

"Refinance Returns" Explained

In order to refinance and not have to bring money to the table, you must have at least 20% equity on a residential investment, or 30% equity on a commercial project. This means if you buy a property for $500,000 and make changes on it that cost $1,000,000 resulting in the property being worth $2,000,000, you have a $500,000 equity position left after what you owe on the property. That $500,000 is 25% of $2,000,000. Therefore, you have a 25% equity position. (I'll give you a formula for this shortly)

If that property is a home, duplex or fourplex you will be able to refinance it without bringing money to the closing. If it is anything with more than four units *you will have to bring 5% or $100,000 to the closing!* (Anything with more than 4 units is considered commercial) So, as you can see it is very important to make sure every deal will have enough equity that you can take the project long-term without a big expense to you.

If you work your numbers well enough at the beginning of your deal you will know that you will be able to either sell in the short-term for a profit or keep the property for long-term for cash flow. What could be better than having both options be viable? Nothing, which is why this section of the deal evaluation is what will give your deal the green light.

P.S. If you can find a company that will give you a refinance loan on a commercial property with a higher loan to value ratio such as 75% then you might consider deals with a bit smaller return. If this is available then you only need to have 25% equity in the property to refinance. Sometimes this type of loan is available on a "residential" commercial property like an apartment building.

The Crucial Formula

Before I teach you how to use the crucial formula you will need some definitions. Please read through them so it is easier to understand the spreadsheets I will show you in later sections.

"Acquisition Cost"- (AC)

This number is equal to the total amount you spend when you purchase the property. It is not just the purchase price but also includes all aspects of purchase, including closing costs, loan costs, inspections etc.

"Cost to Change"- (CTC)

The CTC includes every dollar you spend during the course of changing the property. Some of these items may be architectural costs, fix up costs, development costs or construction costs. In addition you may have to pay utilities, holding costs such as loan payments, insurance, taxes and management expenses. These even include advertising and commissions when you sell.

Sometimes there will be some *income* included in the CTC. For instance if there are tenants currently making rent payments, you will use those amounts to lower your cost to change.

"Future Value" – (FV)

This is the price you will get for the property when you sell it, or the amount it will appraise for if you refinance.

So, here it is, "<u>The Refinance Return Formula</u>":

Acquisition Costs + Cost to Change = Total Acquisition Cost (TAC)

Future Value (FV) – TAC = Your Profit or Equity amount.

Profit or Equity amount, divided by, your FV = Refinance Return

In a nut shell, figure out what your future value is, subtract out everything it will cost to do the *entire* project. Then you divide that remaining amount by the *future* value. You will end up with a percentage. That percentage is your "Refinance Return".

If the number is over 20% and your project is between one to four residential units you are in business. If it is over 30% and it has five or more residential units or is retail, industrial or commercial you are also in business. Write those offers. Get those deals. GREEN LIGHT! GO!

How to Determine the Future Value

The first question that usually comes along following the previous section is "How do I figure out what the property will be worth after I change it to its 'Highest and Best' use?"

Luckily this is an easy thing to do. All you have to do is pretend. Pretend that the project is done and then find out the value of other similar projects or properties that have recently sold.

If the project will take a long time (Over 6 months) I will factor in a very slight gain for an up market (2-4%) and a slight loss for a down market (5-10%). If there are no new projects to compare to, pricing will be a little better than the older projects that are already in existence. People love to buy new things and will pay more for a new home than an older one.

How does everyone else calculate returns?

Most traditional investors take their profit and divide it by how much money they have *spent*, rather than the *future value.* When this is done it shows a higher return. Many look at a traditional 20% return and do a deal. The only problem with that reasoning is now they *must* sell. If they don't sell they will have to bring money to the closing table in order to refinance. That is bad news!

Let me show you how this works. Let's say you buy a piece of property for $500,000 and spend $1,000,000 fixing it up. You would be in it for $1,500,000. If it is worth $2,000,000 fixed up you have a $500,000 profit. Typical investors would say that we have a 33% return. They say that because they had a $500,000 profit and they divided that by their $1,500,000 in expenses, giving them the 33% number.

Our return in this same example shows only 25%. We take the $500,000 in profit and divide it by its new value of $2,000,000. This gives us a 25% return. If this property happens to be a commercial building the owner is in serious trouble if it does not sell. They will have to bring money to the table to refinance out of their short-term loans for construction.

Many investors would proceed with this deal based on the traditional 33% return. We would never have done this deal in the first place. We would have known that it would be difficult to refinance before we ever bought the property. This deal evaluation system will keep you out of trouble. Every property you purchase should profit in the short-term and also work in your long-term portfolio. That way you will be creating wealth and or profits on *every* deal.

Is the "Short-term" a week or what?

The crux of the issue for the sixth step of your deal evaluation is to make sure the deal works in the "Short-term" and *also* in the "Long-term". But how do you know what the "Short-term" is? Is it a week or is it ten years? The "Short-term" is simply the time it takes for you to sell the property for a profit at some point *before* you complete the changes.

This might not make a lot of sense yet as we have not started our discussion about "Flixers". We will get there soon. It is literally Step #8 of "The Foundation to Success". For now just know it means you do *not* end up holding this property in your "Long-term" portfolio.

Will every deal have the same "Short-term" time? Absolutely not. Every deal will be different. For instance, if you buy a fourplex in order to do a condo-conversion, the short-term may be 6 months. That is an estimate of the time it will take to do the *paper* part of the conversion. In order to do your "Short-term" evaluation you need to decide what the whole complex would be worth at *that* time if an investor came in and finished the physical work and sold the units themselves.

Another example is if you buy a lot with a small home on it where you can build a 15 unit condominium complex. In this case the short-term may be the time it takes you to get the full plans through the city and approved for building permits. At this point the value you are looking for is the price a *builder* would pay for the property.

So, the very first thing you have to determine is, "How *long* is the "Short-term" on this particular deal?" In most cases it is the time it takes you to get to a turning point or milestone where someone wants to buy the property from you and finish the work themselves to make a profit.

Once you determine the short-term for your project you can start with the numbers. You want to get as close to actual income and expenses as possible. But don't worry! We have an *amazing* tool to help you through this process.

Remember:

- Every deal is different and every city has different costs.
- Most, but not all, of your costs will be included on the form.
- Make sure you put together all of the costs necessary for your area and project.
- Get more than one opinion on these costs if they are not regulated fixed costs.
- Real estate agents, Title companies, Loan officers, Contractors, Architects, Engineers, Surveyors, Inspectors, Property managers, and Appraisers, etc. will come in very handy at this point. They will help you understand the costs of *your specific project.* (See "Power Teams")

Note: This might be a good time to make some notes on your "Spark of Inspiration" List in Appendix 2. Especially in reference to people who may be interested in investing. Anyone you know who is in any of the specific fields mentioned in the previous paragraph is a good candidate.

Just Plug in Your Deal and it Spits Out Your Returns

This form shows an example of buying a home on a lot which is zoned for 15 condos. (Sound familiar?) The home is occupied and you will receive rent during the time you own the property. We assume you will buy the distressed home for $129,900 and then sell each brand new condo for $225,000. This will give a value of $675,000 to the land for a builder. If you are wondering how I came up with that number, there are two ways to calculate it.

First take the $225,000 per door and multiply it by 15 doors. This results in a total future value of $3,375,000. In a *typical* market a builder will pay up to 20% of the future value of a project for the raw land with full permits and plans. That is how I arrive at $675,000.

You can use this calculation as a baseline but in addition you should always find similar properties that have sold recently in your market place. This is the second way to arrive at your short-term number. Get comparable solds and assume you will be able to get close to those same prices.

In our example we are going to also assume you complete everything needed to get the property permitted and plans drawn for a builder. And finally, that it will take you six months to make those changes and find a buyer who is a builder. At this point the builder buys the project from you and thus it is a "Short-term" deal. *You* did not finish building the project or keep it in your "Long-term" portfolio.

So let's put in some numbers and see what happens. Is this a good deal or not?

(See the "Short Term Deal Evaluation" on the next page)

Short Term Deal Evaluation

EXPENSE SUMMARY

Time Money Needed: 6 Months

Purchase price	$129,900	Cost of property
Escrow fees 1%	$1,299	1% of purchase price
Recording fees	$130	Get from your title company
6 months property taxes	$1,500	Get most recent info from your tax district
Hazard insurance	$1,000	Get estimate from insurance agent
Total Acquisition Cost (TAC)	$133,829	Add above 5 items

COST TO CHANGE

Architect/Engineering fees	$20,000	Get 3 bids for each
Upgrades or fix up costs	$1,000	No upgrade, just maintenance
Appraisal	$750	Get 3 bids
Survey	$5,000	Get 3 bids
Legal work for condo paperwork	$10,000	Get bids from attorneys
Permits	$2,500	Check with your city and county for costs
Inspections	$500	Get bids
Advertising	$2,000	Assume 4 months advertising and marketing costs
Development, roads, infrastructure, utilities	$0	Not needed in short term
Management	$2,000	Get bids if needed
Miscellaneous	$2,000	Repairs, maintenance, landscaping, etc.
Utilities	$500	Calculate months when you pay or vacant.
Sub-Total Cost to Change (CTC)	$46,250	Add above 12 items
Contingency (20% of CTC)	$9,250	Multiply CTC by 20% (Do not share this with builder)
Escrow fees 2nd sale 1%	$6,750	Ask your title company
Recording fees 2nd sale	$250	Ask your title company
Real estate commissions 2nd sale 6%	$40,500	Multiply the future value by 6%
Total Cost to Change (TCTC)	$103,000	Add the CTC and the above 4 items to get TCTC
Debt Service (DS)	$9,004	(TAC + CTC) x 5% Assuming you pay 10% on the money for 6 mo.
Total Project Cost (TPC)	$245,833	(TAC + TCTC + DS)

PROFIT SUMMARY

Future Value (FV)	$675,000	Analyze value of land for 15 units
Rental Income	$6,000	Add up total rent collected for 6 months
Gross Profit (GP)	$681,000	Add above 2 items
TOTAL DEAL PROFIT (TDP)	**$435,167**	GP - TPC
"Refinance Returns"!	**64.47%**	TDP/FV is "Refinance Return" (Want minimum of 30%)
Traditional Returns	177.0%	TDP/TPC is the "Traditional" way to calculate returns

Now that you have gone through the numbers what do you notice? Is this a good deal? Should you run out the door and make an offer? Or if you are already under contract do you know yet if it is a "for sure" deal? No, you don't.

On the surface this deal looks fantastic. It is showing over a 60% return based on "Refinance Returns" and over a 170% return based on a traditional investor's calculation! Why would I say "Do not do this deal yet" if it is such a profitable deal?

This is only the "Short-term" profits. You have not yet calculated your "Long-term" profits or equity position. "The Foundation to Success" says, "Make sure you will make money in the short-term *and* long-term or don't do the deal!" This is critical because if it won't work in the long-term for *you* it won't work for someone else either therefore it's not a good deal.

I want to mention a couple of extra ways you can use this form before we go on to the "Long-term". First, you can work it *in reverse.* In other words, you can put in the future value and the expenses and the percent of profit you want and then it will calculate how much you can pay for the property.

Why would this be important? How could you use this tool? It could be used when you are dealing with a seller that won't give you a price at all. What do I mean? Well, you have learned how to find sellers that do not have their property on the market. Some may say, "Make me an offer." This is one way you can do just that. Figure out all of your expenses, the future value, and your desired return and out jumps your price!

Finally, you can play with the numbers on the evaluation form based on what *terms* you want to negotiate. This is where it becomes clear how terms can make or break a deal.

Another creative use for this tool is when a seller is firm on a price *and* terms yet the form does not show your desired returns. When this happens you will know to MOVE ON! It is that simple. Do not waste any more time on that deal. Find the next one, they are everywhere now that you know how to look.

You should use this form *every* time you come across a deal you think has potential. Remember you are always looking for at least a 20% or more refinance return on residential, and 30% or more on commercial.

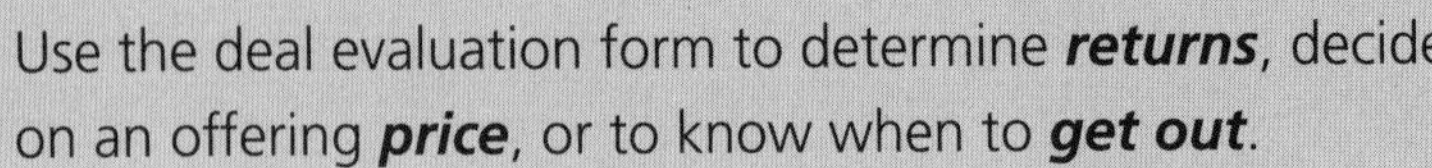

> Use the deal evaluation form to determine ***returns***, decide on an offering ***price***, or to know when to ***get out***.
>
> **~Mike Watson**

The Deciding Factor to Do Your Deal or Not

Finally we have reached the top of the mountain for deal evaluation. I'm glad you have made it this far. I promise that after you do a few of these you will get faster and faster at them. Just keep plugging in those numbers and one day very soon you will be able to look at a property and know it is an incredible deal.

Now that you know your "Short-term" time frame, let's determine the length of time for your "Long-term" plan. When I say "Long-term" I mean the project is *complete.*

First you need to determine how long it will take to get any permits to build, drawings made, utilities put in, inspections, conversion paperwork done, all development, remodeling, construction, etc. Remember to include the time it will take to *sell* the properties to new buyers. If this is a development or addition project an architect will come in very handy right now. Most of them will have been through the majority of these processes in your specific city and have a clear idea of how long it will take to get through each step.

When you determine this time frame add on *at least* 30 percent more time than you expect. For example, if you have been told it will take 6 months to go through the city, and then 8 months to build and you think it will take 6 months to sell for a total of 20 months I would say your long-term should be at least 26 months. To be completely on the safe side *double* the time you predict. Remember, "Conservative Analysis leaves Liberal Profits."

After settling on a time frame you will go through the same process as the short-term of determining your expenses. Get your bids and insert them in a "Long-term Deal Evaluation Form". By the way, your best bet for bids is to talk with builders and contractors who have done these types of projects in the past. Hopefully you will have one on your "Power Team".

The point of this evaluation form is to help you make a decision as to whether or not the project has any chance of working in the long-term. If it does then it is worth going under contract. This form will help you *make your decisions* and will also help keep you on track through the transaction. You will be revising it on a weekly if not *daily* basis during the whole deal. It is a fantastic tool!

On this form we assume an extended closing where we get the project part way through the city prior to ownership. Then we assume 18 months to build and sell.

(See the "Long Term Deal Evaluation" on the next page)

Long Term Deal Evaluation

EXPENSE SUMMARY

Time Money Needed: 18 Months

Purchase price	$129,900	Cost of property
Escrow fees 1%	$1,299	1% of purchase price
Recording fees	$130	Get from your title company
18 Months property taxes	$4,500	Get most recent info from your tax district
Hazard insurance	$12,000	Get estimate from insurance agent, may need builders policy during build
Total Acquisition Cost (TAC)	$147,829	Add above 5 items

COST TO CHANGE

Architect/Engineering fees	$20,000	Get 3 bids for each
Upgrades or fix up costs	$1,275,000	Consider 1000 sqft properties x15 at $85/ft to build
Appraisal	$2,500	Get 3 bids
Survey	$5,000	Get 3 bids
Legal work for condo paper-work	$10,000	Get bids from attorneys
Permits	$2,500	Check with your city and county for costs
Inspections	$2,000	Get bids
Advertising	$10,000	Assume 10 months advertising and marketing costs
Development, roads, infrastructure, utilities	$75,000	Get bids from road/utility/landscapers
Management	$2,000	Get bids if needed
Miscellaneous	$5,000	Repairs, maintenance, landscaping, etc.
Utilities	$5,000	Calculate months when you pay or vacant.
Sub-Total Cost to Change (CTC)	$1,414,000	Add above 12 items
Contingency (20% of CTC)	$282,800	Multiply CTC by 20% (Do not share this with your builder)
Escrow fees 2nd sale 1%	$33,750	Ask your title company
Recording fees 2nd sale	$3,750	Ask your title company
Real estate commissions 2nd Sale 5%	$168,750	Multiply the future value by 5% (Discount for volume)
Total Cost to Change (TCTC)	$1,903,050	Add the CTC and the above 4 items to get TCTC
Debt Service (DS)	$156,183	(TAC + CTC) x 10% Assuming you pay 10% on the money for 12 mo.
		Only need construction money during construction
Total Project Cost (TPC)	$2,207,062	(TAC + TCTC + DS)

PROFIT SUMMARY

Future Value (FV)	$3,375,000	Do market analysis for end product, 15 new condos
Rental Income	$6,000	Add up total rent collected over 6 months
Gross Profit (GP)	$3,381,000	Add above 2 items
TOTAL DEAL PROFIT (TDP)	**$1,173,938**	GP - TPC
"Refinance Returns"!	**34.78%**	TDP/FV is "Refinance Returns" (Want minimum of 30%)
Traditional Returns	53.2%	TDP/TPC is the "Traditional" way to calculate returns

Take a minute to analyze the data on this form. The same assumptions exist as before except you are taking the project all the way to completion. *Now* do you go forward on this deal? With the information we have gathered and analyzed so far, I would answer with a resounding "YES!" You have found a deal that works in the short-term if you do a "Flixer". (Sell it to a builder for a quick profit) It also works in the long-term if you build it and sell to the people who will ultimately live there.

But here is the best part, "It even works if you *can't* sell it!" With these equity/profit numbers you will be able to refinance onto a long-term loan and hold it in your "Long-term Portfolio" for an equity position and positive cash flow without having to come to the closing table with *any* money. The time has come to GO FOR IT!

Note: If the project is longer than 2 years you may want to have an even higher percent return to accommodate the time issue. In other words, you might want a 40% return if it takes more than 2 years to complete. This way you will get a 20% return *per year*. However, as long as you have that 30% equity position you will be able to refinance.

FREE Online Resources

The Short Term and Long Term Deal Evaluation spreadsheets are available on my web site for FREE!
Go to **mikewatsoninvesting.com/bookextras** and click on the "Deal Evaluation Form" Here you will find a blank spreadsheet. Save it to your computer and plug in your numbers on your deals. Change it to fit your market and requirements on each deal and your long-term deal evaluations will be simplified.

How the *Market* can affect Your Evaluation

When I am teaching my Boot Camps I will usually have someone hold up their hand at this point and say, "What if the market is declining during your deal?" This is an absolutely valid question. The answer you should remember is this, "Will the property have a positive cash flow? If it does then it will most likely work out fine. That is because your back up plan is in place."

That said I would like to go into a little more explanation of down markets. The truth is that markets are usually down because there has been no affordable housing for some time. Property prices rise in a good market to the point where people can't afford to buy starter homes anymore. This causes the market to turn into a soft or down market as property sales slow.

When this happens rents can go up fairly dramatically. Research shows that high price markets starting to drop in price are typically followed by increases in the rental markets. This is because people can't afford to buy. As landlords realize less people can buy and more will rent, the monthly rents will inevitably go up. When rents go up, cash flows will improve dramatically for those who own property with fixed payments.

People with long-term portfolios will benefit in improving markets through appreciation and equity growth. They also benefit in down markets when their assets become far more *cash flow rich* due to the increase in rental income.

The second thing to focus on in down markets is the "Highest and Best" use. The best use in these markets is *affordable housing*. If your project is compellingly affordable to the "End User" it will have a very high chance of success.

As an example, let's assume you want to buy a house on a half acre lot where you can put 12 condos. The smart thing to do is to determine what the sales price would have to be per unit on a 12-unit condominium complex to be profitable. If that price is *at or above* current entry level housing you should *not* buy that property, especially if it doesn't have positive cash flow. However, if you could offer your completed units at "affordable entry level" pricing for your area and for 15% less than the lowest priced similar units you will more than likely be able to sell them even in a bad market.

Most people don't realize the best deals sell in a bad market. People still have to buy and sell property. You just have to remember that in a down market "only the best priced properties are assured of selling".

Keep the following things in mind for your evaluation if you are in a downward moving market.

1. Terms

You are getting ready to learn about terms in great detail. Within the section on "Seller Financing" you will find a plethora of terms you can use to make any deal work. Study the ones I introduce and then get creative with your deals. In a down market sellers are much more willing to be flexible with terms. Use that willingness to make your deals work phenomenally!

2. Rents

In a bad market more people have to rent. They may have less cash, plus they may have foreclosures or bankruptcies on their record. When there is a higher demand for rentals in an area where prices were very high for entry level homes the rents *will* go up until it is possible to buy again.

In other words rents will rise until they get much closer to the cost to own. Once they get nearer to that number they will begin to taper off again. If you own property with renters during a down market there is a good chance your rents will go up during that time. Therefore, your cash flow will be higher. Keep this in mind with your evaluations.

3. Prices

When people *have* to sell their property and there are no buyers what happens? It is a simple economic principal. Prices drop. Not only do they drop, but sellers will accept low offers all day long. They will offer incentives and bonuses. Ask for *the world* in a bad market. Get rock bottom prices or move on to the next deal. You are in the driver's seat. There are deals everywhere.

4. Building costs

When there is a glut of contractors needing work, the cost of construction goes down and goes down fast. If these people don't have a job they may not eat. Make sure to get bids redone *frequently* in a down market to make sure you are not paying more than necessary for construction. Make your deal evaluation reflect these better prices for more concise profit determinations.

5. Something is always selling

Something always sells. Even in the worst market something is selling. There is not a city that has had *not one sale* over any length of time. The key is to find out *exactly* what it is that is selling. Keep track of *every* sale in your "Area of Expertise". Once you determine what is selling, find a way to *create* more of that product. Incorporate this process into your choice of deals and evaluations.

Only a Few Are so Lucky...

You have now learned the six main steps of how to evaluate your deal.

1. Determine The "Highest and Best" use of the property.
2. Compare your purchase price with your appraised value.
3. Evaluate your current and possible future, cash flow.
4. Explore and exploit terms.
5. Determine the "Future Potential" of the property.
6. Evaluate your short-term and long-term plans.

The seventh step is one that not all people are able to use. If you qualify, consider yourself lucky because you can make more money than anyone else! Step number seven is as follows:

7. Remember to ask, "Is there any Professional Application?"

More specifically the question you want to ask yourself is, "Do I have a job where the professional application in the deal will make this a more attractive investment?"

What I mean by a professional application is this. If you are a loan officer you may be able to make quite a bit more money on the transaction by doing the loans necessary for yourself and for buyers at the end of the project.

Some other examples would be a contractor who can do the construction for a much lower price than most, a property manager who can do all of the management or a real estate agent who can make a commission when they purchase and save on commissions when they sell.

There are many professions who benefit when a real estate investment is made. You always want to ask yourself, "Is there a professional application during the investment that will increase my profits?" If there is, make sure you take it into account when you are evaluating your deal.

This idea will resurface again when we talk about "Flixers" and "Power Teams". It is a super-powerful inside way to *sell* your properties with lightening speed! It is also a conversation starter to invite key professionals to be on your "Power Team".

Are *all* of the steps necessary?

Some have told me that the seven steps of my deal evaluation are overkill. Here is the thing, I want to make sure that *every* deal you do is *profitable*. Therefore I have created a deal evaluation system that is as bulletproof as I can make it. I have inserted all of my experience from 14 years of investing and packed it with a punch. It is yours for the taking. I believe you make your money when you buy. If you do your deal evaluation and buy correctly you have a much higher chance of success.

The good news is that once you know your "AoE" and start to do a few evaluations you will find that it will only take you 30 minutes or so to evaluate a property before you make an offer. I don't suggest you do every single portion of every step of this evaluation prior to making an offer. I suggest you do a quick evaluation and then *make an offer.*

Some people like to do a lot more extensive research on the property before they write a contract. There are a few problems with that theory. First of all, most sellers don't want to disclose much to someone who doesn't have a vested interest in the property in the form of a contract and earnest money. They think, "Buyers without a contract are not serious." Honestly, they have a point.

Secondly, the longer you wait to make an offer on properties, especially the good ones, the more likely it is that someone else will come along and make an offer on the deal before you do. Now you did all that work for *nothing!*

Thirdly, most people won't spend money on professional property condition research such as surveys, appraisals and environmental studies if they don't have the property under contract. If this is the case how well are you really evaluating the property before you go under contract anyway?

The trick is to determine as best as you can that the property works conceptually and then *write an offer!* You should have a clear understanding of what the seller wants, what the property is and what it can be in the future. You can then write compelling contracts and begin your due diligence (Technical word for "property condition research") period earnestly. You should include in the contract as much as you can in the way of contingencies and buyers due diligence time so you can do the proper evaluation.

By going under contract it *forces* you to get more serious about your evaluation and protects you from losing the deal to another buyer. Let's write some offers!

> "Do good evaluations but don't get caught up in ***analysis paralysis*** or you may never make an offer in time to get the deal.
>
> **~Mike Watson**"

STEP 5

BUY THE PROPERTY USING THE TWO OPM'S

STEP 5

BUY THE PROPERTY USING THE TWO OPM'S

How to Make Incredible Offers

We are now ready to move on to Step #5 of "The Foundation to Success". It is to buy the property using the *two* OPM's. In this section I will teach you how to negotiate to an *ultimate* win/win. I will also show you how to buy properties all day long without a *penny* out of your own pocket! You probably still don't believe me on that one though you soon will.

But let's not get ahead of ourselves. The first thing you have to do is know how to write excellent offers that people will respond to. If you are an active real estate agent you have most likely written many offers and are familiar with your local contracts.

If you are not a real estate agent what do you do? How are you going to get the contracts you need? How are you going to learn the language of the industry? My strongest recommendation is that you get an exceptional real estate agent on your "Power Team". More on that later but for now you will want to *hire* an exceptional real estate agent.

How do I define an exceptional real estate agent? In my opinion the only exceptional real estate agents are those who are doing deals the way *you* are going to do them. Therefore they have either been to MWI events or studied MWI material.

There are real estate agents in my programs who have been studying this method of property investing for years. They are knowledgeable in these techniques and will be a huge help when you start making offers and doing deals.

If you are unable to go to an MWI event to meet someone you should get on my web site at www.mikewatsoninvesting.com and go to the "Forum". There you can search for a real estate agent in your area. There are real estate agents in *most* cities that are actively learning or using "The Foundation to Success".

If you are unable to find one who has experience in these techniques you should interview several real estate agents in your area. In your interview focus on the following things; Have they ever bought property for *themselves*? Do they have an *open mind* about investing? Are they able to be as *passionate* about investing as you are? Do they have or are they willing to put together their own "Red Button Statement"?

If they have these qualities then they will most likely be open to reading this book and to learning this process. If they are unwilling to learn these investing techniques your investing success will be greatly affected. Keep asking and you will find someone who is as excited about investing as you are. *They* are the right real estate agent. Only an exceptional real estate agent will have the ability to write an incredible offer.

In order to understand how to write incredible offers you will need to have a working knowledge of how to use the two types of "Other People's Money". An incredible offer is one that incorporates these techniques into a "4-Offer Spreadsheet". I will walk you through the process.

The *1st* kind of OPM (Other People's Money)

Why is the term "OPM" (Other People's Money) such a buzz word in the investing world? Why does it even matter to you? In my opinion you should *always* use one or both of the types of OPM's.

Why? Because if you do, you will increase your personal profits exponentially! When you do not use *your* own money and yet you still make profits, the actual returns are *infinite.* Zero money coming out of your own pocket on any positive return you earn equals infinity, no matter how you calculate it.

The first type of OPM I am going to discuss is actually going to be your own money. Why am I calling it OPM then? Because it is money you are not currently using to create income. Or I should say, "It is money that is *not* working for you."

If you decide to use true "other" people's money on deals you need to check with your State *and* the Federal SEC (Securities and Exchange Commission). There are rules for raising capital in your state and any state in which you raise capital or do a deal. Follow the rules to the letter as raising capital can be an offense punishable by *jail* if you do it wrong. That said, if you make sure you are raising funds correctly you *can* teach other people how to use these same techniques and you can use those funds for your deals.

Returning to our talk on using money that was not previously being used, I'd like to explain a bit further. What do I mean by "not being used"? I mean you are quite possibly sitting on hundreds of thousands of dollars that is *wasting away.* Every day you do not tap into those funds and use them to *create income* is a day you have lost money.

If you have equity in your home you have a potential source of cash for deals. You can pull a "Line of Credit" on the equity and get that money out. It will cost you interest to use it but just count that as interest expense when you are doing your deal evaluation.

I suggest you use equity in your home on a deal because if you just let your equity sit it does not *exist.* (We will talk more in Step #7 about equity and how it works.) What I mean by this is that if the market drops you will lose that equity. Therefore it does not exist.

The only way to make equity *real* is to access it and use it. The two ways you can make equity real are by taking out a line of credit or by selling the property. I prefer to access it by doing a line of credit. Then I can use that money on deals and still *own* my asset.

Another place that people do not realize they have capital for real estate deals is in their IRA accounts. In most cases you are able to tap into that money and use it for real estate transactions. In addition a self-directed IRA allows investors, under certain guidelines, to invest in *other* people's real estate projects. Just like equity in their home, most people's mutual funds, retirement accounts and IRAs aren't performing well or at all. If you are able to offer a better investment secured by real estate for people with these kinds of techniques it can be a real win/win opportunity.

This may sound peculiar but it is true. Most people who are *smart* with money don't have much money *sitting* in the bank. What I mean is this; there is a *cost* to having money at your fingertips. When you borrow it you typically pay interest and when you hoard it you are not using it to *make* money for you. Both of these options cost you money!

For example, is it smarter to have $100,000 in a bank account making 2% interest or in a Money Market account making 4.5% interest? The common answer is the latter. So, I ask you, "Is it smarter to have your money in an account making 4.5% interest or in a deal that will make you 20, 30 or 40% returns?

This whole concept should be an incentive to you and others to put that *cash* to work. Make it work hard so you won't have to. If you find a deal, find cash, either your own or someone else's!

> "Don't ***waste*** your money! If you have funds that are not working ***hard*** for you find an incredible deal and ***put them to work.***
>
> **~Mike Watson**"

What was the *return* on your home equity last year?

I touched briefly on this subject but it warrants a bit more clarification. One of the questions I will often ask in my Boot Camp is, "What was the return on your home equity last year?" Most people say something like, "My home went up in value by $50,000 last year. So I guess I made $50,000".

The interesting thing is that their answer didn't answer my question. I was asking them about the *return* on their equity, not how much their equity was. An increase in value is a return on ownership, not on *equity*.

At this point they are usually starting to get a little frustrated so I ask them, "Did you take your equity out and do something with it to make you money?" If they answer yes I ask them, "Where did you invest it and what was the return?"

For the vast majority of people, the answer is, "I didn't do anything with my equity." Or, "I took out a home equity loan and *spent* the money and now I have payments." Both of these answers are a travesty!

This means that the largest portion of America's homeowner's net worth is sitting unused and unprofitable or is *costing* them money. Not only that, this equity is diminishing in value over time due to inflation. Once you understand these concepts getting this money out and investing it starts to makes a lot of sense.

Here is the icing on the cake. If you find a fantastic deal, you can then offer someone a 10% or 12% return on their money. (This is higher than the 7-8% they will pay for the line of credit.) The people who invested with you are now getting positive CASH FLOW having done nothing but a little paperwork! And, you have just funded your deal. You have turned a win/win into a win/win/win. Now *that* is what I call outstanding investing.

If you are interested in learning more about raising capital for your deals, MWI offers an intensive course on the topic. In that Degree Camp I go over the rules and regulations of my state and the federal SEC, how to talk with potential investors and ways you can share your profits.

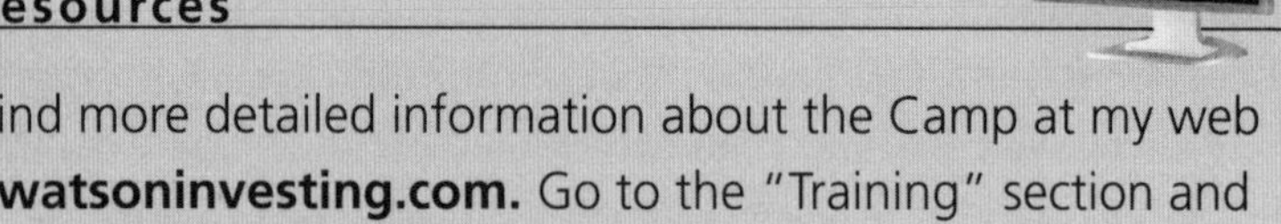

Other Resources

You can find more detailed information about the Camp at my web site **mikewatsoninvesting.com.** Go to the "Training" section and then click on the "Raising Capital" Degree Camp.

I also have a FREE audio clip you can listen to on my web site that demonstrates how to talk with someone who might be interested in investing in your projects.

FREE Online Resources

To access the free Capital Raising audio,
go to **mikewatsoninvesting.com/bookextras**, and click on "Capital Raising Role Play Audio".

Is it smart to use cash or privately raised capital to buy properties?

Some people think that paying cash for a property is foolish. They think it is smarter to get as much leverage on a deal as you can. In some ways that is true but here are some *other* things to consider about using cash.

1. Cash offers look strong and are enticing to a seller. A seller thinks a buyer with cash can, and will perform. Cash offers are often accompanied by quicker closings and less contingencies (such as loan approvals and/or appraisals). Read, "No brain damage for going through the loan process!" Since the seller thinks you are a strong buyer and you can close faster you can get *better terms* from the seller. The most common concession you should get for paying cash is a *discounted price.* (See the cash offer on the "4-offer spreadsheet" coming later in the book.)

2. Cash purchases result in a free and clear property after purchase. When you own properties free and clear they become assets you can borrow against or use as collateral. In other words, "They have equity that you can access over and over for deals, whenever you need money!"

3. When you pay cash you do not have to deal with *banks*. I had a student recently ask, "Why would you pay more for a loan from private capital or for your own line of credit, than you would pay a traditional bank?" The answer is this, "I avoid all of the paperwork and red tape that comes with working with traditional lenders. In addition, the closing cost of private money can be much lower than it is for a loan from a bank." Believe me paying a higher rate is worth every penny.

4. If the capital is your own you will lower your debt service on the subject property and have better positive *cash flow!* You will have this awesome cash flow until you refinance the property or use it for collateral in another deal.

5. When you use a bank loan you are required to buy the bank a title insurance policy to protect their investment. This policy can cost you as much as 1% of the loan amount or more. This is an additional expense you may not be required to incur with a cash closing. Check the rules and regulations of the areas in which you do business.

When you raise private capital (money from other people) and use it for your deals it has all of the benefits of cash. However it has some differences. The first is you owe someone those funds and often you will owe much higher rates of return. This may affect your cash flow in the long-term, if this is the case make sure you are able to refinance so you can get a lower long-term rate and return the funds to the private investor in a reasonable amount of time.

So let's take a look at the advantages of raising private capital over getting a loan from a bank.

1. Private money doesn't show on your credit report or reduce your credit score. You always want to disclose your private debts to financial institutions, however they don't show on your credit.
2. Profits can be shared with private investors if you choose, thus making the transaction more of a win/win deal for you and your investors.
3. Private money loans are easier to move from 1st position to a subordinate position at a later time if necessary.
4. Private money loans are easier to move to another piece of collateral if needed.

5. Private money loans can have much easier payment methods and terms.

Based on these benefits I will choose raising private capital or cash over doing a loan with a bank in most instances. For me there is not an issue of using my own or other people's money for deals.

Often people start my program who have no money, credit, work history or other resources. They tend to feel disadvantaged because of their economic situation. They think they can't do deals because they can't get loans. What I say to them is, "Even if your only option is for private money, which is very expensive, you should still look at deals and see if you can make profits and equity positions. If you can, then go for it!" Your finances will improve as you do deals and the money will get easier and cheaper. Plus, if you find a remarkable deal, the money will find you!

> "If you find a remarkable deal, the money will find you! If not, call me.
>
> **~Mike Watson**"

Does paying cash lower your return?

Paying cash can lower your return if it is not *your* cash. If you raise private capital at a 10% interest rate to pay "cash" for your deal and your bank would have charged you 7.5% you will have a lower return on your transaction by 2.5% per year of the investment.

However, if you pay cash on a property you should expect at *least* a 10-20% discount below what the seller would have taken as a regular financed sale. This will more than offset your extra expense in finance costs. In addition you may not have to pay as much in the way of closing costs when you get a loan from private resources rather than a bank. Bank loans usually carry some heavy costs to get the loan. You may pay 2 or 3 points right at closing.

Paying cash is a quick way for you to buy a property. However, owning a property free and clear is not a long-term strategy you should engage in at the early stages of investing. If you pay cash for a property, "Create and Enhance Equity" by changing its use and then refinance your cash investment back out. Then you will have a nice equity position left from the value you created.

Finally keep this in mind, the higher interest rate you pay for this cash deal will only last for 1-2 years at most. Once you refinance the cash back out you will then get to use your cash again on the next investment. How much is cash worth if you can use it over and over again by refinancing it out of a property?

Consider the following example:

Let's assume you have $1 million dollars with which to purchase property. This may have been attained from equity in a home or from an IRA (yours or other people's). Then you purchase a property for $800,000 which has an impressive "Higher and Better" use. You spend the other $200,000 in cash on your carrying costs and the "change of use" costs.

When the deal is finished the property is now worth $1,500,000! At this point you can go to your bank and say, "I would like a 70% first lien refinance on my property at its new and improved value." The bank can give you a loan for $1,050,000 (70% of $1,500,000). This $1,050,000 loan gives you your *$1,000,000 dollars back, puts $50,000 in your pocket and leaves you with $450,000 equity in your newly fixed up or changed property!*

Read that again! This is the power of CASH!

After you have gone full circle through a deal and refinanced you will have your capital back to do this *again*. Plus, you will also still have a cash flowing property with no mortgage insurance (lower payments) and a $450,000 improvement to your net worth!

This new equity you have in the property can also be used as collateral in other real estate deals or loans. You can do this process over and over again if you use cash. All in all, cash has some incredible benefits when you use it to buy real estate.

The *Unbelievable* 2nd Type of OPM

You have now made it to one of my absolute favorite parts of this whole program! The second type of OPM is "Other People's *Mortgages*" In other words it is seller financing. Seller financing is the *holy grail* of real estate investing. Let me say right now that if you really understand how to use seller financing your life will be changed. I can say this with complete confidence. It is that powerful.

Why do I say seller financing is the ultimate way to do deals? I say that because it has the financier sitting right in front of you from day one. Your *bank* is staring you in the eye.

I have investor students who started out paying cash for properties and getting loans from traditional lenders who will not even *do* a deal now unless there is some portion of seller financing. They just won't go back. Here is the best part, they don't have to and neither do you. I intend to teach you the ins and outs of seller financing so well that you will be able to use it on every deal.

I am so sure of seller financing as the ultimate real estate investing tool that I almost always buy with seller financing *and sell* with seller financing. This one technique is the most powerful tool you will ever have at your disposal with real estate investing. It will *explode* the number of deals you will be able to do and your profits.

I have a confession to make at this point. I have led you down the path of "The Foundation to Success" and have taught you the importance of finding the "Highest and Best" use for property. But here is the truth. All I have ever taught you and am ever going to teach you is how to *think differently*. If you can grasp seller financing the way I teach it, you *will* have learned how to think differently. When you learn how to think differently you will know how to make *any* deal work. You will be among the elite in the world of real estate investing. Your success will be certain.

Why does seller financing force you to think differently? Why is seller financing so incredibly powerful? For the same reason that a tree is so strong. A tree is not strong because of its roots or trunk. A tree is strong because it is *flexible*. Seller financing is the most flexible instrument you will find in any type of investing. With seller financing all of the rules are made up between just you and the seller. Imagine the possibilities.

> "My ***ultimate*** goal is to teach you how to ***think differently***.
>
> **~Mike Watson**"

Your options are unlimited.

The basic idea behind seller financing is that the seller will act as the bank in some manner. They will either finance the whole transaction or a portion of it for you. Here are just a few examples of how this can look. I challenge you to think of more as you read.

1. Free and Clear Seller Financing:

This is my favorite type of seller financing because it is the most flexible. Why? Because when the seller owns the property free and clear they are completely free to finance the *entire* purchase price.

Another reason is that it is the simplest form of seller financing. There are no other people who need to be involved. You can utilize *any terms* that both of you agree on.

Note: This financing is usually secured by a Trust Deed and Note. Most states have promulgated forms your real estate agent can use to write offers on these properties. A title company will usually draw up the Trust Deed and Note to be signed at closing.

2. <u>Equity only Seller Financing</u>

This kind of seller financing is almost as spectacular as the first. This is where the seller finances their *equity only*. In other words you get a first lien with a bank (Usually 70 or 80%) and the seller gives you a second lien on some *or the remainder* of the purchase price. This happens when the seller actually has some equity in the property.

For example, let's say you find a home on a lot and the sales price is $200,000. The owner has a loan of $100,000 on it. You can go to a bank and get an 80% loan ($160,000). Then the seller can give you a loan for the balance owed. (see chart below)

When it is all said and done you will be paying the bank a payment and the seller a payment but you may have been able to buy the property for *no money out of your pocket!* And the awesome thing is that usually the seller is thrilled because you paid off their loan and gave them some cash at closing. They are now getting the best of both worlds; cash at closing *and* payments over time.

Buyer's **$160,000** Loan from Bank		
$100,000 Seller's Original Loan ***(paid off by Buyer's $160,000 Loan from Bank)***	**$60,000** Cash at closing to Seller	**$40,000 Equity Seller Finance** Loan to Buyer
$200,000 Purchase Price		

3. "Subject to", "wrap" or "blanket" financing:

What these mean is that the seller has a loan right now on the property that the buyer will "wrap" (like a blanket) and assume without consent from the existing mortgage company.

This is not for the faint of heart. (Read more on this in the "Due on Sale Clause" and "Rules of Wrapping" sections.)

Note: The paperwork usually used to wrap existing financing is called an *All-Inclusive*-Trust Deed and Note. Check with your real estate agent, Title Company and even an attorney if you want to attempt this method.

4. Combo Seller Financing

In a nutshell this is a mix of the two above methods. In other words the underlying mortgage is "wrapped" *and* some equity is financed by the seller. This happens when there is a loan on the property but the owner has more equity above the loan and is willing to seller finance that equity. In this case the buyer would not have to get a new loan at all.

5. Purchase Options:

In the previous examples the sellers are acting as the bank *after* closing. In this scenario the seller is acting as the bank *before* closing. Yes, you read that right. Here is how it works. The seller gives you the right to buy the property within a certain amount of time. During that time you do some of the initial evaluation and changes. As a result you have NO carrying costs until you actually close on the property.

The beauty of this is that by the time you close you will most likely have a new buyer. "Purchase Options" may be *years* in length and in most cases they will require a *large deposit*. Keep in mind, if you need to make changes to the property that require you having your name on the title you will be somewhat limited with this option.

6. Extended Closing:

An extended closing is similar to the "Purchase Option" except it may not be as long and may not require as much of a deposit. Again the negative thing about this is your name is not on the title so you may not be able to do *some* of the changes.

That said, I tend to use the "Extended Closing" technique quite often. I like to minimize my carrying costs and this is an effective method to do that if you don't need your name on the title to start changes.

Here are some reasons why a closing could be extended:

1. You need time to get your financing.
2. The property requires physical improvements (finished or on paper) during the feasibility time.
3. Your due diligence on the property and the conditions take an extended amount of time. In some cases, such as with larger developments, this is routine.
4. The seller doesn't want to move out immediately.

Extended closings can lower your carrying costs significantly. Keep this technique in mind in your negotiations if it fits your deal. You might as well get as much done as possible when someone *else* is still paying for the property!

There is one more "Seller Financing Closing" technique I think is worth mentioning. I teach a method that is similar to the "Extended Close" and it is called the "Open-Ended Closing". An "Open-Ended Closing" gives you the same benefits of the "Extended Closing" but for an open-ended period of time.

The way you decide on a closing date is that you *tie it to a milestone*. For instance, you say, "Closing will be 7 days after the city approves a change of zoning." Or "Closing will be 21 days after final plats are approved." Or you could say, "Closing will be within 48 hours of all units being occupied."

You can tie a closing date to *anything*. I had one project that did not close for nearly a year because the closing was tied to something that ended up taking much longer than I originally thought. Had I been paying interest on a loan on that property it would have hurt the deal tremendously. Because of the "Open Ended Closing" it did not matter at all.

If you are doing a deal based on a change that is not *guaranteed*, always use an "Open ended Closing"

> "Extended closings and Open-Ended closings can save you thousands of dollars in carrying costs and literally save a deal.
>
> **~Mike Watson**"

7. Seller partnerships:

What is a "Seller Partnership", and why would I say a "Seller Partnership" is a form of seller financing? This is when the seller stays involved with the deal *during the change of use.*

When this happens the seller puts the property in the name of the buyer *without* charging the buyer for the property until the changes are complete and the property is re-sold. At that time the seller will get the money for their property *and* their portion of the profits.

Essentially the seller is bringing or offering the property as their contribution to the deal. This is a sensational option because you have *no carrying costs* on the property itself during purchase, changes and sale! Talk about saving a ton of money. That is what I call seller financing.

8. Seller Finance Boomerang

I named this technique the "Seller Finance Boomerang" because essentially any cash you put into the deal boomerangs right back to you. Let me explain.

In short, this is a form of seller financing where the seller finances the *changes* to the property. You pay cash, one way or another for the property. Right after the closing the seller *loans that cash back to you* and you pay them an interest rate return for that cash. You are basically raising capital from the *property itself.*

You then use that cash to do the changes to the property and pay the seller their money back with interest when you re-sell the property. They are happy because they got to make *income* during the time of the changes in the form of interest. Therefore they end up making more on the deal than they otherwise would have.

They can boomerang as much or as little as they wish back to you for changes. (Hey OPM is OPM.) You might as well use the cash you raised to *buy* the property *and* pay for the *changes!*

Still not sold on Seller Financing?

At this point you may have some questions like, "Why would a seller actually offer me seller financing?" or "Am I really better off getting seller financing?" Let me go over a few more items that may help you grasp the importance of this technique.

Seller financing is the *absolute* best form of financing available because there is *nothing* better for both the buyer AND the seller. The seller gets the benefit of making *more money* than they would have, by being the bank. The buyer gets the benefit of not having to worry about working with a bank. And finally *you* get to negotiate all of the terms to make everyone happy.

I have said before that the power of seller financing comes from the fact that it is flexible. It is flexible because all items of the deal are negotiable, not just the price and time for closing.

Here are *some* of the things you can negotiate when you use seller financing:

1. The amount of time until the first payment.
2. The amount of down payment.
3. If the loan can be assumed.
4. If the interest rate will change over time, up *or* down.
5. If part of the property can be released upon partial payoff. (needed for when you do condo-conversions, subdivisions or unit additions)
6. The length of time you will make payments.
7. The amount of interest paid and when it is paid.
8. The number of points, if any, that are paid.
9. How the loan is amortized. (how many years you pay it out)
10. If there is a prepayment penalty.
11. Payment amounts.
12. The timing of payments: quarterly, monthly, or yearly.
13. The amount of payoff. (you can tie the payoff to circumstances if necessary)
14. Whether or not the seller will subordinate the loan to another loan. (you need this in order to get a bank first lien)

You will think of many more when you begin to practice Seller Financing.

Note: It's a good time to go to Appendix 2 and write some notes about some terms you want to learn more about or attempt to use in a deal.

Here is another reason to love seller financing; it is the easiest way to buy property with *no money down!* This is what you do. Get a seller to finance a portion of the property. Find a bank that lends based on deals rather than people. (They are out there, usually they are the smaller local banks, talk to them *all* if you have to!) Prove to the bank that you will create equity in the property with your changes. Then have the bank finance the balance of your purchase price.

What does this mean? NO MONEY DOWN! In addition, when the seller finances some of the purchase price and you show equity growth, most banks will have lower qualifying standards for their part of the financing.

Those are the major reasons for using seller financing in your deals, but amazingly there are even more. Next I want to split out the benefits to the seller and to the buyer. I hope you are starting to think differently about how impressive seller financing is.

Here are some of the benefits for *the seller:*

1. The closing can happen very *fast*, pretty much all that is needed is a title policy.
2. Seller financing can provide cash at closing *plus* income over time.
3. Capital gains taxes can be spread over time since all proceeds won't be claimed in one year. They may not even have capital gains until the *end* of the whole loan if you pay them "interest only".
4. *All buyers qualify!* This creates more demand for their property and thus the seller can get a higher price.
5. If the property has to be reclaimed usually the values will have risen and they will have made money the whole time anyway via the payments they received.
6. It is easy to sell the property, even one that is otherwise difficult to sell for some reason or another.
7. They can make a *higher return* on their money when they loan it to the buyer than they could on other investments such as money markets or bank accounts.
8. They have *no property management* even though they have cash flow. In most cases the cash flow from the seller financing is *more*

than their net rents were previously.

> Seller financing is ***better for the seller*** than it is for the buyer!
>
> **~Mike Watson**

Here are some of the benefits for ***the buyer:***

1. *All* buyers qualify! There are no standard qualifications. The seller may ask for something to feel more comfortable but usually these things are minimal. If you are the seller ask for a credit report and check to make sure they do not have a solid history of bad credit.
2. It is *easy* to close. You don't have to get appraisals, surveys, inspections etc. In some cases you may still want to get these things but they are not required.
3. The buyer does not have to go through the typical red tape of a loan with a bank.
4. Closings can occur very *quickly*. The main thing you need that takes time is a title policy. On some properties you can get a title policy in a matter of two or three days.
5. There is *no mortgage insurance*. This can potentially save you thousands at closing and in the months to come.
6. Sometimes a seller will sell *because* you let them seller finance. They understand the benefits and would prefer to finance their equity and get more money than with other uses of that equity.
7. The closing *costs* are low. There are no lender's fees, points, etc.

8. It is possible to invest with *little or no* money down. You can negotiate any terms you like so why not go for little or no money for a down payment. Combine the types of seller financing above and you can accomplish this on almost every purchase.
9. You can *negotiate* terms with seller, unlike with a bank. You could end up paying zero interest or not making payments for several years.
10. You can re-sell the property easier if the loan is a simple assumption. If the seller agrees to allow the loan to be a simple assumption then in essence it is a non-qualifying loan for the next buyer. This can create *more value* in the property and an easier sale for you.
11. You can raise capital by doing the seller finance boomerang.

You should be starting to realize why seller financing can make or break a deal. No, actually at this point you should be starting to think, "The benefits of Seller Financing are ASTOUNDING! I have to do it!" If you are thinking this, you are right they are. Go for it!

> "Seller financing is the ultimate tool in Real Estate investing because it is the most ***flexible*** type of purchasing power that exists. Learn how to master it and nothing can stop you, ever.
>
> **~Mike Watson**"

No pay no stay!

After I instill the many virtues of Seller Financing to my students invariably one of them will stand up and say, "I think seller financing sounds awesome. I think it sounds so fantastic for the seller that when I sell *my* properties I want to seller finance them to a buyer. My only concern is what if they don't pay *me*?"

This is a valid concern. That is why I suggest you do not *ever* finance any of your *debt*. Only finance your equity. Your risk goes *way* down when you only seller finance your *equity*. Let me show you how this might work.

Let's say you own a property that is worth $500,000 and you owe $300,000 on it. When you sell it the new buyer gets an 80% first mortgage on the $500,000 sales price which is $400,000. The $400,000 proceeds from the loan *pay off* your $300,000 original indebtedness and put what is left of the $100,000 after closing costs in your pocket as cash. You walk away from the closing with no more debt plus cash in your hand.

In addition you extend a $100,000 loan (the seller financing portion) to the buyer as a second lien to their first lien. Notice that this note consists only of your *equity*. If the buyer stops paying, you lose your cash flow but you will still have your trust deed position and an asset on which you can foreclose.

Some investors actually look at a second mortgage that *isn't* being paid as an opportunity for *profit*. They hope the buyer won't pay so they can foreclose on them. The first thing they do is contact the mortgage company who has the first lien to try to buy *that* mortgage at a *large* discount from its face value. If they succeed they take the property back through foreclosure and *sell it again* to someone else for a *second profit.*

It is a lot of work to go through this process, but it can be far more profitable than if they had sold the unit for cash in the first place. This is because they most likely got a higher price for *offering* the seller financing. I don't suggest you hope your buyer doesn't pay; I just want you to understand it can be a profitable situation if it does happen.

If you had owed $500,000 on this property and seller financed the entire $500,000 then you would be in a whole different situation. If the buyer quits paying, *you* would still owe the payment for the underlying loan, and you would not have had your first mortgage paid off. In addition you would not have taken any cash from the sale to use somewhere else. This would truly be a risky endeavor!

> "When you are the ***seller*** only offer seller financing on your ***Equity***.
>
> **~Mike Watson**"

How to Get the *Seller* to "See the Light"

At this point you are probably chomping at the bit to do some seller financing. But your excitement is only one side of the equation. How do you get the seller to feel the same way? How do you get them excited about offering seller financing to you?

Honestly, the answer to this question is; first *understand* and then *explain* the benefits to them. Most people do not understand why seller financing is so incredible. When *you* understand why it is such an incredible tool and then present your "4-offer spreadsheet" (coming soon) it will usually become clear to them why seller financing is a phenomenal opportunity.

All that said you may run into some resistance. Over the years I've noticed a few themes that sellers have who are leery of seller financing. Here are some of the objections you will run into and some effective ways to handle those objections.

Reason why they won't seller finance	Your Solution
1. Seller doesn't understand why they should finance.	Educate seller using previous list of benefits
2. The seller doesn't trust you.	You can offer to give them other properties as collateral, have co-signers, pay a higher interest rate, pre-pay some payments, etc. Find out what will make them feel comfortable and if it is reasonable, give it to them.
3. The seller is worried about receiving their payments.	You can offer the first few months of payments as earnest money or offer to pay them at closing.
4. They want you to prove you qualify for the payments.	See #2
5. They worry you won't take care of the property	Talk to them about how you will create or enhance equity and that it will *increase* the value of the property.

6. They worry about you making little or no down payment.	Put a down payment in a trust account to prove you have cash.
7. They are worried about their capital gains.	Let them know they won't have to pay until they realize the returns (check with CPA).
8. They need a down payment for their next home.	Let them stay in the property during the call time. They can rent from you. Usually you only need the money for 6-12 months.
9. Seller thinks they won't qualify for another home.	Same as #8.
10. Worried about the "Due on Sale Clause"	Don't cancel their insurance, pay taxes, and make sure the the payment is made (see "Due on Sale" section).
11. Loss of tax advantages	Increased income and no property management off-sets the tax advantages.

Four Solutions for Seller Financing Objections

Here are the four main things you can talk about when a seller is concerned about doing seller financing. In almost *all* cases one or more of the following four solutions will solve whatever their concerns may be. Study them and have them in your arsenal for negotiating.

- Occupancy: Have them stay in the property until you pay them off. That way the seller will not have to get a new loan for another property until this one is paid off. In addition they can make sure the property is cared for since *they* will be the one living there.

- Term of call or balloon: Don't do *long-term* seller financing. If you keep the balloon time frame under a year you will help the seller feel more comfortable. Most seller financed properties can easily be sold or refinanced within 180 days of closing as long as there are significant alterations that "Create and Enhance Equity."

- Collateralization of other real property: This is you saying, "If I don't make my payments, not only can you take the property you sold to me back, but you will be able to take *another* property too!" This gives the seller recourse that can be extremely painful to you. You should of course, *always* pay your payment.

- Additional Co-signers: What is a seller going to say if you tell them, "I'll have 14 people sign on your loan and share the responsibility for repayment"? There is implied strength in numbers. They will most likely be thrilled that they can go after 14 people if payments aren't made. One benefit for you and your co-signers is that a seller financed mortgage does *not* appear on the co-signers' credit reports.

If after you have explained all of the benefits and attempted to ease the sellers mind in regards to seller financing and you are still unable to get them to offer seller financing then the last option is to attempt to get an *extended closing*. This in itself is a form of seller financing, as previously explained.

When will an extended closing work?

The absolute best time to utilize an "Extended Closing" is when any changes can be done *prior* to actual ownership. For instance, can a portion of the process go through the city without your name being on the title? Sometimes this can still be done with the current owner's permission. Check with your city to find out.

Imagine doing repairs and or updates to a property *before* you own it. Why would you want to? Wouldn't this be a risk? The first answer is, "You would want to do this in order to avoid carrying costs." The other answer is, "Yes, there is some risk." Here is how to lower that risk.

1. Record your sales contract at your county courthouse so the seller cannot back out of the contract without repercussions.
2. Put wording in your contract that if the seller does not close, they owe you for all monies spent on the property.
3. If you are going to do interior work make sure there are not tenants in the property.

There are many reasons why you would want to extend your closing period. Some of those reasons are when: you need to get permits to build or demolish, you need time to get capital from investors, there are repairs you could do prior to closing, there are zoning change steps you could take, or architectural work you could start. Finally an opportune time to do an extended closing is when the seller wants to stay in the property while they build another home. If your transaction has any of these elements, then an extended closing could be *very* valuable.

FREE Online Resources

I have a FREE audio clip of a role play demonstrating how to talk with a seller about seller financing.

Go to **mikewatsoninvesting.com/bookextras**, and click on "Seller Finance Role Play Audio" to get a sampling of how to explain seller financing in a way that will show the seller the incredible benefits they will receive from seller financing.

Some Examples of When to Use Seller Financing

I recommend you use seller financing on *every deal you do*. Here are a few scenarios that will start to expand your mind and spark some new ideas:

Here are some specific opportunities where seller financing is especially beneficial:

1. If you have a distressed property you are having trouble selling, it will sell faster if you advertise with seller financing available. This is especially the case if you offer 100% seller financing with low or no down payment.

2. You can help Pre-Foreclosures and Notice of Defaults because they can now sell quickly.

3. If a seller is behind on payments seller financing could give them a way to get a buyer to make their loan good so they avoid foreclosure.

4. It is appropriate to use seller financing when the seller wants to be an investor. They will be excited to feel like they are part of a big deal by offering financing. They will also get good returns (like every investor should).

5. When a seller faces a heavy capital gains burden by selling the property, they can defer the tax to later years and/or spread it out over time.

6. If a seller wants long-term income (this is the ultimate reason for you to offer seller financing when you sell *your* properties).

7. If you find a property that is being managed poorly or has high vacancies, typically that owner will be very open to seller financing. They like passive income and obviously don't like management.

Can a seller *really* finance 100% if they have a loan on the property?

Yes, there are ways to get 100% financing from the seller even when they have a loan on the property. I mentioned something called a "wrap" earlier in the "Types of Seller Financing" section. Wrapping is an informal way for someone to "assume" a mortgage without permission. There are some pretty big benefits for a buyer to do this. The best benefit is they don't have to qualify to assume the loan *or* qualify for a new loan. Another is that they do not have all new loan fees.

If you want to try this technique first talk with a title company and see if they will help you through the process. If they will and you want to attempt this method here are some tips for you to follow.

First and foremost, check with your state to see if there are any rules or laws *against* "wrapping" a loan. If there aren't then you can move forward. Make sure the terms of your new loan (the "wrap" or "blanket loan") match the terms of the seller's current loan fairly closely.

For instance you do not want to do a loan with the seller that will pay off in 10 years when *their* loan doesn't pay off for 14 years. The seller will be stuck with a loan and no payments coming in and *no property*. This is one of the reasons why it is important to do *short-term* seller financing especially when you wrap a loan. When you do, completely avoid this issue.

The following are what I call "The Rules of Wrapping". Follow them *every time* if you decide to wrap a loan.

1. If you are worried about wrapping loans DON'T!

2. Never wrap government financing such as FHA and VA loans, under any circumstances. Unlike some other loans, government financing has potential penalties to the *buyer* for wrapping mortgages.

3. Make sure the payment is made on time to the seller and to the mortgage company. This is best achieved by having a third party accept the buyer's payments, make the mortgage payment and send everyone a receipt.

4. Get a *new* insurance policy on the property and do not cancel the old one. Make sure you account for this when you do your deal evaluation. The cost will be insignificant compared to the benefit of this type of financing. By doing this you will make sure the seller's lender and the seller are all covered if something happens. Use YOUR insurance if something happens with the property.

5. Make sure the taxes are always paid up to date. If the current loan has an escrow account then you should include those amounts on your loan with the seller. That way you are paying the taxes to the

seller, he pays them to his lender and the lender pays them to the taxing authority.

6. If you do wrap a loan, only do so on short-term properties, (six months or less). This is accomplished in the "Foundation to Success" by purchasing the property, putting it immediately back up for sale, creating and enhancing equity in the property by achieving a "Higher and Better" use. Once this happens the property will either sell for a profit or it will be refinanced for an equity position. Either way, the "wrapped" mortgage will be paid off in a short period of time.

The Most Common Question of All

During the "Wrapping" section of my camps it is almost a guarantee that someone will go up to the microphone and say, "What about the 'Due on Sale Clause'?" Most loans have a "Due on Sale Clause" though not all do.

The "Due on Sale Clause" is known in my Camps as the "*Don't* on Sale Clause." I call it that because I don't recommend that you do "wraps". There are so many options to purchase property using your own funds, other people's funds and other forms of seller financing that I consider "wraps" a last resort. That said, I'll do my best to explain how the "Due on Sale Clause" works.

This well-known clause is something lenders put into a mortgage note that says something along the lines of, "If the buyer ever sells the mortgaged property then they agree to *pay off* the mortgage at the time of the sale."

The mortgage companies put this in to protect themselves from people wrapping their mortgage without their permission. The clause basically states that the lender has the right to call the mortgage due and payable if they find out the property has been sold and the mortgage has not been paid off in full. The lender can then demand the mortgage be paid off in full and if it isn't, they have the right to begin foreclosure proceedings on the property.

The funny thing is that despite a lender's ability to call mortgages due and payable, people still continue to "wrap" mortgages.

It is a personal decision whether or not to participate in this kind of financing, however no one should do it if they are not willing to accept the associated risks. If people still choose to use this tactic, they should do so with their eyes wide open to the potential pitfalls associated. The pitfalls are that you may have a lender that calls your note due immediately. Or, in some cases you may have broken laws. Stated bluntly, "*Don't* wrap mortgages if you are not prepared for the consequences." I'll discuss several ways you can be prepared in later sections.

The fact remains there are strong emotions that go both directions on this subject. If you decide this is a way you would like to purchase property I recommend the following:

1. Follow the rules of wrapping in the previous section!

2. Get a "Due on Sale Clause" from a lender and review it thoroughly to understand exactly what a lender's perspective and language is in the clause.

3. Call a mortgage company and ask them about the practice and their perspective on the program.

4. Plan a good exit strategy if you wrap a mortgage and that loan gets called due and payable. Three of my favorites are:
   a. Have a refinance package ready at all times with your lender. If the mortgage is called due and payable, you can refinance very quickly and the "wrapped" mortgage can be paid off before a foreclosure takes place.
   b. Make sure that you have enough profit in your deal to allow

for a handsome discount if you need to sell the property quickly. Cutting the price will help enact a quick sale that will pay off the mortgage.

c Have an emergency "Go To" private lender in place at all times. This will allow you to pay off the called mortgage very quickly with private funds. You'll be able to do this quickly if you get in a pinch.

5. Only wrap mortgages on properties that have a "Higher and Better" use. This will allow you to have the ability to quickly sell for a profit or refinance for an equity position.

6. "Create and Enhance Equity" as fast as possible after purchase. The sooner you can sell or refinance, the less chance there is of a lender calling a note.

7. You might consider waiting to record the sale until you are ready to re-sell or refinance. Check to see if this is an option in your state or if you are required to record the change of title immediately.

8. Carry a large slush fund to be able to pay off any mortgage that is called due. Some of the investors I know would respond to a due and payable notice with the comment, "Send me wiring instructions and you'll have your mortgage paid off by this time tomorrow."

Some time ago I was teaching this topic to a group of people and one of my students raised his hand and proclaimed, "I don't feel good about wrapping mortgages and I just couldn't do it." I said, "If you feel that way definitely *don't* wrap mortgages. There are risks involved and the technique isn't for everyone."

Several weeks later he came to class and said, "I found a property and wrapped the mortgage and I'm *sick* about it. I feel so bad about it that I can't sleep at night." I asked him why he did it. He said, "I thought it was a good deal." I told him to make sure to make the payments and sell it for a profit or refinance it for an equity position as soon as he possibly could.

The next week he called me and said, "I was so nervous about wrapping the mortgage that I called the mortgage company and told them what I did." After I recovered from my shock I asked him what happened. He said, "They said I shouldn't have wrapped the loan and that I will be hearing from them." By this time he was pretty upset.

Just over a week later he received a letter stating that they *could* call the mortgage due and payable at any time. Imagine getting this kind of letter especially when to begin with you were nervous about the transaction.

However, here is where the story is now. Over 24 months have passed since he wrapped the mortgage and it has not been called due. This result is *not* guaranteed, but it illustrates that mortgage companies are in business to make a profit. They do this through the lending of money and the receipt of timely payments, not by calling in their loans.

It is virtually impossible to cover all of the information on seller financing options in this book. I am working on a book where the only topic is "Seller Financing" but until it is available you can check out my three-day Degree Camp on "Advanced Seller Financing Techniques".

Other Resources

You can find more detailed information about the Camp at my web site **mikewatsoninvesting.com.** Go to the "Training" section and then click on the "Advanced Seller Financing" Degree Camp. For those of you who can't wait for my next camp or book, I also have one of my live Seller Financing Degree camps available on CD!

How to Develop and Present Your Offer

Now that you understand the two "OPM's", raising capital and seller financing, let's move forward to how you should present your offer.

When you make an offer to buy another person's property it should be in earnest. Many people write contracts and then look for reasons to *get out* of the deal. Why would they waste their own time and the time of the seller? I teach investors to take a different approach. I teach them to work diligently to find reasons to *stay* with their contract and purchase the property. This is how *incredible* investors succeed. Let me show you how this works.

Here is how to best present your offer:

1. If there is an agent involved with the seller take a little time to talk with them. I suggest you even meet with them and the seller. This is when you want to find out what the sellers most pressing needs are.

2. Write your contract as conservatively as possible. In other words give yourself leeway on everything; price, terms, time frames, repairs etc. At the same time make sure you address and cover the seller's needs. You can accomplish both of these at the same time using the 20 additional negotiating terms (see list in next section).

3. Write contracts that give you plenty of ways to cancel and receive your earnest money back.

4. Don't make your offer too one-sided or you may have a hard time getting the contract accepted. Instead, write lots of ways to get out of the contract, but all of them should have solid time lines with which the seller can identify.

5. Make sure you have ample time to do your feasibility studies. This is your inspections, environmental reports, soil reports, etc (in other words your due diligence).

6. If for some reason you need more time or information ask for it prior to the end of the feasibility time frame or get out of the contract. Do not have your earnest money go "hard" (seller keeps it for sure) without knowing this is a fantastic deal!

7. Work as hard as you can to get through your due diligence and still end up with an exceptional deal.

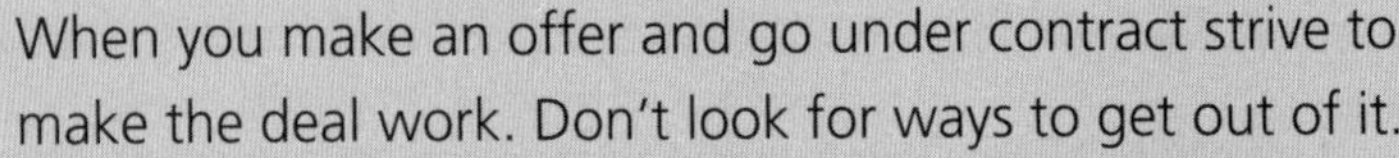

> "When you make an offer and go under contract strive to make the deal work. Don't look for ways to get out of it.
>
> **~Mike Watson**"

20 Negotiable Terms *Other* Than Price

When you are getting ready to write an offer, give the seller what they want and then build the rest of your terms to make the deal attractive for *you*. Typically the seller's main concern is the price. Remember there are ways to make a full price offer work if the seller is willing to do seller financing.

Here are some ideas of terms to ask for:

Will the seller...

1. Take a lower interest rate on their seller financing?

2. Give you an adjustable rate on their seller financing? (up or down whichever suits your deal best)
3. Allow you to make interest only payments?
4. Allow you to have no interest and make principal payments only?
5. Allow you to make quarterly or yearly payments rather than monthly?
6. Let you make no payments until the call period?
7. Let you amortize the loan over a long period? (like 50 years)
8. Let you have your down payment back to use on the change or other deals? (follow your "raising capital" rules)
9. Put on a pre-payment penalty? (this means you don't have to pay it off until the end of the pre-payment time)
10. Release the "Due on Sale Clause?"
11. Allow their financing to be assumed by a qualified person?
12. Allow their financing to be assumed by someone without qualifying?
13. Allow their financing to be assumed if they get a higher rate or points?
14. Allow the loan to be split up, (splintered) and assumed? (necessary in the case of a conversion or addition of units that are to be sold separately)
15. Sign a subordination agreement allowing a different person or entity to be the first lien? (necessary if you are getting a bank first lien)
16. Extend the closing date?
17. Allow you to do changes prior to closing?
18. Allow for a small or no down payment?
19. Pay for some of the cost to change?
20. Pay for closing costs?

Use these terms and others you learn or create to make any deal work for both the buyer and seller.

What are "Vital Clauses"?

When you are ready to make your offer, make sure to get help and supervision from an expert. I also strongly recommend you study and even *memorize* your contracts so you are completely familiar with them. Your ultimate success in real estate is proportional to your ability to write and understand real estate contracts.

Before we go any further with clauses and language, I want to make it clear that the examples you find in this book should be reviewed by your attorney and real estate broker (if applicable) before you use them. Always make sure they work in your state. Real estate laws are *not* universal.

Simply stated "Vital Clauses" are clauses you should include in almost every offer. The only time you would not include them is if you intentionally leave them out. You might do that to make your offer stronger because you are getting a *really* low sales price. If there are no extenuating circumstances with your negotiations use the majority of the "Vital Clauses".

(The first five "Vital Clauses" start with the phrase, "Buyer's offer and earnest money are subject to..." The others do not.)

1. All financing being approved by the buyer.
2. Financial partner's approval of the contract / property / financing.
3. Buyer's approval of all due diligence (please find a more extensive list of due diligence below) and seller's disclosure on the property.
4. City or County's approval of zoning change/site plan/engineering/use change/building inspection/special use permit/overlay/building permit/occupancy permit/use certificate/condominium conversion etc. (where applicable)
5. Buyer's approval of the appraisal.
6. Buyer is in the business to profit and offered to partner

with the seller. Seller refused in order to receive their funds sooner. ALWAYS put this one in when you use the "4-Offer Spreadsheet" (will be discussed shortly).

7. If you are a real estate agent and you are the buyer or seller, always disclose that you are a licensed real estate agent representing yourself only.
8. Acceptance of any one offer makes all other offers made by buyer null and void. This is necessary when you use your "4-Offer Spreadsheet" to make offers.

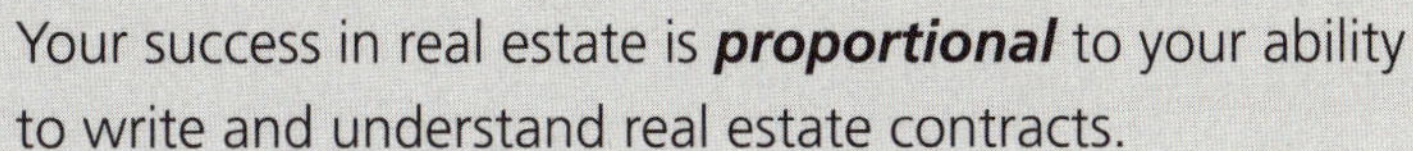

> "Your success in real estate is ***proportional*** to your ability to write and understand real estate contracts.
>
> **~Mike Watson**"

The Ultimate Tool to Uncover a Seller's Needs

It's time to make an offer! Or should I say, it's time to make *four* offers. This doesn't mean make four offers on four properties. I'm saying you are going to make four offers on *one* property.

Why would you make four offers on one property? The reason is to determine the seller's needs. It is very important to determine these prior to going under contract. Once you have established the seller's needs you will know *exactly* how to negotiate.

For instance, if the seller wants to have their money very *fast* you can negotiate more on price and terms. If all they care about is getting *full* price then you can negotiate on when you close or whether or not seller financing is an option.

How exactly does making four offers tell you what the seller needs? When you make multiple offers the seller can decide which terms will or will not work for them. If you make sure *all* of the offers work for *you* then you will be able to create a win/win situation at the end of your negotiations.

The easiest way to make four offers at once is to create a spreadsheet of the four offers on one page. I will show you one that I've taught my students to use. You can modify it to fit each of your transactions.

Here is a synopsis of the spreadsheet:

Offer #1 is an all cash offer. This will be your lowest offer. I will explain how to arrive at this price in a later section. Cash carries with it a cost. You cannot afford to pay cash unless you are somehow compensated for that cost through the price.

Offer #2 is a small amount of seller financing (usually 20-40%) with the balance being cash or a loan. Put this option in so the seller can decide if they want to make a little more money on the property over time. This offer can be a little higher purchase price. The sum of the payments you will make to the seller are outlined. This shows the seller how beneficial seller financing can be for them compared to cash.

Make sure the seller understands that if you do end up holding the property long-term then you will refinance their loan and pay them off. Typically you will ask for 1 to 2 years of seller financing and offer a balloon payment. Whether you sell it or refinance it, they get their full amount at that time.

The only time you would do long-term financing with the seller is if they are adamant about getting long-term income. In that case make sure you get a good interest rate to cover your loan in case you end up keeping the project long-term.

Offer #3 is a large amount of seller financing. (Usually 75-100%) Give them your highest price on this offer because it is the easiest type of purchase for you. There are no loan costs, no lender points, no appraisal, loan paperwork, red tape, qualifying, etc.

The interest rates stated are just suggestions. I would play around with them and see what works for you on a deal-by-deal basis. The monthly payments are also just a suggestion. Some investors offer to pay quarterly or yearly or even less frequently. In addition you may wish to pay principal and interest (instead of principal only as shown). This option will trigger the seller's capital gains tax though, so why make your payment higher?

Offer #4 is the offer to partner with the seller. You make this offer to see if you can do the deal without having to buy the property up front *or* pay for the changes out of your pocket. Yes, you read that right. If the seller chooses to partner with you then you will ask them to put the property in your name while you execute the "Change of Use". If they want to get a maximum return then you also ask them to pay for all of the changes. When you sell or refinance you will pay them the full price for their property, return the money they paid for the changes, and give them a portion of the profits.

The other reason to always offer to partner with the seller is to help protect you later. Always mention in your final agreed upon contract that you offered to partner with the seller and they refused in order to get their money sooner (remember this from "Vital Clauses"). That way when you sell the property again in the future they cannot come back to you and say you should have paid them more money for their property. This doesn't typically happen when you are up front with the seller all along, but it is nice to be covered just in case.

On the next page is the example of the Spreadsheet: The first column shows an item of the contract, the second shows the terms of the first offer, and the third shows the terms of the second offer. (The 3rd and 4th offers are on the next page.)

Numbers tell a story. Spend some time studying the numbers so you can understand the reasoning and intent of each offer. Take special notice that we show the seller how much *extra* they will make if they seller finance!

Sample "4-Offer Spreadsheet" Offers 1&2

Contract Element	#1 Cash Purchase	#2 30% Owner Seller Finance	
Total Price	$220,000	$235,000	
Cash Down Payment	$220,000	$164,500	
Financing	n/a	$70,500	Seller 2nd lien
Seller Finance Income	n/a	**7%** interest only payments Full payoff within 12 months Monthly Interest =	$411.25
		Total Interest =	$4,935
Cash to Seller at Closing	$220,000		$164,500
Gross Profit to seller	**$220,000**	**(Price+Interest)**	**$239,935**
Timing of Profits to Seller	At closing	Within 12 months	
Earnest Money	$3,000	$3,000	
Closing Date	7 days after permits approved	7 days after permits approved	
Response Deadline	Before 01/01/09	Before 01/01/09	
Feasibility Period	45 days	45 days	
"Vital Clauses"	Rejected partnership Buyer's partner to approve … Contingent on Permits	Rejected partnership Buyer's partner to approve … Contingent on Permits	

Sample "4-Offer Spreadsheet" Offers 3&4

Contract Element	**#3 90% Owner Seller Finance**	**#4 Seller Partnership**
Total Price	$250,000	*$250,000 +% of profits
Cash Down Payment	$25,000	n/a
Financing	seller 1st lien $225,000	n/a
Seller Finance Income	**8%** interest only payments Full payoff within 12 months Monthly Interest = $1,500	n/a
	Total Interest = $18,000	n/a
Cash to Seller at Closing	$25,000	n/a
Gross Profit to seller	**(Price + Interest) $268,000**	**Unknown**
Timing of Profits to Seller	Within 12 months	Within 24 months
Earnest Money	$3,000	$0
Closing Date	7 days after permits approved	n/a
Response Deadline	Before 01/01/09	Before 01/01/09
Feasibility Period	45 days	30 days
"Vital Clauses"	Rejected partnership Buyer's partner to approve … Contingent on Permits	* Paid to seller when re-sold or refinanced. Will also be paid back all "cost to change" plus a 40% split of profits.

FREE Online Resources

I have decided to offer this form for FREE in a spreadsheet format you can modify to fit your own needs.
Go to **mikewatsoninvesting.com/bookextras**, and click on "4-Offer Spreadsheet". Here you will find this blank spreadsheet. Save it to your computer and plug in your numbers on your offers, then go buy some properties!

How to Determine Your Offering Prices

How do you know what price to offer? Here is the beauty of this system. If you have completed your short-term and long-term deal evaluations, you have already determined the highest price (#3 offer) you are willing to pay.

From the short-term and long-term deal eval forms which one has the *lowest purchase price* to give you your required returns? That lower number is the *highest price* you will want to pay for the property. Take that price and make it your Offer #3 on your spreadsheet. Offer #3 is the one with the *most* seller financing, therefore it is the one where you can pay the highest price (because ideally your costs are the lowest).

The lowest price you will offer is the cash price (offer #1). That is because *cash is costly*. You will either have to pay loan fees and interest to a bank, or to an investor who helps you buy the property. Only offer a cash price that makes up for these expenses you will incur.

One way to determine the cash price you offer is to take the highest price and reduce it by at least 10%. Quite often you will have to pay much more than 10% for money. If you have to pay more than 10% for private capital adjust your cash offer accordingly.

If you are using your own cash and there is no interest to yourself, I recommend you still price your own money at private market rates. That way you can profit on your deal *and* make money on your money. Remember smart investors put their money to work for them!

> "Make sure your cash offer is low enough to cover the ***cost*** of your cash.
>
> **~Mike Watson**"

Offer #2 which has the smaller amount of seller financing will be somewhere between #1 and #3. This price should be based on *how much* seller financing the seller is willing to carry for you.

Offer # 4 where you are asking them to partner with you, should be the same as the highest price offer for their property. This is because they are essentially putting the property into the deal *free* of carrying costs.

The reason for making all of the offers is to find out the needs of the seller. By making four different offers with different terms it opens up a conversation with them about their needs. You can then adopt the offer to meet those needs and add terms in your favor to make the deal work for you. A "4-offer spreadsheet" is a fantastic tool to find and meet the needs of both parties.

What to Do Once You Are Under Contract

At this point you have learned how to find a property with a "Higher and Better" use and how to negotiate a win/win with the seller. So let's assume you have gone out and done these things and are now under contract. What's next? You are now officially in your "feasibility" or "due diligence" time frame. It's time to roll up your sleeves and do the hard work needed to determine if you are actually going to buy the property in a month or two. The clock is ticking for when your earnest money will become non-refundable. Get to work as *quickly* as possible.

Here are some of the items you will need to do during this time frame. (Please understand the list will be extremely different based on what *type* of property you are considering. I suggest you seek expert advice to determine exactly what information you need to gather and what inspections or reports you must have.) Your due diligence should include proper inspections, tests, appraisals, surveys etc. needed for your area and property type. In addition if your project will need to go through the city or county for any type of approval it would be prudent to make a trip there and get their opinion on your plans NOW!

Don't be a buyer that buys something with a huge problem when you could have discovered it during your due diligence. In addition don't be a buyer who complains about costs associated with this part of the deal. I have heard investors say "Why don't I just save the due diligence costs and use those funds to remedy any problems I find out about later?" This is an extremely *risky* way of thinking. People unwilling to do correct due diligence should not be investing. They are just one mistake away from financial ruin.

> "Start your due diligence ***immediately*** and do correct and ***thorough*** due diligence or do ***not*** invest.
>
> **~Mike Watson**"

Here is a short list of items you may need to do during your due diligence. Some of them will apply to your project, others will not. Some items may be missing from this list entirely for your *area* or *type* of deal. (This is where a local real estate agent comes in very handy.)

1. A building inspection
2. A mold inspection
3. Asbestos testing
4. Testing for radon and other gases
5. Check for sink holes
6. Inspect for faulty plumbing and leaks
7. Address any foundation problems
8. Termite inspection
9. Verify the property is up to current building code for the area
10. Soils tests and reports
11. Review of title policy for problems
12. Review deed restrictions to see if you can do your project
13. Review of HOA conditions and costs if applicable
14. Analyze utility costs (both current and proposed)
15. Verify property tax costs
16. Ingress/egress issues for a project
17. Lead based paint inspection
18. Environment studies
19. Hazardous materials report (Phase One Environmental)
20. Property located on wetlands
21. Endangered plants or animals on property
22. Applicable zoning and use permits
23. If all past work was done with a building permit
24. Study any financial documents affecting the ownership like rental contracts, leases, easements or encumbrances

It may seem repetitive but I highly suggest you have a real estate agent handle your contracts and offers. Real estate agents help orchestrate all of the necessary items to be completed during feasibility (due diligence) and up until closing. They also will help you decide how and if you need to *renegotiate* at any point.

The vast majority of the time you *will* renegotiate between when you first go under contract and when you close. Every property has a history and problems to go with it. Don't *back out* when you find problems, negotiate! The seller is going to have to deal with the problem with *any* buyer. Why not with you?

After the feasibility phase your agent will help you with the rest of the contractual items that need to be completed. Some of these items are; loans, survey, appraisal, title commitment, repairs, renegotiating, amendments, addendums, inspections, setting appointments with tenants for all of this and much more. In addition they will go over the closing statement with you to make sure all the numbers match the contract and will coordinate and even go with you to the closing.

> "When you find problems don't back out, ***renegotiate*** to make the deal work.
>
> **~Mike Watson**"

STEP 6

EXPOSE THE VISION!

STEP 6

EXPOSE THE VISION!

Now that you own it, what's next?

Now that you have found and purchased your first deal what do you do next? According to Step #6 of "The Foundation to Success" the very next thing you do is "*Expose* the Vision!" (Immediately put the property back up for sale). You might be wondering why I suggest you put it up for sale immediately. The reason is this; if you know it has a "Higher and Better" use, you want to let the world know about it as fast as you can. It is time to "Expose the Vision!"

Remember when I talked about the value of the property going up at the exact moment you *realize* there is a "Higher and Better" use? Here is your chance to quickly capitalize on that increase in value.

In order to *realize* the value of what the property *can be* you must put it up for sale. The trick is not to just put it up for sale and sit back and do the "Three P's." (Put a sign in the yard, Put it in MLS, and Pray)

Instead you are going to do two things almost simultaneously. You will put it for sale to *actively promote the "vision"* and you are going to *enact the changes* as fast as you can. Actually if you are really smart you have already started the change process before you even own it.

But I am getting ahead of myself. The very first things you will do are put the property on the market and create a marketing plan. The crux of this plan is to promote the property for what it will *become.* You are going to announce to the world that *they* can either come do the project or *you* will.

Some people say, "I'm going to do *all* of the changes and then sell it. That way I will make *more* money." The truth is they have no idea if that is true. They might go through all of the changes, hit lots of bumps along the way and do a ton of work. And even then they may not make a larger profit than if they sell quickly. The smart thing to do is to put it on the market with a nice profit built in. If it sells great, if not you will do the whole project.

Let's learn *how* to "Sell the Vision" and *who* you should sell it to. The best buyer out there is the "Next User". This concept alone has the ability to make you millions!

First you have to understand what I mean by the "Vision". The vision is what you have uncovered as the *"Higher and Better" use* of the property. For instance, on our "Awesome 15-unit Condo Deal" the vision was a fully functioning 15-unit condo complex. Here is the key; most people do not have the tools that *you* now have to know that a property could be anything *more* than it is *right now*. So once you have found that higher use you want to tell everyone about it.

The best way to expose or sell the vision is by getting drawings made, and by having floor plans put together. This way you can literally show people what the "Higher and Better" use is. By having renderings created and getting those out to people along with detailed information on what the property can become, you will make it *easy* for them see your vision.

Who is going to buy your property?

The most important person who needs to receive this information is the "Next User". What I mean by the "Next User" is the next person who will *do something* to the property. For instance it could be anyone from an architect, an engineer, a surveyor, or an inspector, to a contractor or a painter. Why does it matter that these are the people you focus on? It matters to them because they have the benefit of our

7th step of the deal evaluation. They have a *professional application* which makes the deal juicier for them than anyone else!

P.S. That last paragraph is so important to your success with selling your property I would like you to read it again.

Here is a real life example of how this works:

One day very early in my investing career, while overseeing work that was being done to a fixer-upper home, I learned a great lesson (Those "good" old days of lots of work for not much profit were an excellent time for learning).

At that time I did put the property on the market *before* the work was done. But my justification was I wanted to lower carrying costs by having a buyer ready to close right when the work was finished. At that point I didn't realize the power of "who" to market to. I put the property up for sale based on the "fixed-up" price, because I knew I was going to do the work. Or at least I *thought* I was…

While I was at the property checking on the painter's work, an agent showed up with a buyer. Later the agent called me and said, "The buyer is very interested in buying the house. Would you consider selling it for a discount with *no more work* done to the property? The client does sheet rock work and can finish the work himself." I was a little nervous about the idea, but I said, "Make an offer and I will consider it if the offer is good enough."

I was *shocked* to find that the offer on the property was high enough to net me over *half* of my fixer-upper *profit* without having done much work at all! The buyer was willing to pay more for the property because he didn't know how to find another one like it and he could do the majority of the work himself. By doing the work himself he would end up with a nice equity position at the time he *bought* it. Talk about win/win!

I turned this event into a major marketing strategy. (More on this in the "Flixer" section) The point is that the "sheet rocker" made more money (or ended up with more equity) on the property than the average buyer.

I used this same technique with our original "Awesome 15-unit Condo Deal" deal. I didn't buy the distressed old house on a .63 acre lot and put it back up for sale as a distressed old house on a large lot. I listed it as a 15-unit condominium project *in progress* and proceeded to sell the vision to builders of condo-complexes! ("Next Users")

> "The "Next Users" are the best buyers for your project because they have a ***professional application*** that makes the deal worth more to them than anyone else!
>
> **~Mike Watson**"

Exactly How to Market to the "Next User"

The "Next User" is the next person in line to do work on your project. For example, if you are doing a carpet and paint rehabilitation, you should contact all of the subcontractors who will be working on the project and see if any of them wants to purchase the property at a greatly reduced price from the future value. Then they can do the work themselves for a profit. (This still leaves a handsome profit for you!)

If you are tearing a house out like our "Awesome 15-unit Condo Deal" and putting in a condominium project, the "Next Users" initially would be engineering, architectural, excavating and contractor firms. They would be the next group of people advancing the project along. Many of them work on other people's *investments* enough that they often have investment aspirations of their own.

The main thing you will want to do is to find out *who* you will need to complete the project. Those people will have a vested interest in purchasing the project from you. They definitely have a "Professional Application" that makes the deal more attractive to them than to the average investor.

Create a *database* of these "Next Users" and whenever you put a property up for sale you will have your lists ready to go. Send them a quick fax or email "Exposing the Vision" and asking if they want to:

1. Bid your project?
2. Partner with you on your project? (You can raise capital for the use change this way, many builders partner with investors)
3. Purchase the deal from you?

If you put a set of building plans for a 15-unit condominium complex in front of a group of builders, the vast majority of them would be extremely confident and capable of building the project. However, if you asked that same group of builders to go find a property legally zoned for a 15-unit complex, put it under contract and close on it, most wouldn't have a clue what to do or where to begin. Your job is to simply find these opportunities and make them available to those who wish to profit by bringing the projects to fruition.

Where to Find All of these "Next Users"

Most professionals such as architects and engineers belong to local groups of their profession. Typically you can join these groups as an affiliate member and have access to the other members and their contact information as a part of your membership. These organizations will also help you learn more about who these professionals are and what they do.

When you put together your database of these types of businesses and individuals wherever possible include addresses, phone numbers, fax numbers and email addresses. This will make your communication with them faster and easier.

My *favorite* method of finding key "Next Users" is to use the city development office. Go and ask for a list of the last 25 or so projects that have been approved and built in the area around your project. These plans and projects are *public* information. Have them pull the plans and make copies for you. Most cities charge a very reasonable fee for this service. Next take the plans and copy the key professional information from them such as the architect, engineer, contractor, subcontractors, excavators, landscapers, etc.

After going through this list of projects you will have an outstanding list of prospects for your campaign. Not only can you sell projects to those professionals or partner with them, you can also hire them to work on your projects if you end up building your entire project.

The other benefit with creating your database this way is that these people have successfully taken a project through the city to completion. Their experience and insight with your city's development process will be invaluable to your project!

As you go through these projects try and *match up* the property you have for sale with people that built *similar* ones in the past. They will be the one's most interested in your project.

Milestones and "End Users"

Before I move on I would like to mention what I call the "End User". This is the person who will own the property for the *long-term* after it is completed. This can either be a builder or investor who is going to own a whole complex or a person who is going to buy just one unit and live there.

I like to start to market to "End Users" relatively soon in my marketing plan. That is because many people will want to buy these properties early to make more money or have a larger "say" in the development. In the case of an owner occupant I will start to market to them as soon as I have approved permits to build. Owner occupants sometimes like to buy prior to completion in order to select design and color options.

I especially do this if my project isn't very long. For instance in some areas you can complete a condo-conversion in a matter of days. In that case your "Next User" may actually *be* the "End User".

I still create my databases for "End User" marketing but they are a little different. If you are marketing to an "End User" that could be an owner occupant, you can create a database of tenants that live in the area. You can also create a database of real estate agents that work in the area of your project.

Send these people periodic updates to your project. Let them know every time there is a milestone. As a matter of fact you want to do this when you are marketing to anyone. Whenever you hit a milestone in your project "re-drip" on them. Send out an announcement of the milestone such as, "Full Exterior Remodel Complete", or "Final Plat approved by the City!" When you drip on people you generate a buzz around your property and a sense of urgency for someone to make an offer if they have any interest in buying.

> "Re-drip" on your "Next" and "End" users whenever you hit a milestone in your project to create a sense of ***urgency*** to buy!
>
> **~Mike Watson**

You *still* want to do *all* of the Work First

Many times I get to this point of my presentation and I have a student stand up and say, "I still want to do all of the work before I put it on the market." And the reality is you could. The reason I suggest you put the projects up for sale immediately is so that someone has the *chance* to purchase the property thereby earning you short-term profits. Most investors don't want to wait a year or two to get their first check. Some of these projects take significant time and money to get all the way through. You can learn a lot from short-term deals and get *paid* at the same time.

The beauty of "The Foundation to Success" is that if you purchase enough properties and get them started in the system, some will sell for short-term profits and others will go to completion and yield much larger long-term profits.

The short-term money is *now* money and the long-term money is *then* money. It is always best to offer the property for sale at each step in the process and allow the *market* to decide if it is a short-term deal or a long-term deal. Don't try to force a sale or stop a sale. The market is more powerful than you are and it will always win.

> "Don't try to force or stop a sale. The market is more powerful than you. Just follow "The Foundation to Success" and profit!
>
> **~Mike Watson**"

Put away that hammer.

One of the other questions I get quite often is, "Will someone *really* buy it if I haven't done anything to the property?" The truth is, if you are following "The Foundation to Success" properly it will be virtually *impossible* for you to not to have done *something* to the property. That is because "The Foundation to Success" says to put the property up for sale and then *immediately* start the changes to the "Highest and Best" use.

In many cases changes will start prior to you buying the property. Many investors will accomplish large amounts of work during their own feasibility and purchase contract period.

All that said; let me answer the earlier question. A buyer will buy the property when you have done no or a very small amount of work because you are selling it as something *different* than it was previously. Also, you will be pricing the property at a point where the next buyer can finish the work and still have an equity position or profit.

One of the most remarkable things about "The Foundation to Success" is this step. I say this because you are creating a true win/win situation for *everyone*. You helped the previous seller win with a sale and terms. You win by making a profit. The next buyer will win with a good equity position for themselves. Not to mention all of the people who will benefit by doing work on the property.

Many people just need help finding opportunities. They will pay good money for these opportunities as long as the purchase price plus their work and costs will still yield a good profit. Remember, these professionals will usually pay *more* for these projects than you might because it will usually cost them *less* to do the work than it would have cost you.

It's worth *how* much?!

How do you know what price to put on the property when it is time to sell? Once again, it will be extremely helpful if you completed the "deal evaluation forms" during your due diligence or earlier. The price you are going to ask now was determined in your original deal evaluation.

One way you can price your property is to use the "Long-term" deal evaluation "Future Value" price. When preparing advertising you would offer a discount from that price based on what work may be remaining. The discount you should allow for a buyer will lessen as your costs increase and the work draws nearer to an end.

Another way to find your price is to use the price you determined in your *"Short-term"* deal evaluation. Decide on the next *key* time when a buyer would be interested in the property. For instance, one milestone would be when you get your building permit. Then do a fresh market analysis to see what builders are paying for lots per door in your project area. Change your price accordingly just before completing each milestone.

Advertise for Attention!

Here is how you can use your advertising and drip campaign to best get the attention of the buyer. First you have to determine who the "Next Users" *are*. Then pick *which* "Next Users" you will focus on for each ad. Or if it is a short time period for your "use change" focus on the "End User". Then I will show you a sample of an ad you can use to attract their attention.

First let me show you the traditional method for advertising so you can understand how my method differs. Using the example of the small home on a big lot "Awesome 15-unit Condo Deal" a person unfamiliar with the "Higher and Better" use might market this property as follows:

> *"Great home with fixer-upper potential. Home needs lots of TLC and has plenty of room to grow. Large detached garage on a big lot. Close to freeways, shopping and schools. Will sell fast, don't miss out! Bring your best rehab clients. Structure appears to be solid. Square footage is an estimate only, buyer to verify all information."*

This is an average advertisement that would get average results. You are no longer an average investor. Here is how you can advertise the property in order to *attract* the right buyer. Do not advertise it for what it *currently* is but for what it *will* be. Note you identify your "Next User" right at the beginning and then you talk in their language.

> *Attention Investors, Contractors, Sub Contractors, "Do It Yourselfers" and Handymen; this is a 15-unit condominium project in process. Buy now and do the work yourself for a profit!*
>
> *The zoning is already in place and the preliminary site plan is being drawn. Rough site plan has already been submitted and approved by city staff. Once the project is approved and platted, building permits will be pulled and the sales price will be increased.*
>
> *Call now for preliminary renderings and city submittals. The sooner you call, the better the price you will get!*

As you can see, the two ads will draw considerably different buyers and solicit considerably different offers. The fun part about the two very different ads is that they are advertising the exact same property!

Have some fun with the ads for your deals. People respond to something that is out of the ordinary. Catch people's attention. Show them *they* can make a profit and then you will too.

Once you put the property up for sale it's time to get down to the business of "Creating and Enhancing the Equity" in the property. As amazing investors we don't sit around and wait for appreciation or a buyer. We force appreciation immediately through changing the use.

> "Average advertising will get you average results. Catch the buyer's attention by showing them how ***they*** can profit and watch your properties fly off the shelf!
>
> **~Mike Watson**"

STEP 7

CREATE AND ENHANCE EQUITY

STEP 7

CREATE AND ENHANCE EQUITY

What to Do With Your Equity

Step #7 of the "Foundation to Success" is to "Create and Enhance Equity" (Change the use and *explode* your profits). When you change the use of a property you massively boost its value and therefore, your *profits!* Of course you do have to change it to a "Higher and Better" use for this to happen.

Let's talk briefly about what Equity is and what it can do for you.

Here's a quick definition of the word Equity:

- Equity is the position of value in a property located between the property's current market value and its' indebtedness. In other words, if you own a property and have a $200,000 loan on the property and it is worth $300,000 then you would have $100,000 of "equity" in that property.

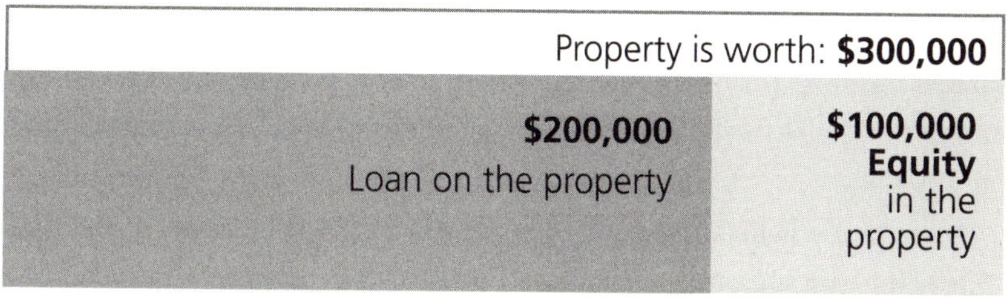

Property is worth: **$300,000**	
$200,000 Loan on the property	**$100,000** **Equity** in the property

If you do not have a loan on it then you would have $300,000 of "equity".

Two things to note about "Equity" are:

- Equity is real, but not realized until you access or use it in some manner. If you do not have direct access to your equity to put it to work for you, then for all intents and purposes it does not exist. So how do you gain access to the equity?

- The ways to access your equity include: selling your property, or getting lines of credit, mortgages and collateralization against the equity. Until you do one of these things you do not really "HAVE" your equity.

Yes you read that right, until you *do something* to access it and then use it, equity doesn't exist. It can vanish in a very short time if the market drops. Once it vanishes you are not ever guaranteed it will return. Therefore it does not exist until you do something with it.

Since I said your equity doesn't exist until you use it you might be wondering why we stress "creating" it and "enhancing" it. Well, it's so you *can* use it. You can sell the property and realize the equity as profit. You can use it for collateral on a loan to get cash with which to invest. You can take out credit lines on the equity.

If you have equity in a property you will most likely have a positive cash flow if you decide to lease it. When you have equity in a property you can sell that property and easily seller finance the equity to someone. If you do that you will not only get the equity at some point in the future but also *interest* on that equity! (or passive income) If you get enough interest for long enough you could double or triple your profits on any deal.

All of these reasons are why you invest in the first place. Therefore "Creating and Enhancing Equity" is one of the vital steps in your process. Without equity you may not have positive cash flow. Without equity you do not have a way to access more cash. Without equity you may not even be able to sell your property without losing money. Equity is everything. So let's "Create and Enhance some Equity"!

> "If you use your equity wisely you can double or ***triple*** your profits on every deal.
>
> **~Mike Watson**"

Start NOW! (Or even earlier)

Some people ask me, "When should I start to 'Create and Enhance Equity'?" Honestly the moment you are able to, is the best time to start. And more importantly continue with the process as quickly as you can and don't stop until a buyer makes you stop or you have sold the property or the project is *done!*

Why would you start so early, go so fast and not stop? It's simple, "Because if there is never a buyer, or if a potential buyer fails to purchase the property, you want to be as far along in the process as possible for the next buyer, or for you, to finish the project". The further along you are on the project when a buyer shows up, the more money you will make.

Finally, the most important reason is because when you get things done quickly you lower the time you own the property prior to completion. This way you lower your holding costs and therefore create even *more* equity. Move quickly!

You might ask, "Shouldn't I wait to see if it sells 'as is' before I make any changes?" The answer is, absolutely not. Once the property is for sale immediately begin the steps to take the property from what it is and begin to transform it into what it can become. The more you get done the easier it will be for a buyer to see your vision.

In our original example of the "Awesome 15-unit Condo Deal", we bought a house on a large lot, exposed the "Higher and Better" use and then hired an engineer to draft a site plan for the condominium complex. We asked for and received a simple design with the building footprint, the parking, setbacks, and simple landscaping.

When we had these plans we could meet potential buyers in front of the house and show them a drawing of what the property could become. (Remember, this is one of the ways you expose the higher and better vision you have for the property.)

The plat clearly showed the buyer that the use change was *in motion* and would take place *whether or not* they bought the property. It showed them they could buy it and make some money for themselves, or not buy it and you would keep all of the profits. When they saw this it gave validity to the project and a sense of urgency to the buyer.

(Another reason builders like to buy our partly finished projects is because they have less to do themselves to have a buildable project. In essence, they wouldn't have to *start from scratch* with the city, architect or engineer.)

Fortunately or unfortunately, depending on how you like to build wealth, the property got an offer and sold for a nice profit. Had it not sold, we would have continued with the step of "Creating and Enhancing Equity" until the project was far enough along for someone to buy the property and finish it, or until the project was *complete*. If we had continued with the platting and other work on the project, we certainly would have continued to raise the price to reflect any new work that had been done.

One of the main reasons you want to start the use change as soon as possible is you want to keep *momentum* going on your project. If you buy something, put it on the market and let it just *sit there*, you will find that buyers don't just come knocking at your door. On the other hand if you are busily changing the property into a higher use they will want to come buy it because if they don't *you* will be the one making all of the profits.

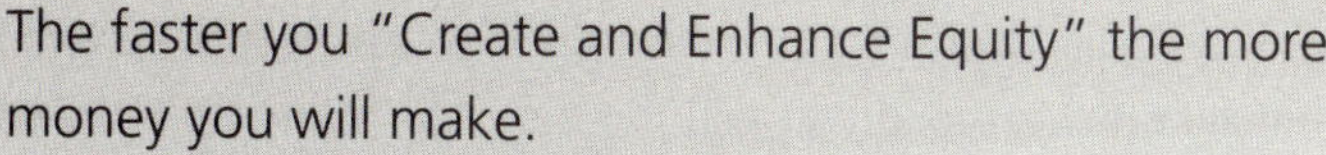

> "The faster you "Create and Enhance Equity" the more money you will make.
>
> **~Mike Watson**"

The 5 Ways to Make Your Property worth *Much More*

We have talked about how to increase the equity of your property throughout the book but never as a full package. Now, here is a list of the five types of "fix-up" strategies you can use to "Create and Enhance Equity". (Remember "Creating and Enhancing Equity" is just "fixing-up" the property in some way to change it to a "Higher and Better" use.)

1. Conceptual Fixer-Upper – Value is increased using *concepts* only ("Expose the Vision").
2. Paper Fixer-Upper - Value is increased through *paperwork* only. (subdivisions, conversions).
3. Income Fixer-Upper – Value increased by increasing the net income (increase rents or lower expenses)
4. Terms Fixer-Upper – Value is increased by offering better terms to make a property more appealing to future buyers (offer assumable seller financing).
5. Physical Fixer-Upper – Value is increased by physical changes (new buildings, change floor plans, add square footage, cosmetic, etc.).

You might have your doubts about number 1, the "Conceptual Fixer-Upper". Let me explain how just *exposing* the "Higher and

Better" use creates equity. It does so by exposing a more *valuable* property. When you do that you will enable more people to see the true potential and therefore you will increase the value by increasing the *demand* for the property.

The best way to expose the higher use of the property is to put it back on the market and announce through your marketing that you are "in the process of making the change to the new use". Describe the better use *well* and the buyers will come.

When you "fix-up" a property by doing a condo conversion, a lot split, or a subdivision to increase the density or the number of owners, you will increase the value of the property. These are all considered "Paper Changes" because in order for the change to happen all you need to do is the *paperwork*.

When you increase rents and/or decrease expenses on a property you literally change the net income and thus its value. An appraiser will give a property a higher value based on its new net cash flow. This is especially true for income producing properties of five or more units.

The amount the property will change in value is usually about $10,000-$15,000 per $100/month you increase cash flow. As you can see this can be an extremely lucrative way to "Create and Enhance Equity". I suggest referring back to the section on how to increase rents and decrease expenses earlier in the book for how to go about this.

I have talked a lot about how terms can make or break a deal. But I've not talked about how they specifically increase the value of a property. When you buy a property then turn around and offer seller financing, (especially with zero down or low qualifying standards) you instantly increase the pool of buyers who can invest in your property. This will automatically increase the value of your property. As a matter of fact whenever you offer seller financing you should *raise* the price of your property. It makes that much of a difference. Even appraisers will give a higher value to a property with favorable financing terms.

Finally I want to talk about actual "Physical Fixer-Uppers". These can be anything from a simple fixer upper to the addition of thousands of square feet of office space. Physical changes can drastically increase the equity of a property. Always make sure the cost of those changes is *less* than what the end product is worth.

> "You can change the value of a property significantly by simply ***exposing*** a higher and better use.
>
> **~Mike Watson**"

20 ways to "Create and Enhance Equity"

Within these five categories of "fixer-uppers" there are thousands of different ways to change density (increase equity). Each of these different "density" changes will have specific steps for you to follow. With several of these types of changes your city, architect and or attorney will have the guidelines for you to follow. As you go through this list put any of the ideas that appeal to you on your "Spark of Inspiration" list. That way you can later look into them further.

1. Conversions - The changing of any type of multi-unit property into condominiums. This can be done with apartments, horse stables, mini-storage units, office complexes, mobile home parks, marinas, parking lots, or literally anything that can be split into smaller units. (These are considered "Paper" and sometimes "Physical" Fixer-uppers)

2. Square Footage Fixer-Uppers - This is where the property is small but there is room on the lot to add on to the structure.

Make sure the comparable sales show a high enough price for the end product to still make a profit from the cost of the addition. (Physical Fixer-upper)

3. Floor Plan Fixer-Uppers - In this instance the floor plan is obsolete for some reason such as having no living room, dining area or only one bathroom in a four bedroom home. It could also be a property that is very dated and needs to have modern features added or removed such as, high ceilings, dishwasher, utility room, popcorn ceiling, poor paint colors etc. (Physical Fixer-upper)

4. Income Fixer-Uppers – Here you find a way to increase rents and/or decrease expenses. I discussed this technique in the deal evaluation section. (Income Fixer-upper)

5. As-Is Condominium Conversions – Here you convert a property to condos but do not remodel it. That way you can sell the units at a lower price point than others. This can be a good move in a market where there is literally no affordable 'first time buyer' housing. There are tons of buyers that want to own and don't care if the property is remodeled. There can be a LOT of profit on this type of deal. (Paper Fixer-upper)

6. Basement Finish Outs – This is where there is an unfinished basement you can finish out with more bedrooms, baths and/or living areas. Basically this is a way to add on square footage for a low cost. Wherever you can find cheap square footage you've found a good candidate for a "Finish Out". (Physical)

7. Attic Finishes - and patio finish outs. See above. (Physical)

8. Development - Here you take a vacant lot and build or add units to existing structures. This could end up being just a

paper change if you do not get to the point of breaking ground. Otherwise it will encompass almost every kind of "Fixer-upper" on this list. This is the most complex form of a fixer-upper.

9. Planned Unit Developments (PUD) - A PUD is usually a development that follows the zoning for the property in question, but doesn't meet all of the development standards. The project and developer overcome these limitations by building additional amenities. A PUD is essentially a "master planned community" that takes advantage of the best zoning available. (Paper, physical, conceptual)

10. Remodeling – This is used in areas where there is a high price per square foot on sales prices. The best thing to do here is to find areas that are selling for high prices. Then get some good bids on how much it would cost to remodel kitchens, bathrooms, bedrooms, living areas and exteriors. Then look for properties in poor condition that are being sold at a much lower cost per square foot than homes are selling for in the surrounding area. (Physical)

11. Bedroom/Bathroom Additions - These are frequently used on obsolete floor plans. Only do these when the area around it has homes with the same or more bedrooms and baths than what you are planning to have once you do the addition. Otherwise you could create an "Obsolete" floor plan yourself. (Physical)

12. Landscaping/Amenities Additions - When you make a property more enjoyable and pleasing to look at you will add value to it. (Physical)

13. Subdivision - By taking raw land and subdividing you are adding "units or tax ID numbers" and thus value. Make sure your finished lot prices will be at a value where a builder will still be

willing to buy them. Find out how much it costs to subdivide by going to your city or talking with an architect or engineer. (Paper)

14. "Flag" Lot - Essentially this is a miniature subdivision. You will change one large lot into two. (Paper)

15. Lot Line Adjustments – These can be used to re-configure lots that are obsolete, create more lots or better sized lots for development. Your plat maps will expose some astounding potential for these types of deals. (Paper)

16. Annexation - In most cases if you find a property that will be annexed (moved into the city jurisdiction) the zoning will change to a higher density after it gets annexed. Cities have maps that show where they next intend to annex. You can get a copy of that map and just buy something in their path. Obviously make sure to find out how it will be zoned if you want to use this technique. (Conceptual)

17. Additional Unit Addition/Conversion – In this situation there is already a structure on the property that you will convert to have additional units within the same structure. (Conceptual, physical)

18. Enclosures - When you take a porch, carport or deck and *enclose* them for more square footage. Get bids on what this will cost as these are a bit more pricey than the attic or basement finish outs. (Physical)

19. Pop-Tops – This is when you take the roof off and add a second or third floor. By doing this you add square footage on a property without encroaching on any setbacks or increasing the amount of area of the lot you are covering. Those can be

critical development issues. Always remember you can add on going up. (Physical)

20. Use Change – For example, when you change a residential home in a commercial area into a commercial property. Many times this will be found in your "Future Land Use Map" or just by driving around and seeing something that doesn't fit its zoning. You can make a fortune with this technique just by exposing the better use! (Conceptual)

The whole point of "Creating and Enhancing Equity" is to take a property the way you find it and change it into what it can become as *quickly as possible.* In the meantime you will have it on the market announcing your change.

Your intention will be to finish the project in order to have a huge equity position, but you will gladly sell it along the way for a smaller profit and a faster turnaround if someone tears it out of your hands. Remember that "The Foundation to Success" says to let the market decide if the property will sell in the short-term or if you will hold it in your long-term portfolio.

One final thing I want to say here is that I have given you many ways to "Create and Enhance Equity". I suggest you pick two or three that interest you and go out and look at a few properties that might have some potential. Have some *fun* with it.

Once you have done that then you can do some checking at the city or with an architect or attorney to see what *exact* steps are necessary for the type of "Fixer-Upper" you want to try in your area. You can start to compile the "costs to change the use" for when you evaluate a specific deal.

What should you do first?

When you are actually making your changes what do you do first? Do you paint the outside? Do you get your permits? Do you add on amenities? The timing of your changes really depends on what type of property you are modifying.

For example, if you are taking a single family home and doing a square footage and/or floor plan fixer-upper you should start with resolving any *hazardous* issues.

Next you should remedy anything that is not up to *code*. You can finish with any *cosmetic* items that will *not* be affected by your floor plan change or addition. While you are doing those things to the current structure you should *submit* for your building permit for the addition and floor plan changes. Here is a quick example.

A few years ago I purchased a small home that my team found while door knocking in our "AoE". The home had been lived in by a widow for some time. The widow passed away and for four years her son kept the home vacant while he was living in another state. We got an excellent price on it and began a cosmetic and floor plan fixer-upper.

Following Step #6 of "The Foundation to Success" we *immediately* put the property back up for sale. We listed it at the finished value and offered a "massive" discount on the property for anyone that wanted to buy the home "as is" and fix-up the property themselves for a profit.

One problem we had with the property was that the original front steps were wood and had rotted away. We hauled them off and had not yet replaced them when the first few buyers looked at the home. They did not seem interested.

We decided to do the stairs early on because of the hazard/code issue. We had an offer on the home within days of putting in the stairs. I learned a real lesson about people needing and wanting to feel safe about the home they are buying.

If you are buying a piece of land for new construction or to subdivide, you should immediately go to the city and start with the *entitle-*

ment and *zoning* processes. Once you are comfortable with the due diligence get the owner's permission, if possible and start these things during your contract period. With land, you will want to get as much of the paperwork done as soon as possible so you can start building structures or moving dirt. That is because with land you will not have any rental income to help with the carrying costs.

As mentioned previously it is important for you to learn the city requirements, process, and fees for doing a subdivision, prior to going into the time where you will possibly lose your earnest money. This process and cost should be part of your original evaluation so you know *what* you have to do and *when* and *how long* it will take.

Working with an architect at this point will help you determine exactly what will fit on the property. Always make sure to explain to the architect that your goal is to *maximize density* by either maximizing the number of units or square footage. You should get a very good feel for what you can put on the property during the feasibility period.

If you are buying a property where you are going to do a condo conversion you should speak with a local attorney who is familiar with the process. He or she will help you determine the steps you need to take in order to facilitate the change to condominiums. These regulations vary greatly from area to area. In some places you can convert in a matter of days. In others it takes over a year. In a few areas conversions are not even *allowed*.

It is smart to figure out the requirements in your area prior to making an offer. This will make your time line and cost to change become much clearer. Make sure you know what your city, county and state require for conversions.

Get out of my way!

One of the things you will run into during your change process is *tenants* in your property. This will affect the changes you can do and when you can do them. They can most definitely be considered "In

Your Way" on some deals.

During due diligence, the seller, as a part of the seller's disclosures, should provide a copy of *all* leases affecting the property. This could be tenants, people using the property for storage or even easements. During due diligence make sure you are comfortable with the lease agreements.

When you buy a property you assume the terms of any lease attached to the property. Leases can have an adverse affect on the property. For example, if a tenant has a 15 year lease agreement and you want to build on the property you couldn't take out the existing unit. You would have to take care of the lease and therefore the tenant. If you do find a property with a "bad" lease here are four options you have:

1. If you know about a lease that hurts your deal <u>before you negotiate</u> then write an offer on the property that requires the seller to negotiate the *end of the lease* with the current tenant. This will force the *seller* to work it out with the tenant prior to you purchasing the property.

   If you find out about the lease during due diligence and you are already under contract, write an *addendum* telling the seller to remedy the lease to your satisfaction or you will *cancel* the sale based on the adverse effect of the lease.

2. You can purchase the property and wait until the tenants move out. Remember, when you need building permits or entitlement work done, tenants will pay rent and *help you cover the debt service* while you do the necessary paperwork for your project.

   Some partners and I are currently doing a condominium conversion on an 11-unit apartment complex. The condo conversion paperwork will take 4-5 months. Upon writing a contract we discovered the tenants all had month-to-month leases. This was perfect as it allowed us to do the conversion and get the rents at the same time. Those rents are paying for the majority of our carrying costs. When the units are ready to sell we will see if the tenants want to buy their unit. If they don't we will give them a 30-day notice to vacate.

Keep in mind you could do lots of work on the exterior of a property with a tenant in place. The main things you cannot do are physical development and interior remodel work.

3. Another option is to *buy the tenant out* after you close. Sometimes the deal is so good you will take it even though there may be a bad lease. You should talk to the tenants and see if they are willing to move early. A free month's rent or two can go a long way toward getting a tenant to move early. Don't forget to factor this in to your projected expenses when you evaluate and before you purchase the property.

4. That last option is to *not buy* the property. You should try your best to negotiate before you let this one happen, but a bad lease really can make a deal not work.

> "Make sure any lease on the property does not adversely affect your deal.
>
> **~Mike Watson**"

Bring in the Backhoe

On many of your deals you will need to remove a structure. Once you determine it *can* and *should be* removed the first step is to talk to your city or county building department. Most municipalities require a *demolition permit* before structures can be removed. Get an application and find out what the requirements are for a permit. I recommend you determine these requirements during or before your feasibility. (Sound familiar?)

You may be required to have a hazardous materials inspection of the property before anything is torn down. Most dumps and landfills are becoming picky about the type of materials that they will accept. One of the main concerns in the inspection will be asbestos. If it is found during the inspection, then a hazardous waste removal expert will most likely have to come in and remedy any hazardous material issues.

Another concern will be that all utilities are turned off to the house and disconnected before work starts. You can imagine the fun a gas leak would present while a house was being torn down. After you meet the conditions you will be issued a demolition permit and a contractor can be hired to remove the structure.

Another option you have other than demolition is to *move* a building. You may want to check for companies in your area who will remove a home for free if they get to keep the structure. They take it and sell it or put it on another lot and sell it. Check your area for "house mover" type companies. This could save you a pretty penny in demolition expenses.

Should you *ever* change the price?

During the time you are "Creating and Enhancing Equity" you will have two ways you can price your property. The first way is to list the property at its future and *final* sales price. Then you offer a massive discount for anyone who wants to buy it and finish the work themselves for a profit.

This first method offers two distinct advantages. First you won't have to adjust the price as you finish each phase of the project, because it will already be priced at its future finished value. As you proceed with work and transform the property into its "Highest and Best" use, you will begin to be *less flexible* with that "massively discounted sales price."

Once your work is done, your finished sales price should be an excellent value for someone to purchase.

The second advantage to this pricing system is that during the work phase it will attract people who want to finish the work, your "Next Users". But it will also attract your "End Users" by continuously advertising at the "End User" price. When the work is done, the property will attract *only* "End Users".

The other method is to change your price at each milestone as we discussed before. Either method works, though I prefer the one where you offer it at the final price with a discount. This is because your buyer can easily get a feel for the equity they will have in the property if they buy it at a discount. In its own way this is another method of "Exposing the Vision". You are exposing the vision of the *end value*.

The *Only* 3 Times You *Stop* "Creating and Enhancing Equity"

Never *ever* stop working on the property until one of these three things occurs. Number one is if a buyer comes in and *demands* that you stop the work. This may happen if they want to change what you are doing. I am hesitant to stop work in this scenario unless I have a significant earnest money deposit. And even then I like a portion of it to be non-refundable because if they do not buy the property then you have wasted your time.

Remember, the further you are along on the "Change of Use" the better chance you have of getting a buyer. This is partially because it gets easier and easier to see the final vision of the property.

Number two is always stop work if a buyer *closes* on the property. In this case it is obvious to stop as you no longer own the property.

Number three is to stop working on the property when the work is *complete*. That means the change to its "Higher and Better" use is done. At this point you are free to sell it to "End Users", via traditional methods or seller financing, or keep it in your long-term portfolio. Congratulations, you are well on your way to being a Real Estate Tycoon!

> "Don't stop your "change of use" for ***anything*** except a check, a sale, or a completion of a project!
>
> **~Mike Watson**"

STEP 8

SELL THE PROPERTY FOR A PROFIT

STEP 8

SELL THE PROPERTY FOR A PROFIT

It's time to cash in on your hard work. YES!

Step # 8 of "The Foundation to Success" is to sell the property for a profit. (Short-term *fast cash*) You have done your work to find your area, you have found a deal, bought it, put it on the market, started your change and now have a buyer. Congratulations, you are about to complete your first "Highest and Best Real Estate Investment!"

I will talk a little later on how to negotiate your deal, when you should accept an offer, etc. But for now I would like to go a little more in depth into the technique I touched on briefly in the marketing section called "Flixers".

To understand "Flixers" correctly, you need to understand what a flip and a fixer-upper are. A flip is when you buy low and sell high as *quickly* as possible without doing *any* work to the property. The way to make money on flips is to buy for discount and sell for market value. A fixer-upper is when you buy low, *completely* improve the property from what it is to what it can be and then put it on the market and sell it for a higher price. A "Flixer" is a *hybrid* of the two.

A "Flixer" is a property we buy, expose the future vision of, begin the work on and sell prior to completion of the work. The person who buys the "Flixer" will finish the work and make a profit.

I want to talk more about this technique because it is quite literally what you will do on every deal that you sell in the short-term. Otherwise it becomes a long-term deal you sell to "End Users" or hold in your portfolio. A "Flixer" is what you call a "Sale for a Profit in the Short-term".

The main difference between a fixer-upper and a "Flixer" is that the "Flixer" allows another person (the buyer) to make a profit on the property. This is essential to understand so you will know how to sell your deal. Always leave enough money on the table for the buyer so it will make sense for them to finish the work. Also, you may see why it is so important to market to people who can do the work themselves. They can profit more than *anyone* else.

To better illustrate this point consider the following examples:

Example Number One:

When I started doing fixer uppers I would go and find cosmetically distressed houses, buy them cheap and fix them up for a profit. I had the same crew of subcontractors that would come to each home and do the work for me.

I had one contractor who would come to every project and would bug me over and over to sell him the property. At first I was offended that he would try and *take* my deal. I told him deal after deal just to do the work and leave the investing to me.

Finally after he had pestered me over and over again I told him, "On the next deal if you want to buy it, just make me an offer." I figured this would get him off my back and we could get the investment done. He showed up with an offer a few days later that was high enough to pay me my acquisition price plus *over half* of my finished fixer-upper profit without having done *any* of the fix-up work. I was shocked, stunned and amazed. I could make over half of my profit and not do or pay for anything!

I didn't understand why *he* would pay that much more than *I* would for the same investment. The first thing I realized was he only knew what I was selling the house for when the work was done. As "The Foundation to Success" states, I bought the house, put it back up for sale again at the future fixed-up value and then began to "Create and

Enhance Equity".

To determine his offer, he took the future value of the house, subtracted out his cost and what profit he wanted to make on the deal. I learned two things. First of all, he was willing to do the deal for a *smaller* profit because he was already there working on the house anyway. Therefore he would get paid for his *work* and get paid a *profit* on the investment. He considered himself a double-dipper at this point. Secondly, he could probably get better pricing on the fix up than I could. I ended up selling him the house and it was quite profitable for both of us.

Example Number Two:

Recently I was speaking to a large room of investors, agents and contractors. During my camp I asked them, "How many of you could take a set of approved blueprints on a 10-unit condominium project and confidently build that project yourself or with your contractor." Almost 100% of the hands in the room went up.

Next I asked them to raise their hands if they were knowledgeable enough to consistently locate the piece of land they could build it on, entitle the property, draw the plans and finance the project. Almost no hands were raised the second time.

What I learned was that builders, agents and investors wanted to build, but most lacked either the ability to do projects or the time for all of the preparation work. Because of this it is very profitable to find properties where projects can be built, buy them, begin the work, and then sell them to someone else who will come in and finish the projects.

Example Number Three:

Years ago I was selling new homes for a builder. One day he called me and said, "I have a new subdivision I want you to start selling for me." He gave me an address and I drove to the site. As soon as I got there I noticed a construction trailer in the middle of 10 acres of fenced farmland with a cow hanging out. I was kind of confused. Where were the homes? I walked into the trailer and asked the person who was there if we could go to the new subdivision. He said, "This is it!"

So I tried a new tactic, I asked him if the plat was approved through the city. He responded by saying the plat was preliminarily approved, but that the city had given him written permission to take reservations. He then showed me a copy of the preliminary plat that I would be showing to buyers. There was absolutely nothing done on the site. The curbs, roads and streets weren't even shown. The utilities were not brought in or anything. We had a fenced field of weeds with a cow and I was supposed to sell *homes*.

Trying to buy a little time I asked, "Which of the current models in other subdivisions are we going to be selling and building in this subdivision?" He happily exclaimed that we basically had all new models to build. I then asked him, "So you want me to sell homes we haven't built on lots that don't exist?"

He said, "Yes."

I said, "I don't think that is possible. How do you sell a home that doesn't exist on a lot that doesn't exist?"

He asked back, "Well, how good are you at sales?"

It was pretty funny because with that question he hit my "Red Button Statement" at a time when people didn't believe in me (this was a long time ago). I told him to give me the plans. By the time we got a building permit on the first home, I had 29 of the 35 homes sold. The sale of those homes was an important lesson to me that *people will buy properties based on a vision.* This is what makes a "Flixer" work. We find a property the way it is, expose the vision of what its "Highest and Best" use is, and then sell to people who want to do the work for a profit.

In summary, a flip is bought and sold before *any* work is done. A fixer-upper is a property that you buy, do *all* the work to and then sell for a profit or refinance for an equity position. A "Flixer" is a property that we buy, *start* the work on and then sell to someone else who wants to *finish the work themselves for a profit.*

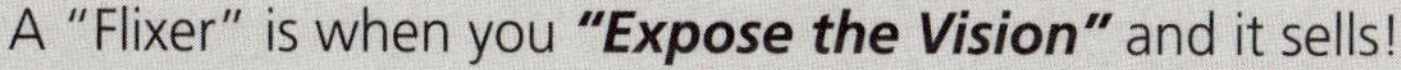

> A "Flixer" is when you ***"Expose the Vision"*** and it sells!
>
> **~Mike Watson**

So you really, really want to finish a project?

Many investors have told me, "I really want to finish a project because I will make more money on it." I have a soft spot in my heart for them because I know they see the value of long-term deals. But my answer to them is always this, "Do not try to force the property to sell or *not* sell. Let the market decide." But, I also like to throw in these reasons for why it is smart to sell some deals in the "Short-term".

1. A quick profit will help you have the cash to *fund other deals.*

2. A quick closing will build your confidence and allow you to have financial proof that your system works. This will drive you to work harder on finding other deals.

3. You can use the proceeds to pay off properties for future credit lines to use again and again.

4. You can do *more* deals when some of them are short-term deals. How many quick deals could you do in the time it would take to complete a 15-unit condominium construction project? What could the profits be on all of those quick deals?

5. A quick check helps you improve your life financially. Most people consider investing because they want to improve their lives. Getting a quick check will certainly help you *begin* that process.

6. A quick deal helps you have *proof of your success* to use when you want to raise capital for your next deal. One of the first things people ask about is your experience. It will be good to be able to show them some complete deals where you have made a profit.

   Early on, I started meeting people that I was going to raise capital from at my *current or recently finished investments.* I would start the appointment with a tour through the property and show them what I was doing, how I was doing it and what my profits were. I also liked to show them my "Area of Expertise" book and my "Deal Binder". This helped people understand how my investing worked and gave them confidence in me to help them make profits as well.

The other thing to keep in mind is that you don't just have to do *one* deal at a time. You could get four of five of them going at once or even *more.* I have several investors in my camps that are doing *over fifteen deals* at one time. Some of them will sell in the short-term and some will be held for long-term wealth. Investors who are able to do *both* will prosper on a very high level.

When you get an offer, do you sell or not?

When you get an offer here is what you should consider:

1. How profitable is the current offer based on all the time, risk and involvement you have had on this deal?
2. What is the likelihood of another offer coming in at a higher price and how long would it take for that to happen?
3. How badly do you want to keep the property in your long-term portfolio? If you want it badly enough, you may not sell for

almost *any* price.

4. How many other deals do you have going? Is this your only deal or are you working on 15 of them?
5. Do you have other income coming in or is this it?
6. When is your bank or private financing *due* compared to your closing time? If you have loans coming due soon it might be more compelling to sell.

The reality is I like to make money. I like to sell properties quickly for profits, but I also really like to hold projects long-term for the bigger money. My perfect reality is to do enough projects that I am always selling properties in the short-term *and* keeping some for the long-term. This provides me fast cash profits, the long-term residual income, and improved net worth. This is the best of both worlds.

Negotiating Tip

I recommend that you use an expert when you negotiate, such as a licensed real estate agent and/or an attorney. There are a lot of sections in most purchase contracts and many beginners are not experienced enough to properly represent their own interests.

The expense of a professional will more than likely save you from a lot of exposure, additional risk and problems that could have been avoided. Most will also *save* you a lot more money with their negotiating skills than they will cost you on the transaction.

Negotiating is just coming to a win/win agreement between two parties. Closely review any offer you get. Put pen to paper and determine exactly how much you will make based on all expenses you have spent and will incur to sell. If you are happy with the offer, take it. If not, manipulate the terms to make them work for you.

Negotiating is all about terms. Review the sections on "Terms" and you will be able to create a win/win for you and the buyer.

If you would like more information about contracts and negotiating tactics I offer a Degree Camp on that topic. We spend 3 days going over terms, "Vital Clauses", "4-Offer Spreadsheets", negotiating and contracts themselves.

Other Resources

You can find more detailed information about the Camp at my web site **mikewatsoninvesting.com.** Go to the "Training" section and then click on the "Contracts" Degree Camp. I also have a live Degree Camp available on CD if you prefer that format.

How to Have Cash Flow with *No Property Management!*

One of the terms you can negotiate when you *sell* is "Seller Financing". I highly recommend you do this, just like I highly recommended you get seller financing when you bought the property. We have now come full circle. This is one of my favorite methods I teach. It is when an investor (you) has done a deal using the "Foundation to Success" and has a buyer who wants to do seller financing. There are so many benefits to *you* the investor in this scenario.

First you are able to ask a *higher asking price* on your property when you sell. Second, you will make more money than you would have because you will receive *interest over time* in addition to a higher sales price.

If for some reason your property is difficult to sell, seller financing may create a market for a buyer who might not otherwise have considered buying. And finally the biggie, you can have passive income *without* property management.

So let's talk a little bit about how this will work. Let's say you buy a 16 unit apartment complex and complete a condominium conversion. Next you sell 4 of those units. Then along comes the buyer for the 5th unit and she wants you to provide some seller financing.

If you obtained seller financing when you bought the apartment complex and convinced the seller to allow their loan to be *assumed and split into smaller amounts* then you can offer that loan (split or splintered part) directly to the next buyer. In addition you can offer your equity as a *second lien* and have the buyer pay you residually. This would be how you get long-term income without property management.

But what if you did a long-term bank or mortgage loan on the unit and have to pay it off when you sell? Well there are a couple of scenarios. You can allow the buyer to come in and wrap your loan. (Make sure you follow the "Rules of Wrapping") Then you can offer them a second lien on the property and have them pay you interest on that lien. Second, you can have the buyer get a new loan that *pays off your loan* on the property and then you could give them a second lien where they pay you interest on your equity.

One of the cool things about a condo conversion is that you could sell 12 of those units and then own the other 4 outright (with no loan). In that case you could offer up to 100% seller financing on the remaining 4 units with no issues at all. Again, long-term cash flow, and no property management, the best of both worlds!

Here is another example:

Let's assume you buy a lot for $200,000 and do a short-term loan with a bank for $140,000 and put $60,000 as a down payment. Next you do what it takes to subdivide the property into 4 lots that are worth $100,000 each for a total value of $400,000. During this time you have the property on the market.

Next let's say a builder buys the property from you for the full $400,000 price. You can offer them seller financing in the following way. You could have them get a 70% first lien in the amount of $280,000 which would pay off your loan of $140,000 and pay you back for the down payment of $60,000 you made. It would also pay you $80,000 (minus your change and closing fees) more at closing!

Now look what is left. If you offer them a 30% second lien, in the amount of $120,000. This lets them buy the property for *zero down!* You will then get interest payments on the $120,000 loan you extend them *plus* you will get the $120,000 loan back when they refinance or sell.

It can be an awesome option for you to offer seller financing when you sell. If that builder had needed to put 30% down on a development they may not have been able to buy the property at all. So once again you all win!

> "An exceptional investing technique is to Seller Finance to a buyer. That way you make long-term passive income with ***no*** property management.
>
> **~Mike Watson**"

Uncle Sam

You may be wondering about taxes and what happens when you sell for a big profit. Before getting involved in real estate be sure to consult a professional Certified Public Accountant (CPA) and a good Tax Attorney. They will be able to instruct you as to the tax laws and implications of your specific situation and investment.

Typically when you sell a property, the gain from that property is taxable when the property sells and the gain is *received.* For example, if I sold a property to a cash buyer I would be taxed on my gain because I *received it all at the closing.* The tax would be due and I would pay it at my next tax deadline.

However, if I sold a property with a seller-financed note, I would be taxed on the portion of the gain I received at the closing, but not on the gain I would receive in the future (seller financed portion). I would be taxed on that part of the gain *as I received* it in the monthly payments over time.

In the previous example with the lots, I would receive $80,000 worth of gain at closing which would be taxable at that time. I would give the buyer a $120,000 loan seller financed either with interest only payments or principal and interest payments. If I received *interest only* payments, my interest would be taxable at my *ordinary* income tax bracket, but there would be no capital gains tax until the call time because I haven't received any more of the gain.

If I received principal *and* interest payments I have to pay ordinary income tax on the interest, and capital gains tax on the principal as it was received. For these reasons it may be smart to let your buyer pay you with interest only payments. That way you can defer some of your tax burden to a later year.

Remember, the best thing to do is talk with a CPA to find out what your tax burden will be on any investment.

I just want to sell, sell, sell!

I've had students say they don't want to do any long-term projects. That is fine. Everyone should do what they want. But here is the truth. Long-term wealth requires long-term assets. It may seem obvious but if you don't *keep* anything long-term, you won't *have* anything in the long-term.

Many people make a lot of money in the short-term but end up spending it and then have to make more money to keep going. The goal of this system is that one day you won't have to go find any more deals. I want the result to be that the deals you find and improve *pay for your life.* (I'd prefer this to happen sooner rather than later)

True wealth doesn't happen until you have assets making money for you in the form of residual passive income. This is one of the big requirements for *retirement.* One of the not so great skills Americans have developed is to spend more money than we make….no matter how much money we make. Long-term assets help overcome that tendency by producing *continual* income without additional effort.

Long-term assets also provide the opportunity for tax write-offs through interest, management, maintenance and capital expenses. In addition, most people are able to depreciate their properties, thereby sheltering their income. This may not seem significant but let's take a look at an example.

Let's assume you own a property that is worth $1,000,000 and it provides $20,000 a year in net rental income. Check with your CPA but most people can also write off about $40,000 of the value of the property. Therefore you do not end up paying taxes on the rental income or on $20,000 of other income. (Qualifications apply)

Additionally, long-term assets can appreciate over time, though we look at this as a *bonus*, and not the reason for investing. Real estate over time will usually outpace inflation in appreciation. In the long-term that appreciation can add up to a nice bonus to your net worth.

Lastly, long-term assets can provide massive equity positions for credit lines and cross collateralization. As your equity positions grow when you pay off your mortgages and have appreciation, your assets become ripe for credit lines. You can use credit lines to get cash for more deals.

All in all, the reasons for owning property long-term are overwhelmingly compelling. Make up your own mind and do what is right for you. But keep in mind sometimes *you will not have a choice.* It is always best to have the long-term as an option and to *make sure* when you evaluate, that every deal works in the long-term.

So what exactly does happen when your property does not sell in the short-term? This is the part of investing that frightens most investors. They think, "I'll find a property and sell it for a profit after I put carpet and paint in it. If it sells I will make a pretty good profit.

Wait a minute.....what if it doesn't sell?" The reality of an investment property *not selling* keeps a lot of potential investors away from the business when in fact this is what they should be *hoping* for.

The beauty of "The Foundation to Success" is that in this situation you still have an exit strategy. Step #9 of "The Foundation to Success" is refinance for an equity position.

STEP 9

REFINANCE FOR AN EQUITY POSITION

STEP 9

REFINANCE FOR AN EQUITY POSITION

> "Long-term ***wealth*** requires long-term ***assets.***
>
> **~Mike Watson**"

The Particulars of Refinancing *Revealed*

Remember the whole premise of "The Foundation to Success" is that you find a property with a "Higher and Better" use, put it up for sale for a short-term profit and then begin to "Create and Enhance Equity". If the property does *not* sell in the short-term, then you complete the changes that take it to its "Highest and Best" use.

Once this is done, you have a property that is worth a lot more than the price you paid plus the money you spent changing it. Because it is worth more, you will have quite a nice equity position in the property. It is now time to follow through with Step # 9 of "The Foundation to Success" and <u>refinance for an equity position. (Long-term strategy for Passive Income)</u>

If you remember, when you do your deal evaluation you *don't pro-*

ceed on a deal unless you will be left with a resulting equity position of at least *20% of the future value* after all purchase price, costs to change the use, and sales costs are factored in. (30% on commercial deals)

Because you now *own* the property, are on title and have this much equity, you can go to your bank and refinance the project with *no money out of your pocket.* If you have an equity position of 20% on a residential property (30% for commercial), you can get a new first mortgage for 80% (70% commercial).

This new mortgage will pay off your investors or purchase loan plus the costs to change and leave you with only a first mortgage (typically a long-term loan with better interest rate). This loan won't have mortgage insurance and you will have a fantastic equity position. You will now have a property with a fighting chance for nice positive cash flow that will most likely appreciate over the years and can be a fantastic tax shelter.

The awesome part about this system is that if you borrowed private capital, got bank financing or had the seller finance your deal, (or any combination of those three) you could have bought the property with *no money down.* Once you refinance, you still will not have put *any* of your own money in the deal. "The Foundation to Success" is truly a "*no money down*" program for buying property *and* holding it long-term!

How to Hold Property in Your Long-term Portfolio

I would like to go through an example of how this works. Let's consider again my original "Awesome 15-unit Condo Deal" for the explanation of this part of the system.

I bought the house for $129,900 and sold it shortly thereafter as a 15-unit condominium project "in process" for $210,000. I made over $65,000 in profit after closing costs and carrying expenses. Most investors think if I didn't sell the property I would have a single-family home that wouldn't rent for enough to cover the mortgage payment and I would be stuck.

But as "The Foundation to Success" says, I *always* continue the "Creating and Enhancing Equity" step until the condominium project is *complete*. Let's see what the numbers may have looked like had I *not* sold it in the short-term.

(These are a very simple estimate of costs to demonstrate the idea.)

Purchase Price $129,900
Costs for Engineering and Architectural Work $75,000
Carrying Costs of Loans (Property/Construction)..... $85,000
Site improvements (Curbs, Utilities, etc.)............ $175,000
Building Costs (15 units x 1000 sq ft. x $80/sq ft.) $1,200,000
Sales Costs (Commissions, closing)................. $240,000

Total Costs $1,904,900

Let's assume the value of each brand new condominium is $225,000. Therefore, with 15 of them, my finished project is worth $3,375,000. I have approximately $1,470,100 in profit if I sell the whole project. ($3,375,000 - $1,904,900). *Or I have $1,710,100 in equity if I don't sell.* (I wouldn't have to pay the $240,000 in sales costs.) If decide to keep the property I will refinance the property as follows:

With a $3,375,000 appraised value, I should be able to get a 70% refinance loan of $2,362,500

If I use those funds to pay off all of my costs of $1,664,900 (remember no sales costs), then I will get $697,600 cash in my pocket at the time of the refinance.

$2,362,500 (Refinance Loan)
<$1,664,900> (All actual costs)
$697,600 (Cash to seller at refinance)

In addition, after the refinance I would be left with a 30% equity position in my property. This would be equal to $1,012,500! (30% of $3,375,000) I would have a property that just made me a millionaire, in fact, almost a multi-millionaire on *one deal.* ($697,600 in cash at the refinance, plus $1,012,500 worth of equity) With $697,600 of cash in my pocket I would be set to run that property quite well as a property manager/owner.

Here is the net result to my life:

1. Increased my net worth by $1,710,100.
   ($697,600 + $1,012,500)
1. I have an asset with no mortgage insurance.
2. I had a handsome cash-out payday.
3. I own a depreciable asset to shelter my income tax.
4. I put a property in my portfolio that grows in value while it pays for itself.
5. I generate a monthly positive cash flow from the rents.
6. I can use my 30% equity position as collateral for other financing or for a possible commercial credit line. (I can do more deals!)

I imagine many of you are now thinking that selling the property for a profit of $66,000 in 70 days wasn't such a good deal after all. This system is so *good* it makes it hard to decide whether to sell for a profit or refinance for an equity position. That is a fantastic situation to be in as an investor. If you do your deal evaluation well you have always got an exit strategy that works, even if that includes *not exiting.*

How do you decide to sell or keep the deal?

The answer is, let the market decide for you. Literally, you should put the property up for sale and if it sells, it is a short-term deal. If it doesn't sell, it is a long-term deal. If the deal works in the short-term and the long-term, does it really matter when it sells? Most of the students I teach would really like a property or two to sell in the short-term so they can get some fast income.

I try to convince them that if they do *enough* deals, some will sell in the short-term and some will sell in the long-term. Imagine if I had bought *ten* of these homes instead of just one!

Typically it is a good idea to do just that, as many of the homes in the immediate area could have the same or similar zoning and "Higher and Better" use potential. If you had 10 properties you were working on and 5 sold in the short-term and 2 sold in the long-term, and you held 3 in your long-term portfolio, imagine how your life would look. You would have an amazing year with outstanding income *and* you would have built incredible long-term wealth!

What to Do *After* You Refinance

You have three options after you refinance. The first is to leave it up for sale just like it has been. In addition you can offer it for sale with seller financing. If you choose this option I suggest you raise the price. Or, you can rent it out and hold it in your long-term portfolio for cash flow. Here is how this process flows.

Once again I am going to go back to the "Awesome 15-unit Condo Deal". Assume it had not sold and that I continued on with entitlement, platting and building permits. Once I had my building permits I would have built the condos.

During all of those steps I would have kept the property on the market. Each time I hit a new milestone I would have announced that milestone to the "Next User" and given less of a discount on the final price. Most likely it would have sold at several points for a larger and larger profit.

Had it not sold and I ended up with nearly built condominiums I would have started to offer them to the "End User". I would have then sold as many single units as possible to individual "End Users" and profited even more. Obviously if I had to sell the 15 units in bulk at any time in the process, there would have been a bulk discount. Selling the units separately would yield an even higher profit.

I would also offer the units for sale with some seller financing for the buyers. I really like this option. (Remember to only offer to seller finance your *profits*.) If I owed 70% on the units for acquisition costs and costs to change, I would have a 30% equity position. I could offer the units for sale with a seller financed lien of 20% or less. This would allow the buyer to get an 80% first lien of their own, avoid mortgage insurance and have a lower payment than they would have, had they done a 100% owner occupied first mortgage.

Because the buyer's first lien was 80% and I only owe 70%, I would get all of my costs paid off at closing. In addition I would get a 10% profit check (minus closing costs) and a note receivable for as long as that buyer pays on *my mortgage.*

This is truly the best kind of residual income. I call it *property-less passive income.* With it I will receive passive income without having to manage a property. Essentially I become a bank and just collect interest checks!

If some or all of the units still didn't sell I would then lease them out long-term for positive cash flow. In addition to that cash flow I will have at least a 20% plus equity position thus increasing my net worth.

It is that simple, evaluate conservatively, follow through to the end, offer the property for sale the whole time, and let the market decide what will happen. "The Foundation to Success" literally gives you a way to make more and more money as time goes on.

> "Follow "The Foundation to Success" ***as it is written*** and it will lead you to vast wealth.
>
> **~Mike Watson**"

At this time you have all of the basic techniques to get you through a deal using "The Foundation to Success". That said, I do not think it is a good idea to do this whole system by yourself. I sincerely believe in working together. The benefits of putting more than one mind together far outweigh the profits you will share. That is why my final step is about "Power Teams". A "Power Team" is a group of real estate investors that work together to achieve a common goal of investing success. The group pools their time, talents and financial abilities in their pursuit of success. It is a system in which you will teach others how to find these types of deals, and capital.

I will get to "Power Teams" in a bit but for right now I want to go into some detail on a couple of questions I get in my boot camps. In addition I want to share a few of my *favorite* programs that have developed from using this system. Read on for some *extraordinary* "bonus" material. At the end I will give you a "Quick Start" plan of action to jump you right into the thick of investing quickly and easily.

Development Made Easy

At this point in my teaching I usually get a lot of questions like, "How will I have time to do all of the work to go long-term on a project? And even more important, how will I make sure to do it right?"

There a couple of things you can do if a project you are looking at ends up having a development stage in the long-term. The first one is to make sure the project works extremely well as a "Flixer". That way there is a very small chance you will go long-term if you market the property correctly. This will allow another professional to see the vision of your project and come in and pick up where you left off.

If you do sell your project I suggest you get permission from the buyer to follow the project through to the end (as an observer) so you can learn the ropes for your next project. As a real estate agent, I usually won't sell a project to a builder or developer unless they consent to let my team sell it for them when it is built out. That way I can stay in the project and learn. Also, it shows that I believe in the project. Most buyers appreciate this.

The second thing you should do is hire a partner or do a joint venture with someone who has quite a bit of experience in whatever type of development you are doing. You should check at the city development department and see what other similar projects have been done and then research the key players. Then contact them and see if they have any interest in partnering or doing a joint venture. If your numbers work fantastic for you it will be easy to find someone who will want to share in the profits.

Again, relying on another person's expertise is a smart way to take care of your project and learn at the same time. Using these people is a big bonus due to the fact that they have already performed with success in your city or county. Each time you do a project you will learn more and more and eventually be able to handle it yourself.

Another fantastic way to manage a development deal is to form an incredible "Power Team". By loading up your team with qualified real estate professionals in all of the ancillary parts of real estate, you will have capable people at your fingertips to get you through the development process.

Your "Power Team" will be extremely helpful if it consists of people such as developers, engineers, architects, builders, excavators and others who will have worked many times on similar projects. Their expertise will help ensure your project is profitable.

The last thing I will mention on this topic is that I partner and consult with students who attended a Boot Camp and all of our Degree Camps. If you are interested in learning about our partnership program, contact our office at 1-866-WATSON-5 to attend a Boot Camp.

FREE Boot Camp Admission!

Buying this book entitles you and a guest to attend a FREE 2-day **"Highest and Best Real Estate Investing" Boot Camp** worth $999!*

See Rules and Regulations on Certificate at the front of this book, on your FREE TICKET VOUCHER.

The "Property Management" Taboo

I have students that tell me they like my program except they don't want to manage rental property. I tell them, "If you are lucky you will *get* to manage the property forever. That will mean your asset is growing, appreciating, providing positive cash flows and tax write-offs." America would be far more stable if we all decided to have long-term income properties.

Having said this, I know property management has a bad stigma about it. I have done property management for years and it is an interesting and trying business to say the least. However, these days, instead of answering midnight calls on clogged toilets, I manage my properties by managing *people* who manage my properties. Managing two or three people is much better than managing a bunch of properties.

I know that everyone doesn't have the benefit of employees just yet, but you can hire a good property management company to do the nasty stuff for you. Since the properties you will end up holding long-term will be truly profitable, you can afford to pay a property management firm if you need to and *still* have positive cash flow.

Everyone I know who has owned real estate long-term is very happy that they have held onto it. The vast majority of them realize how much of a blessing those properties have been in their financial lives. They are glad they went through the hassles of management for all of the benefits they received then and on into their retirements.

On the other hand I have met very few people who were glad that they sold their long-term assets when they did. Most of them look back and wish that they had held them for a much longer period of time to enjoy the benefits that they lost when their properties were sold.

> "Don't let the ***fear*** of property management keep you from all of the benefits of owning long-term real estate. Don't manage properties. Manage ***people*** who manage properties.
>
> **~Mike Watson**"

The "One Hit Wonder" Program

I have a technique I teach that is so incredibly exciting I can hardly contain myself when I talk about it. It is a program that can literally change your life for a very long time with *just one deal.* I call it the "One Hit Wonder".

I have given you a couple of sneak peeks into this technique but it is time to give you the guts of it. For simplicity sake let's use the original "Awesome 15-unit Condo Deal" as our model.

Basically the "One Hit Wonder" program will teach you how to maximize your returns using seller financing when you sell. I'm going to walk through the simple numbers of that project one more time.

The Deal:

Purchase Price	$129,900
Costs for Engineering and Architectural Work	$75,000
Carrying Costs of Loans (Property/Construction)	$85,000
Site improvements (Curbs, Utilities, etc.)	$175,000
*Building Costs (15 units x 1000 sq ft. x $80/sq ft.)	$1,200,000
Total Costs	$1,664,900

**This number is very achievable in any market place with a contractor on your "Power Team".*

- Our hard cost to finish the project to this point comes to $1,664,900
- Divide that total by 15 units and your per-unit complete cost is $110,993
- We assume the brand new units would sell for $225,000 each.

When you sell the units here is how you determine your profits.

With a sales price of	$225,000
*Commissions plus closing costs	<$16,000>
Complete costs per unit	<$110,993>
Net proceeds to you	$98,007

**Low due to volume.*

If you sell all of the units for *cash to you at closing* your total profit will be $1,470,105! ($98,007 x 15 units)

That looks like an incredible deal! But let's see what *else* we could do with that equity. If you structure it correctly you will be able to offer some incredible terms to the buyers *and* take advantage of the full seller financing benefits for yourself! If you have a unit that is worth $225,000 and you owe $110,993 you have a phenomenal equity position. Let's show you some ways to use this equity to *multiply* your profits!

Example #1 (20% Seller Financing)

Let's say you decide to extend the following seller financing terms to each buyer. You will give them each a loan for 20% of the purchase price and they will pay you 10% *interest only* payments for 10 years on that loan.

In this case the buyer will get their own 80% first mortgage from a bank or lender on $225,000 purchase price. That first loan amount will be $180,000. ($225,000 x 80%) Their second loan amount will be $45,000 with you. ($225,000 x 20%) The first thing you might notice is that the buyer now is paying ZERO DOWN. Think your units might sell quickly?

Here is how it plays out:

Their loan of . . . . $180,000 (80% of $225,000)
Commissions and closing costs: <$16,000>
Complete cost of each unit . . . . <$110,993>
Equals at closing to you: $53,007 cash plus a $45,000 note to you!

If you sold all 15 units this way you would end up with a total of $795,105 in cash at closing. ($53,007 x 15 units) And the best part is you would also have $675,000 in notes receivable (15 units x $45,000 per unit).

Because the buyers are all paying you 10% *interest only* payments on those notes you will receive $67,500 *per year* in interest or $5,625 per month! Ideally this will last for the full ten years until your loan has its balloon and then they will still owe you the *principal balance* of the notes.

Imagine what it would be like to do *one project* and walk out of your closings with $795,105 cash in hand and $67,500 in *interest income* per year for ten years PLUS $675,000 in *principal* paid to you when the notes come due in ten years. At the end of ten years when all of the interest is paid and the principal is paid back you would have a total profit on that one deal of:

Total Cash at closings $795,105
Interest paid out to you over ten years $675,000
Principal due to you in ten years. $675,000
Total Profit $2,145,105

This is a perfect example of how seller financing can make you *a lot more money* than if you just sell your project outright in a traditional way. I hope the benefits of offering seller financing are becoming more clear to you.

Example #2 (30% Seller Financing)

If you had instead decided to offer the seller financing on 30% of the purchase price instead of 20% the numbers would change to look like this:

Their bank loan of . . . . $157,500 (70% of $225,000)
Commissions and closing costs . . <$16,000>
Complete cost of each unit . . . . . . <$110,993>
Equals at closing to you. . . . . $30,507 cash + a $67,500 note to you.

If you sold all 15 units this way you would end up with a total of $457,605 in cash at closing. ($30,507 x 15 units) And the best part is you would also have $1,012,500 in notes receivable (15 units x $67,500 per unit).

Because the buyers are all paying you 10% interest only payments on those notes you will receive $101,250 per year in interest or $8,437 per month in property-less passive income! Ideally this will last for the full ten years until your loan has its balloon and then they will pay you the principal balance of the notes. At the end of the ten years when all the interest has been paid and the notes are paid back, you would have a total profit of:

Total Cash at closings	$457,605
Interest paid out to you over ten years	$1,012,500
Principal due to you in ten years	$1,012,500
Total Profit	$2,482,605

Let's compare the different profits from each scenario:

The original deal had a cash profit of $1,401,705. This was the net profit per door of $98,007 times 15 units.

If you did the 20% seller financing as part of the deal the total profit *increases* to $2,145,105. This is almost an extra $750,000 you get by *helping people* get housing.

If you had decided to seller finance 30% of the purchase price to buyers then your profits would have increased *even more* to $2,482,605! By using seller financing you can take a *great* deal and make it unbelievable!

Imagine how your life would be different if you offered seller financing and had either of the outcomes presented above. Now imagine if you did more than just one of these types of projects. Remember that with "The Foundation to Success" you have the ability to offer seller financing whenever you sell. The property-less passive monthly income can become staggering if you let it. Seller financing can change your life!

Passive Income for *Life*

Now that you understand how a "One Hit Wonder" works I want to present another idea that goes a couple of steps further. The most common feedback I get with the "One Hit Wonder" program is "Wow that is incredible! I love almost doubling my profits and getting the income for several years." The second most common feedback I get is, "I want to get income for *life* so I am *not* going to sell. I'm going to hold the property for rental income." That thought is a valid one, but keep reading.

What if I could show you a way to turn the "One Hit Wonder" into *income for life*? Let's take a closer look at some of the finer details. What if when you made the 20% or 30% seller financed loans, you put some additional provisions in them? For instance, what if you added a "pre-payment penalty"? (They have to pay you a fee if they return your principal balance of the loan prior to the call or balloon date)

What would that accomplish? Hopefully the person would pay you for a longer period of time rather than refinance. That way they would avoid the pre-payment penalty. But what if they wanted or *needed* to sell? Wouldn't they just pay off the seller financed loan even if there was a pre-payment penalty?

They might, but what if you made the loan assumable? Then the *next* buyer could take over that loan. If that happened you would have an even better chance of getting payments for the full term of ten years or at least until the prepayment penalty date had passed. (That is a good reason to have the pre-payment penalty for the length of the loan)

But what if you wanted better odds than that? Or what if you wanted the payments to go on *longer* than the term of the prepayment penalty or even past the balloon time? How could you structure the lien?

Here is the ultimate way to set up your seller financing if you wish to accomplish *income for life*.

1. Allow the loan to be *assumed*.
2. Agree to *subordinate* to any other loan on the property.
3. Have the call date *reset* each time someone assumes the loan.

Let me explain why this loan structure is so important. What it does is let each buyer pass your loan through to *any* subsequent buyer. They then assume the loan and the ten year *clock resets!*

Let's say you sell your property for $225,000 and let the buyer have a seller financed note of $45,000. You let them pay interest only so they have a lower payment. (They also don't have mortgage insurance because they have an 80% first lien.) You create a 10 year pre-payment penalty of $6,750. (This is 15% of the loan. That way they most likely won't refinance.) You also put a reset clause in your loan and allow the loan to be assumed.

Typically after 5 years if they decide to sell the property you would have been paid off and your payments would *stop*. Because of how you've now structured the loan another buyer can assume the loan and your payments will continue.

The new buyer's bank doesn't mind because you agree to subordinate to them. (They will be in 'first lien' position on the property) In addition the new buyer now restarts the 10 year clock on the loan and on the pre-payment penalty.

Why would the new buyers be willing to do that? They are willing because it doesn't make a difference to them. They and the previous buyers were only paying interest anyway. Either they are paying the interest or they owe the full amount to you. In addition, if they could not assume your loan they would have to get a different loan and it would also be at least that long. Now the new buyer has a 10 year pre-payment penalty and *you* get payments for 10 *more* years.

One of the times your seller financed loan might get paid off is if one of the buyers paid the loan for the full 10 years. It is rare for someone to stay in a property that long so hopefully it wouldn't happen. If it did, you could go to them and see if they want to keep paying payments (you could even put a renewal option clause in the loan at the beginning).

The other time is if they sell the property and the new buyer does not want to assume the loan. At that point you would get the $6,750 pre-payment penalty paid to you which would at least cover your capital gains tax.

I'm going to go even a little deeper. What if you put a fee of one or two percent on the loan if someone assumes it? And what if you raise the interest rate each time someone assumes it? You would end up with bonus checks every few years plus your payments would go up! So now you have "Income for Life" plus bonus checks and raises. I can't think of anything much nicer than that.

So now you have come to the culmination of my book. The "One Hit Wonder" combined with the "Income for Life" plan has the ability to set you up with passive income for your entire life without property management. This is quite literally "The Highest and Best Real Estate Investment!"

P.S. Keep in mind you can do the majority of the aspects of these programs on *any* deal you do. (Even short-term "Flixers")

STEP 10

PROSPER AND SHARE WITH OTHERS

STEP **10**

PROSPER AND SHARE WITH OTHERS

Step # 10 of "The Foundation to Success" is to prosper and share with others. (Give back and create leverage with "Power Teams"). It is probably the step in which I get the most *resistance* from my students. They say things like, "I am learning this and can just do it by myself" or, "I don't want to have a team until I'm doing a deal" or "I'm a one-person show, always have been, always will be" or *whatever*. My first thought is, "It's too bad you don't understand what you are missing out on." What I usually *say* is, "Start a team. If it doesn't work out then you can always stop."

Creating and leading a "Power Team" can be the *most powerful* part of this system. Do not make excuses and "do it on your own". Be generous and giving. Share this knowledge, it was not meant to be hoarded. You will be immensely rewarded if you do. An organized team of people has an incredible amount of knowledge. Tap into that knowledge and every deal you do will be better. Not to mention you will do many more deals. A "Power Team" is literally *leverage*.

How many professional athletes perform completely alone? I guarantee you there is not one. If the sport they are in is a team sport it is impossible to win the game without the other players. If it is an individual sport then they have coaches, trainers, financial backers, doctors, and even their fans on their *team*. If you want to play the game of investing on a high level you must play on a team.

> "Without ***leverage*** it is impossible to play the game of professional real estate investing. A "Power Team" is the highest form of leverage.
>
> **~Mike Watson**"

Since the first part of step #10 is to "prosper", let's first discuss what it is to prosper. I believe you are not truly prosperous until you have wealth *and* those you care about also have wealth. *Individual* wealth is loneliness.

Here are three areas you may want to focus on in order to prosper. They are '*income/net worth*', '*freedom/lifestyle*', and '*career satisfaction*'. Let's take a quick look at each of these so you can create them for yourself *and* your team.

Income/Net Worth

If you have income that covers your day to day life plus allows you to put money away for later you are doing well with your income. If that income does not require you to work but is *passive*, you are truly prosperous in the area of income.

Net worth is the sum of your assets minus your liabilities. When you have a net worth of at least 50 times your annual adjusted gross income you are prospering in the area of net worth. This should be assets that you can borrow against if you choose to leverage them for other transactions. (This would include real estate notes.)

Freedom/Lifestyle

Most people want to be successful so they can be free. Freedom means many things to many people. Freedom to me means you make decisions based on what is *right*, rather than what is financially necessary.

Lifestyle means taking vacations and spending time with family and friends. It means having *all* of the material things you want in life *and* the time to enjoy them. It also means being able to *serve mankind* financially and with your time.

Career Satisfaction

Career satisfaction means you wake up passionate and excited to go into work because you love your work and the people you work with. Life is too short to be unhappy and unfulfilled in this area.

I am lucky enough to be afforded all of these things because of *real estate investing*. I want all of these things and more for you and those you love. I want you and thousands of others to prosper because of "The Foundation to Success". If you take this system, teach it to others and repeat it over and over you will prosper.

The term I use for "teaching others how to prosper" is called, "Power Teams". A basic idea taught for many years now is that "a team can accomplish more than an individual". This is absolutely true. It is especially true if the team is organized and has a common goal.

I have people in my program who attempt to implement "The Foundation to Success" alone. I also have people who have "Power Teams" of 2-20 or more participants. *Without exception* the people who have a "Power Team" are more successful than those who don't, even if their team is *only 2 people.*

One of the reasons a "Power Team" can achieve more than an individual is simply the "Law of Leverage". This law states, "The highest levels of success cannot be achieved alone. You and your life will never be *bigger than yourself* until you learn to leverage your skills and talents with other people and other assets."

The definition of a "Power Team" is; A group of real estate investors that work together to achieve a common goal of investing success. The group pools their time, talents and financial abilities in their pursuit of success.

What you are going to do is be the leader of the team. You will teach the members of your team how to help you find the following:

1. Distressed Properties (Ones that have a "Higher and Better" use)
2. Distressed People (Distressed property owner = Distressed Property)
3. Capital for Deals

When people are bringing in deals and money I'm sure you can see how it would be beneficial to have a team. The question is, "Why would someone want to be on your team?" The answer to that is simply, to *prosper*. What I mean by that is the people on your team will either be people interested in investing or people who are already involved in real estate in some way or another. You are going to teach them to do their own "Highest and Best" deals. You will do this by doing *your* "Highest and Best" deals and *allowing them* to be involved.

Think about how many people are affected in a positive way when you do a real estate deal. There is the seller, the tenants, the lender, the title representative, the appraiser, surveyor, electrician, plumber, painter, carpet layer, tile company, builder, architect, people who work at the city, attorneys, bookkeepers, accountants, neighbors, and the list goes on and on and on. You have a very big effect on people's lives when you do "Highest and Best Real Estate Investments". You literally enhance and enrich communities!

When you put your team together you will work as a group to find and do deals. Investors who wish to learn will be able to invest their money and learn. Others will be able to 'invest' with their time and expertise. Each person on your team will bring something powerful to the table.

The whole point is for *everyone to profit* from the deals you do and also learn along the way so that they can eventually do deals of their own. It is my dream to have "Power Teams" split off of other "Power Teams". For instance, if you have 20 members and do 10 or 12 deals then after a while one of those members goes and creates their own "Power Team". The "Law of Leverage" just got *leveraged.*

We have a full system of how we recommend you share your profits with your team.

FREE Online Resources

To access this system,
go to **mikewatsoninvesting.com/bookextras**, and click on "Power Team Profit Sharing", and you will get a FREE spreadsheet you can modify to fit to your deals.

What does the "Power Team" do?

Essentially a "Power Team" does three things; they find distressed property, distressed people, and capital for deals. I have already talked about how to find distressed property throughout the book, here now are some ways to find distressed people who may need to sell. When an owner of a property is distressed the property is also distressed. They are not two separate entities. The team looks for these people so we can *help them.* Remember all of our deals are win/win and many people will be helped tremendously by selling their property.

An example of someone who is in "distress" may be:

1. A person who is going through or who had a bankruptcy
2. Someone who is in or has had a divorce

3. Someone who is being transferred for their job
4. A person who has lost their job
5. A person who is or who hired a bad property manager
6. Someone who has had a death in the family
7. Someone with a home in foreclosure or who has already had a foreclosure
8. A person with a 'Notice of Default' on their loan (early stage of foreclosure)

Teach your team how to find distressed *property* and distressed *people* and you will be on your way to incredible investment opportunities. I consider "Power Teams" to be the first and foremost way to find "Non-Compete" deals. These opportunities come from finding distressed people but also from doing your "Area of Expertise" actions.

I have a student who utilizes the members of her team to write all of the letters to owners in their "Area of Expertise". The team member gets paid a portion of the profits if a deal materializes from their letter.

Another fun and *profitable* activity to do with your "Power Team" is to drive around your "AoE" and go door knocking. Sometimes it is easier to go knock on doors if you are in a group. I've gone with as many as 23 people at one time. If you do this you *will* get the attention of the owners!

Many times your team will provide capital for their deals and for your deals. That is because they will be able to make nice returns on those transactions that they could not make anywhere else. They may also have family or friends who want to make a profit from what you are doing. In this way they can bring capital to your deals. If this happens, make *sure* you follow *all* Federal and State SEC regulations for raising capital.

Key Team Member List

I used to have a list of all of the different professions I suggested people have on their team. Such as, architect, engineer, real estate agent, property manager, lender, surveyor, contractor, painter, plumber, appraiser… etc. But recently I have changed my tune in this regard. The main reason for this change is I've seen many of my students have incredible success with "Power Teams" that did not contain these professions.

Now my advice is to have people on your team who are *excited* about what you are doing. Only accept members who are *positive* and *passionate* about real estate investing. You will find that when you are talking about what you are doing, people with these attributes will gravitate toward you.

I have students who have 10 real estate agents on their team and I have students who have Chiropractors and Acupuncturists on their team. Both teams are very successful. That said, there are a few people you may want to eventually find. If you end up doing deals that include any type of development, an architect and/or engineer will be *extremely* helpful. If you end up doing a lot of square footage fixers or conversions, a contractor will be essential. In addition I always suggest that every team have *at least one* real estate agent.

Many investment "gurus" suggest that you buy and sell property without a real estate agent. I believe that is a HUGE mistake. They are professionals who can and will bring *priceless* expertise to the table. They will keep you out of trouble and they will make your deals *easier*. They will know the market and how to sell your properties.

Make sure the real estate agent you choose is willing to learn "The Foundation to Success". If they are sign them up!

A positive ***attitude*** and ***passion*** are more important than a person's profession when it comes to being on your "Power Team".

~Mike Watson

FREE Online Resources

If you go to **mikewatsoninvesting.com/bookextras** click on "Power Team Role Play Audio". We have a FREE clip on how to recruit people to be on your "Power Team".

Starting and Running Your "Power Team"

I could go into a long explanation of how to start your "Power Team" but the truth is all you have to do is open your mouth. Once you start looking for deals, start *talking* about them. Make a list of people you think might be interested in what you are doing and *talk* to them. Have them read this book. See if they want to get together and go drive around some areas. Do "The Foundation to Success" together. That way it is even more powerful and more fun!

I have many students who have had official "Power Team" *recruiting* meetings. They have gone to great lengths to talk to very large groups of people. Several of those students have posted details about those meetings on the "Forum" on my web site at mikewatsoninvesting.com. You can go there and read how they started their team.

More Resources

We also have a "Power Team Start Up" packet you can purchase that has meeting minutes, templates and all the tools you need to create your team.
Go to **mikewatsoninvesting.com/bookextras,** and click on "Power Team Startup Kit".

Most teams meet twice a month to learn and discuss deals. Less than that and your team will feel like they are not in touch with you. I suggest you set up an agenda with a few topics from this book. Your main goal is to teach your "Power Team" the steps of the "Foundation to Success". You can also talk about deals, possible deals or areas of town you are researching.

Once you have a few properties under contract your meetings will get very exhilarating. I have two students in Houston who are currently working on 17 deals! They have a *lot* to talk about at their meetings. The people at their meetings are excited and passionate and are *also doing deals.*

Most of my students charge a fee to be on their team. I highly suggest you do this for two main reasons. First, the participants will be more committed to the team. Second, it will take time for you to run the team and you will have some expenses. You should be compensated for those expenses and your time.

I also suggest that every person on your team read this book. It will be difficult to teach your team all of the concepts in the book without taking up a lot of time. The other benefit is that they will notice things in the book and with properties that you will not. This fact alone is a fantastic demonstration of *leverage*.

I once had a student stand up and say, "I just don't think anyone would want to be on a team with me." In my head I was thinking, "If you think that, then you are right." My answer was this, "Two in five people are interested in real estate investing. If you open your mouth and talk about how excited you are, they *will* want to be on your team."

Keep in mind that passion and excitement are catching. Expressing them draws passionate and positive people into your life.

"The Foundation to Success" can be a tremendous way to help people. You can improve their lives by helping them invest funds they didn't know they had. You can help them by teaching them how to invest. You can also help many people on your "Power Team" just by *doing* deals. This entire system is based on the idea of helping others. I believe it is our responsibility to share our knowledge with others. It is my true wish that you take this incredible system and use it to the best of your capabilities and share it with as many people as you can.

I sincerely hope you have found some value in reading this material. I also hope that you make the decision to *take action* with what you have learned. Find properties with a "Higher and Better" use and change them. Keep in mind the concept of "Highest and Best" use does not just apply to properties. It also applies to people. Make sure that every day you are performing the things that are *your* "Highest and Best" use. "The Foundation to Success" has the ability to change entire communities. Let's make it happen! I *know* you can do it.

> If you have knowledge that can ***help others,*** it is your ***responsibility*** to ***share*** that knowledge.
>
> **~Mike Watson**

"Happy Investing"

Michael P. Watson

INVESTOR TOOLS

MWI Investor Tools

Events

Investing Products

"Highest and Best Real Estate Investment" BOOT CAMP

Congratulations!

By purchasing this book, you also receive TWO valuable tickets to my "Highest and Best Real Estate Investing" Boot Camp!

See the FREE TICKET VOUCHER at the beginning of this book for details on *your* free tickets!

The "Highest and Best Real Estate Investing" Boot Camp is a powerful event that will help you immediately use the techniques contained in this book. It is a two day camp, and is held all over the country. You can find a full calendar of upcoming Boot Camp locations at www.MikeWatsonInvesting.com.

In the place of tickets to my boot camp, your FREE TICKET VOUCHER can also be redeemed for two tickets to any of my "Super Camps". *The "Super Camp" ticket offer is only valid for investors who are new to the MWI system.*

Happy Investing!

~ *Mike Watson*

MWI DEGREE CAMPS

There are eight MWI Degree Camps on advanced investing topics:

Non-Compete Methods Degree Cano

Learn how to find the deals other investors are missing! You don't have to frantically chase after leads, or compete with other investors. At this camp let Mike Watson teach you how to take control of your investing career through Non-Compete methods. You will learn how to become *the* investing expert in your community, and people will come to you with their investment opportunities.

Seller Financing Degree Camp

Create amazing investing deals with seller financing! Seller financing opens doors for real estate investing and offers huge benefits for the seller. By the end of this camp, Mike Watson will have taught you how to easily negotiate seller financing. This camp will build your confidence, create a vision of options, and revitalize your investments.

Creating & Enhancing Equity Degree Camp

Now you can learn Mike Watson's techniques to create instant equity. Mike designed this course to inspire investors to create equity by taking advantage of methods most either never considered or thought impossible. Though the topic isn't new to real estate, you are certain to learn something new at this event.

Foundation to Success Degree Camp

At this camp, we will go into great detail on the simple yet powerful Foundation to Success. You will learn how the Foundation to Success applies to all levels of your career and life.

Flips, Fixers, & Flixers Degree Camp

Mike Watson has created a camp to teach his simple techniques to successfully flip, fix or *flix* a property. How would you like to make a large profit on a fixer-upper without doing any work. Hard to believe? It is very possible, and you better enroll for this camp to learn this technique. This is one of Mike's favorite techniques!

Bus Tour Degree Camp

Get out into the field with Mike Watson and personally visit 20+ of Mike's personal invesmentment properties. These deals represent over one million dollars in profits. This is one of the most impactful camps we do for people because you will see these investments up close and personal. There will be no more denying you can invest when you see these deals!

Raising Capital Degree Camp

Raising Capital is vital to investing in today's real estate market. During this powerful camp learn Mike Watson's techniques, and discover how simple raising capital can be. Students leave this camp excited to raise money for their investments, and you will too.

Contracts Degree Camp

Often considered complicated and technical, the subject of contracts is too often neglected. Understanding contract law is fundamental and essential for a successful real estate investor. At this camp, Mike Watson breaks down this subject into an easy to understand format. Learn powerful techniques for preparing and reviewing contracts to get immediate results.

Super Camps

Mike Watson hosts regular Super Camps covering new topics. Some of the recent Super Camps have been:

- The "EVERYTHING CHANGES!" Super Camp
- The "Retire In 5 Years" Super Camp
- The "Any WHERE! Any TIME!" Super Camp

Super Camps are designed for *new* investors as well as *seasoned MWI students*. They are must-attend events to stay updated on our changing real estate markets. MWI also has Home Study Courses of past Super Camps. Visit our web site to sign up for the next Super Camp!

Mini Camps

The MWI Mini Camps are smaller classes on detailed investing topics. These intimate events are taught by Mike Watson.

Deal Evaluation Mini Camp

At this camp, you will learn all aspects of evaluating a deal. You will learn to put together deal evaluations that are worthy of any lender's standards, and you will turn deal evaluation into a system you can teach to others.

Property Management Mini Camp

Mike Watson defines Property Management as the "most profitable business in the world". He should know! Mike Watson has over 200 units, and has an extremely low vacancy rate. Come learn Mike's techniques and make property management one of the most profitable things you do.

GUTS Camps

The MWI GUTS Camps are limited to a small number of students to ensure the greatest level of personal attention is given to each student who attends. These events are taught by Mike's Pro Coaches.

The Portfolio Tour, Houston GUTS Camp

Be one of the few students fortunate enough to visit the office of J&K Interests and receive two days of training from two of Mike's most successful students, Jim Stephens and Kevin Liu. Visit the partnership properties that Jim and Kevin are partnering with MWI on.

Deal Evaluation GUTS Camp

Imagine the value of spending two days with Josh Escobedo and Ginger Norman of the Deal Maker's Division to discuss each aspect of evaluating and processing a real estate deal! Attend this event and you will receive answers to your deal evaluation questions in an intimate setting. You will complete more transactions in less time by eliminating guesswork when evaluating a deal.

Property Management GUTS Camp

Property management is hailed by Mike as "the most lucrative business in the world". This camp will complement your new-found investments by allowing you to uncover capital and resources available to those who own rental properties. Mike owns 200 units and keep these properties occupied with only two full-time property managers. Sign up for the Property Management GUTS Camp and experience new cash flow and freedom by learning this powerful system.

HOME STUDY COURSES

"Any WHERE! Any TIME!"
Home Study Course

Join Mike Watson and learn how to find and evaluate profitable investing deals in ANY market at ANY time! Includes: 15 Audio CD's, with over 18 hours of instruction with Mike, along with all printed camp materials.

"Retire In 5 Years" Home Study Course

Learn how to retire in 5 years or less! With Mike Watson's "Retire In 5 Years" Home Study Course, you can learn the system that is creating an early retirement for investors around the country! Your "Retire In 5 Years" Home Study Course includes: 16 audio discs, with over 22 hours of life-changing instruction from Mike Watson, with all notes included.

"EVERYTHING CHANGES"
Home Study Course - DVD Set

Now, with Mike Watson's EVERYTHING CHANGES DVD Set, you can take advantage of the same strategies that have inspired hundreds of real estate investors to create lasting change and wealth through real estate investing.

Your EVERYTHING CHANGES DVD Set includes:

- 4 DVD's
- Over 20 hours of instruction with Mike Watson
- Presentations from Mike Watson's most successful students

The "Becoming Your Own Best Client" Home Study Course

A live recording of one of Mike Watson's powerful introductory camps. Mike teaches you how to achieve freedom and become your own best client.

Includes:

- 18 audio CD's
- Over 24 hours of instruction.
- A great way to internalize all of Mike's proven strategies at your own pace! Learn with Mike in your car, office, or at home!

MLS Searches

Top Multi-Family MLS Searches

These are Mike Watson's most productive multi-family MLS searches. Search the MLS with Mike Watson, and watch how he evaluates deals. Learn Mike's secrets to find properties everyone else is missing! Just insert the CD-ROM into your computer, and watch and listen to Mike as he searches the MLS.

Top Single-Family MLS Searches

These are Mike Watson's most productive single-family MLS searches. Search the MLS with Mike Watson, and watch how he evaluates deals. Learn Mike's secrets to find properties everyone else is missing! Just insert the CD-ROM into your computer, and watch and listen to Mike as he searches the MLS.

Books

Liberation - Will You Survive or Thrive?

40 Inspirational quotes and dialog by Mike Watson, with Jennifer Hawkins. Do you notice you are either not taking action or not getting the results you want? Do you find it hard to stay passionate about your life on a day to day basis? Mike Watson is a master when it comes to being passionate and taking action. He truly lives his motto "Err on the side of action". With this book, you can own and access a little part of Mike's strength and motivation every day. Full color, 95 pages.

The Do-It-Yourself Guide to Property Maintenance for Those That *Don't* Do-It-Themselves

Mike Watson presents a new Property Maintenance book by Nicholas Escobedo and St. John Holloway. Book includes:

- When Buying your 1st or your 21st property.... What to find out from the previous owners.
- When emergencies arise and preventative maintenance
- How to save money while maintaining your rental property
- Plumbing: The most common issues that arise
- and more!

60 Days to Success Planner

A powerful daily investment planner developed by Mike Watson. Includes 60 days of daily investment tasks designed to turn you into a successful investor. The perfect way to get started, and stay on track to accomplish your investing goals.

Role-Play Series

Power Team Role-Play Audio CDs

This role-play is a *must-have* for anyone who wants to start a Power Team! Contains 2 Audio CDs. Join Mike Watson at a role-play of an "introductory" Power Team meeting or "Open House". Mike shares his Power Team vision with a room full of real estate professionals. He breaks down Power Teams, and gives the attendees overwhelming reasons to become members of the brand-new team. With this role-play, you will understand how to conduct your own successful first Power Team meeting or Open House.

Capital Raising Role-Play Audio CD

Join Mike Watson on a detailed role-play of a recent Capital Raising phone call. Mike breaks down the investing process with a potential investor, and gives them overwhelming reasons to invest their hard-earned money in his deals. He resolves multiple concerns from the investor, and gets them excited to invest in his deal.

Overcoming Seller Financing Objections Role-Play Audio CDs

Join Mike Watson as he shows you how to overcome common Seller Financing objections. In this role play Mike works with six sellers and gives them overwhelming reasons to seller finance their properties. This role-play is a *must-have* for anyone who wants to master Seller Financing! Contains 2 audio CDs.

Appendix 1: "QUICK START PLAN OF ACTION"

1. Start at chapter one and memorize "The Foundation to Success". I highly recommend reading the entire book again. Repetition is the best way to learn something well enough to be able to master it. Post the ten steps of "The Foundation to Success" where you will see it every day. Some investors even carry it with them.

"The Foundation to Success"

1. Know "The Foundation to Success"
2. Create your "Red Button Statement"
3. Find Incredible Properties (Competing and non-competing methods no-one else is using)
4. Evaluate Properties For Their "Highest and Best" Use (Plus 6 other key characteristics)
5. Buy the Property Using the *Two* OPM's (Never use *your* own cash again.)
6. Expose the vision! (Immediately put it back up for sale)
7. Create and Enhance Equity (Change the use, and *explode* your profits.)
8. Sell the Property for a Profit (Short-term *fast cash*)
9. Refinance for an Equity Position (Long-term strategy for *Passive Income*)
10. Prosper and Share with Others (Give back and create *leverage* with "*Power Teams*")

2. *Create your "Red Button Statement".* Remember this is your guarantee for success. Your "Red Button Statement" will jump start you at the start of your new adventure and again whenever you have a tough day. Keep it in plain sight and amend it whenever you feel the need.

3. Keep it simple. I cannot mention this enough. "The Foundation to Success" is simply a way to find properties with a "Higher and Better" use.

4. Pick 2-3 types of deals that have interested you. Take your "Spark of Inspiration" list in Appendix 2 and decide on a couple of project types to begin to research. Focus on those first until you determine that they work well or don't work at all.

5. Choose an "AoE" that fits well with the 2-3 types of deals you want to pursue. Make an appointment at your city planning or development office and go talk with them. (Remember, initially you want to avoid the "walk-in" department) Tell them you don't *know* anything but you want to *help* the city.

6. Drive around, find something with a higher and better use and evaluate it and *make an offer.* You will LEARN! LEARN! LEARN!

7. Stay connected. When you read this book you probably had moments when you were so excited about finding a deal you almost (or maybe did) ran out to your car and drove around. Keep that level of *excitement* by staying connected to the *Mike Watson Investing program.*

   a. Get on to the FREE "MWI Community Forum" at mikewatsoninvesting.com and read about other investors. Post your own questions, and get answers. I especially recommend the thread called "It Works!"

   b. Go to a "Roundtable" Meeting in your area. There are student investors who lead these and have monthly meetings in many cities throughout the United States. At these meetings there are people who believe in this system and are doing deals based on this information. Most Roundtable leaders do not charge to go to the meeting. Check my web site for dates and times in your area.

c. Go to one of my 2-day " Highest and Best Real Estate Investing Boot Camp" or 3-day "Super Camps". This book entitles you to FREE admission! See the FREE TICKET VOUCHER at the beginning of this book, and then check my web site for dates and locations.

d. Once you attend one of my Boot Camps you are able to attend a Degree Camp. I invite you to come on the journey of *expert real estate investing* by attending one of these events. You will not only get cutting edge information not taught anywhere else but you will be in a room of people who are taking action.

At my Degree Camps I invite student investors to come up to the front of the room and share their deals with the room. Typically we have 20-30% of the students share. If you want to experience a phenomenal level of success it is smart to immerse yourself with others who are *taking action.*

If you can't travel to a Degree Camp then you may find it helpful to listen to one or some of the recordings from my past Degree Camps. I have sets of CD's for 6 of the 8 camps I offer. They are all available at mikewatsoninvesting.com. They include topics like, "Advanced Seller Financing", "Negotiating and the Power of Contracts", "How to Master the *Flixer* Technique" and "Amazing Non-Compete Methods for finding Deals". Feel free to visit our site and check those out. Each one is a recording of a 3 day Degree Camp on that topic alone!

Appendix 2: "Spark of Inspiration" List

Thoughts to include in my "Red Button Statement"

1.______________________________________
2.______________________________________
3.______________________________________
4.______________________________________
5.______________________________________

Types of Deals I Like:

1.______________________________________
2.______________________________________
3.______________________________________
4.______________________________________
5.______________________________________

Area of Town that might work:

1.______________________________________
2.______________________________________
3.______________________________________
4.______________________________________

Vital To Do items:

1.______________________________________
2.______________________________________
3.______________________________________
4.______________________________________
5.______________________________________
6.______________________________________

Terms I want to use in a deal:

1.____
2.____
3.____
4.____
5.____

Random Sparks of Inspiration:

1.____
2.____
3.____
4.____
5.____
6.____
7.____

People who might be interested in Real Estate Investing:

1.____
2.____
3.____
4.____
5.____
6.____

Other classes I want to attend/information I wish to obtain:

1.____
2.____
3.____
4.____
5.____

Appendix 3: Frequently asked Questions

How do I get organized?

If you are a little overwhelmed with all of this, the best way to get organized and accomplish more, is to *hire an assistant.* You may feel like you cannot afford it yet but the truth is you can't afford not to. It is possible to hire an online virtual assistant for $5 an hour or a student from a local university. One of my student investors hired a part-time assistant for $6 an hour. As soon as she had someone in front of her every day, her accountability went up and the deals started coming in the door quickly. I consider this another way to share "The Foundation to Success". As you bring in employees teach them the basics as well. Remember, two out of five people is interested in real estate investing.

Where can I find partners for my investments?

The best place is within your "Power Team". If you do not have a team and do not have anyone you know who is interested in investing in your deal, please call "MWI". I require you attend a Boot Camp and go to all of the 8 Degree Camps, but I have partnered with *many* student investors. If the deal you bring in makes it through our Deal Evaluation and Submittal process and you attend our classes I may just end up partnering with *you.*

The reason I require students I partner with to attend my camps is because I *must* have educated partners. You can read this book and go do a deal but if you attend my camps you will learn about the biggest pitfalls, and you will find ways to make your deals even better. I have a student who stood up in a Degree Camp one day and said, "Had I known two months ago the technique you just now taught I could have made *$80,000 more* on a deal." Get educated and let's do a deal together!

What do you think is the key ingredient to being an incredible investor?

Knowing and implementing "The Foundation to Success" *as it is written.*

Do your concepts work with Commercial Real Estate?

Absolutely! As a matter of fact you will very often find that you are buying residential and changing its use into commercial to create unbelievable equity.

What are the characteristics of incredible investors?

Here are four things I think every incredible investor has in common.

1. They are *passionate* about investing.
2. They have unlimited *tenacity.*
3. They are *willing to learn* a new way of thinking.
4. They have a *desire to help others.*

How do I find a niche?

As you learn about your city and its zoning and development standards and incentives, a niche will most likely expose itself *to you.* Some areas are better suited than others for different projects. Find out what works well in your city and mimic someone who is having success with those types of properties. This will happen naturally when you are assembling your "Area of Expertise" binder. Remember, sometimes a niche will determine an "Area of Expertise" whereas sometimes and "Area of Expertise" will determine a niche.

Where can I learn more about this system?

At mikewatsoninvesting.com, you can find information on MWI Roundtables, Other books, Boot Camps, Degree Camps, Super Camps, CD's, DVD's, The Forum, Coaching etc.

One thing I have not mentioned is that MWI offers very inexpensive coaching. We have coaches available several hours a week that only cost one dollar a day! Check out our support system of coaches at mikewatsoninvesting.com

What systems can I apply to heighten my success?

I recommend you create as many systems as you can within your investing. Systems *themselves* heighten success. Use the systems in this book to assure your success. "Deal Evaluation", "Non-Compete and Competing Methods of finding property", "Short-term/Long-term Forms", "4-Offer Spreadsheet", "Area of Expertise", "Power Teams" and creating your "Red Button Statement" are all outstanding ways to systematize your investing.

Do you recommend doing a 1031 exchange when I sell?

That depends on many factors. Talk with your CPA and see if it is the best way for you to go. If you plan on selling something relatively quickly it might not be smart to do a 1031 Exchange as you might have some tax ramifications.

What happens with taxes when I refinance and hold or sell in the long-term?

I recommend you talk to a tax professional as I am not a tax attorney or a CPA. However, if you are lucky enough to keep your projects long-term you will in most instances, be able to enjoy the tax benefits of depreciation, interest and capital improvement write-offs among other things.

Often the write-offs provided by a building will be quite a bit more than the income provided by that same building, thus providing a lower tax burden overall for the investor. Owning properties is historically a fantastic way to lessen your tax burden over time.

When you seller finance you will most likely owe taxes on the interest you receive. Please make sure you make your CPA aware of all aspects of your transactions.

Do you ever have trouble with neighbors when you increase density on a property?

Yes, but here is what you need to know; *Zoning is law.* If you precisely follow the zoning and development standards, the neighbors may not be happy about what you are doing but they cannot *legally* stop you. If you veer from the exact standards then the neighbors could end up having a say in your project. That is why I suggest you follow the "path of least resistance" and do only what the zoning and development standards allow.

How do I know if I am changing a property to *the* "Highest and Best" use?

You should compare the "permitted", "conditional" and "unpermitted" uses from the "Use Chart" in your "AoE" book. If it is not the highest density allowed (units or number of square feet) then there is most likely a higher and better use. If you are unsure about your analysis, get another opinion. Sometimes architects and engineers or even people who work at the city may have an idea for a property that may even be a higher use than you choose.

What should I do when I get stuck on a deal?

1. Involve others. In other words, hire coaches, consultants, or listen to coaching calls, get on "The Forum" (It's FREE) and ask questions.

2. Heighten your due diligence, actually increase your analysis, prove to yourself the deal will work. If you can't then cut it loose, there is always another deal.

3. Get a partner. Share in the risk.

4. Bring in experts such as builders, architects, permit expediters, people who work at the city etc. This is another way to follow the laws of mimicry. If these people are on your "Power Team" you will most likely never get stuck. You will have the advice you need to make decisions and act.

5. Increase your "Capital Raising" and "Seller Financing" efforts. Bring them into your deal at any time. The terms of your deal can change as your needs change. At least they can as long as you have made sure your due diligence time is long enough, or

that you have clauses that allow you to get out of the transaction. Sometimes, negotiating last minute seller financing or receiving more capital, makes a deal possible that otherwise wouldn't have worked.

I have a student who likes to find deals with incredible "Higher and Better" uses and put them under contract at all costs. Typically they go under contract with cash terms. Then after meeting and working with the seller the investor shows the seller the many benefits of seller financing and they change the terms of the deal.

Use all of the tools provided at any and all times during your deal.

6. Have a "Can Do" attitude. Say to yourself "I will make this happen" if you believe it is a fantastic deal then do whatever it takes to make it happen.

7. Remember "The Foundation to Success" is like a professional baseball team.
   Just like a good coach, put all of the players on the field and follow all of the rules or you will take unnecessary risks of losing the game. It doesn't matter if it is cloudy or sunny outside you still have to put the second baseman on base or else you will most likely lose the game. It doesn't matter if the market is booming or crashing or if you are in Florida or Wyoming, when you invest in real estate, use *all 10 steps* (Until the deal is complete) and follow "The Foundation to Success" *as it is written.*

"The Foundation to Success" is a 10 step system which guides you through the process of how to create huge short-term profits from real estate investing and helps you amass a powerful

Glossary

Addendum - A document that adds terms to a contract. A supplement or addition.

Annexation - The process of bringing land from the outside of a city or county into that city or county's legal boundaries.

Appraisal - A price evaluation of a piece of real property done by a licensed and certified appraiser for a bank, investor or property owner.

Area of Expertise ("AoE") - A physical area on which an investor chooses to focus due to the availability of distressed properties, zoning incentives, highest and best uses and development standards. The investor will initiate a campaign to buy properties in this area for short-term and long-term profits.

Asbestos - A fibrous mineral form of magnesium silicate material used in insulation, fire- proofing and other building materials. It is hazardous to human heath and must be removed (abated) from real estate projects.

Bank Loan - Financing that is provided by a bank or a credit union.

Capital Raising - The act of soliciting money from private individuals for use in investment projects by investors. SEC regulations and guidelines should be closely adhered to in this endeavor.

Capitalization Rate - The rate of return that a real estate investment yields. The rate is determined by dividing an investment's net operating income by the sales price or current value of the property.

Codes, Covenants and Restrictions (CC&R) - These are used to govern owners and their rights in a Planned Unit Development and are encapsulated into a document that coincides with the title of the property. CC&R's are typically created by the property's original owner and passed on to subsequent owners.

Collateral - Something, typically real estate, offered as security for a loan given to an investor. The loan to the investor is secured against the piece of collateral for protection of repayment.

Conceptual Fixer-upper - A property that is fixed up using concepts instead of actual labor. For example, finding a single family home on a .63 acre lot and showing in a drawing how a 15-unit condominium conversion might conceptually fit there under the current zoning and development standards of that city. This is a conceptual value improvement. Investors will pay more knowing that 15 units instead of one house are available on that site.

Construction Loan - A loan from a bank or other commercial institution for the funding of the construction of a real estate project.

Contract - A written legally binding agreement between two parties in a real estate transaction. This document will typically spell out the terms of a purchase, or other items to be performed by the parties.

Conventional Lender - A lender that loans money, or brokers loans to those that loan money under the Federal Freddie Mac/Fannie Mae guidelines. These loans are typically for the purchase or refinance of real estate investments.

Debt Service - The payments made on any debt.

Density - In real estate, density is the term for the number, compactness or size of inhabitants or units that an investor can put on a particular project based on the size of the area involved and the controlling development standards in the municipality. For MWI purposes it also includes the amount of net income the property produces, the number of owners, and square footage.

Distress - A state of not being in optimum condition. Real estate distress can be such things as a property that is not using the highest and best use available, or a property that is in less than optimum shape physically or cosmetically.

Due Diligence - The work performed by a buyer or lender in the purchase of a piece of property that details a property's true condition. The buyer uses this work to decide if the property should be purchased and if the property has been represented correctly by the seller.

Earnest Money – An amount of money a person puts down as a payment "in earnest" that they will purchase the property. This occurs at the time of contract.

Egress - The ability or method to legally leave or exit a property.

Encumbrance - A cloud on the title of a property. For example a mortgage, lien, or easement.

End User - The last person to use a property. This is the long-term owner once a project is complete.

Endangered Species - A species of animal that is endangered or facing extinction due to the loss of or diminished quality of habitat caused by human impact or development.

Entitlement - The act of guaranteeing rights of development on property. This is accomplished by submitting and achieving approval for a project through a city or county zoning process. Once the development request is formally approved and recorded the property is considered "entitled."

Equity - The monetary value found by subtracting a property's debts from the current value.

Equity Position – Ownership of a property that has equity.

Extended Closing - Negotiating and obtaining, through a legally binding contract, the consent to take longer to close escrow on a piece of property than what is considered normal.

Feasibility Period - The contractually allotted time frame in a purchase agreement where the buyer can perform any due diligence items they deem necessary to document and verify the validity of their purchase. This period usually takes place at the beginning of the contract when the buyer's earnest money is still refundable.

Financing - The method of obtaining the money necessary to purchase or refinance a piece of real property.

First Lien - A legal claim one party has against another person's property to ensure the repayment of the first loan, mortgage or encumbrance recorded.

Fixer-upper - A property that will be improved in condition or use, for a resulting improvement in value. This would include converting a property from the current use to the highest and best use available in the zoning code and development standards.

Flag Lot - An infill lot subdivision technique that usually causes one lot to be split into two lots. There is one in front by the street and one behind with a driveway back to it as part of the lot. Usually the back lot of the two is shaped like a flag with a pole.

Flip - A property that is bought below market value and quickly sold for a profit before any work is done to enhance value.

Flixer - A real estate investment where the fixer-upper process has begun but is sold for a profit before the work is complete. A Flixer exposes the higher and better use of a property to others and thus makes the property more valuable.

Foundation to Success - The ten simple steps to follow for real estate investing success. The process by which profits are made in the short-term and equity and net worth are created in the long-term.

Frontage - The part of a property that abuts a public road. It is typically measured in linear feet and a minimum amount is usually needed in most development standards in order to build a project.

Future Map - A map showing the future intention of zoning. Different cities have different names for this map.

GIS Map – GIS is an acronym for Geographical Information Systems. A GIS map is a map that uses and presents geographical information among other things such as roads, utilities and infrastructure for investors to review and evaluate properties.

Gross Operating Income - The annual income that a property generates before any expenses are subtracted.

Hard Money - Private capital that is raised by investors in significant times of need. The money typically must be repaid with unusually high interest rates and costs.

Highest and Best Use – A property which is utilizing its maximum density available based on the underlying zoning.

HOA – HOA is an acronym for Home Owners' Association. This is the group of owners in a Planned Unit Development or condominium complex that come together in an Association to manage and govern their property. HOA's are usually governed by written Codes, Covenants and Restrictions.

Holding Costs - The expenses a property generates during ownership. For example, these expenses can be debt service, maintenance, taxes, insurance and property management.

Incentives - An inducement to action offered by a city or county to developers and investors to encourage development, redevelopment and/or urban renewal.

Income Fixer-upper - The act of fixing up or improving a property, by improving the income it produces, thereby enhancing the overall value and financial return of that property.

Infill - The act of filling in open space. These are opportunities in real estate to fill in unused space with additional density. Often an incentive by a city or county for urban renewal or redevelopment.

Ingress - The ability or method of legal access or entry to a property.

Inspection - The act of viewing, visiting, examining or reviewing a property to determine its condition and desirability.

Interest - A promised return on an investment. The return is usually a percentage of the original amount invested.

Investor - A person who purchases or invests in real estate properties that produce income or profits.

Landlocked Lot - A piece of property that has no legal access. To access this property, one must go across another's property where permission to do so may or may not exist. An example is a property that does not have frontage on a public road or an easement on a private one.

Lead Based Paint - Paint that contains a hazardous level of lead. In 1978 the U. S. Product Safety Commission lowered the legally acceptable amount of lead in paint to 0.06%. Paint used before that time often contained excessive and even toxic levels of lead. Properties built before 1978 should be tested for Lead Based Paint.

Leverage - Securing something large by the use of something small. For example, a small down payment that provides enough leverage to get a large loan.

Line of Credit - A loan set up to access equity in a property. Typically a portion of the equity is made available to the owner. The property with the equity is then the collateral for repayment of the credit line.

Loan - The act by an individual, bank or other entity of temporarily allowing someone else the use of their money.

MLS – MLS is an acronym for Multiple Listing Service. The MLS is a program used by licensed real estate agents to list the homes they have for sale and to gain access to area property information.

Mortgage - The method or instrument used to pledge or collateralize a property to a bank or lender as security that borrowed money will be repaid in the agreed upon fashion.

MWI – Is the acronym for the company, Mike Watson Investing LLC.

Net Operating Income - The income that is left over after you take a property's gross received income and subtract all expenses.

Offer - To propose or show intention of purchasing a piece of real estate by tendering a written contract.

Open Ended Closing - When a buyer offers to close a property in a purchase contract based on a type of milestone other than a date. Examples of this would be if the buyer closes after a zone change, project approval or building permit.

OPM – OPM is an acronym for Other People's Money or Other People's Mortgages.

Option Period - A period of time specified between a seller and potential buyer of a piece of property where the buyer has the option to perform or not on a purchase of that property under agreed upon terms and conditions.

Overlays - To lay or place special zoning or development incentives over the regular zoning and regulations of a piece of property or area of a city or county. The overlay is usually intended to stimulate redevelopment or urban renewal in that area.

Paper Fixer-upper - A fixer upper where the value of the property is improved through paperwork only. No physical labor is done to the property. Examples may be a zone change, condo conversion or a subdivision of the lot.

Passive Income - Income that is achieved through investing that continues to be received after the initial investment is completed. Examples may be rent in an investment building or monthly payments received through a seller finance transaction.

Physical Fixer-upper - A fixer upper where physical work to the investment is required to yield a profit or an equity position.

Plat Map (or Property Plat Map) - A drawing of a piece (or pieces) of property that shows size and dimension of the lot/s. The plat map may also show roads, easements, buildings, utilities and other things.

Point - A real estate fee usually equal to one percent of the loan amount in a real estate transaction. This fee is usually charged in association with the creation of a loan.

Power Team - A group of real estate investors who work together to achieve a common goal of investing success. The group pools their time, talents and financial abilities in their pursuit of success.

Private Capital - Capital borrowed from a private source. This is money for use in real estate deals that does not come from standards places such as banks.

Promissory Note - A written promise to pay a borrowed sum of money. The promissory note will include all of the normal parts of a real estate loan and usually does not collateralize a property as security.

Property Taxes - An amount of money required by the government for its support, facilities and services levied annually against a piece of property and its value.

PUD – PUD is the acronym for a "Planned Unit Development." A PUD is usually a development that follows the zoning for the property in question, but doesn't meet all of the development standards. The project overcomes these limitations by offering additional amenities.

Radon Gas - A natural gas that you can't see or smell that can be cancer causing. The existence of this gas in a real estate property is very toxic and dangerous.

Red Button Statement - A statement that an investor creates that elicits passion, enthusiasm and action in his/her investing career. The statement delineates the reasons for action and serves as an emotional mission statement.

Refinance - The act of getting or replacing existing financing with new financing on a property.

Refinance Returns - The equity position that is left in a property after a refinance takes place. This return is a profit on a property that will be held long-term as equity.

REO - An acronym for "real estate owned". This typically refers to a property owned by a bank or other institution rather than an individual.

Seller Finance - Financing that the seller offers to buyers as a part of the sale of their property. Using seller financing, the seller then becomes the bank for part or all of the buyer's purchase. Terms are agreed upon by both parties and a mortgage is created at the property closing.

Setback - The amount of space required from the front, back or side of a property line to the construction site of that property. The setback acts as a buffer between the building and the street or other surrounding properties.

Short Sale - When a property is sold for less than is owed on the mortgage(s). The property is sold short of, or, for less than, the remaining indebtedness.

Special Use Permit - An authorization or special exemption granted by a city or county on a specific piece of property allowing a use or project outside of the regular approved uses for the underlying zone.

Subdivision - The act of dividing a piece of real property into multiple parcels or lots. This typically requires going through a legal process in the city or county where the original property exists.

Subject To – Using these words with a purchase of a property means the property does not have a "free and clear" title at closing. The buyer agrees to purchase the property "subject to" an existing lien or encumbrance. Another use of the words "Subject To" is with an appraisal. If an appraisal is done "subject to" remodeling, then the calculated appraised price is "as if" the work is complete even though it is not.

Subordination - A clause in a loan or lien that allows another loan or lien to be placed ahead of it in ranking on a piece of collateral.

Survey - An inspection on a piece of land that determines boundaries, dimensions, area, corners and positions for that piece of land.

Terms - The parts of a loan or contract that help determine all of the agreed upon details. Examples would be interest rate, years in the loan, down payment required and closing costs.

Terms Fixer-upper - The act of fixing up or improving the value of a property through the use and offering of terms to make a property more appealing to future buyers.

Title Policy - A contract of indemnity issued to the owner of a piece of property guaranteeing a "free and clear" title up to the face amount of the title policy. Should any previous claims arise against the title of a property, the title insurance policy will take care of those claims.

Traditional Investment - An investment using standard and ordinary practices that yields regular returns.

Traditional Lender - One who loans money for regular or ordinary returns or uses standard financing as a method of creating loans.

Traditional Returns - Returns on investments that are typical or ordinary.

Trust Deed - A written legal document used to secure a loan against a piece of property.

Use Chart - A chart or list of uses provided by a city or county showing which land uses are permitted in given zones in that municipality.

Variance - The ability or permission granted by a city or county to build or use something outside the normal permitted uses or regulations by zoning law or building code. Often times this is done with a legal zone change or written permit.

Wet Lands - Land determined by the U.S. Army Corps of Engineers to be "unbuildable" or uninhabitable due to the constant existence of water. This land will be preserved as such and left in its natural state.

Zone Change - The act of permanently changing the zoning on a piece of property through legal paperwork and process at the city or county.

Zoning - The designation for use given to a piece of land by a city or county. Zoning is legally binding and must be followed when building or developing that piece of land.

Zoning Breakdown - A written explanation of each zone in a city or county's zoning code explaining the intentions of the zone, permitted uses and possibly some or all of the development standards.

Zoning Map - A map distributed by a city or county delineating throughout the municipality, the zoning designations for each area and piece of property.

INDEX